D1191129

Calvin and the Federal Vision

우리 주 예수 그리스도 안에서
사랑하고
존경하는

강 창욱 장로 내외 께

주후 2011년 7월 29일

전정기 드림
JK

Calvin and the Federal Vision

Calvin's Covenant Theology
in Light of Contemporary Discussion

JEONG KOO JEON

RESOURCE *Publications* · Eugene, Oregon

CALVIN AND THE FEDERAL VISION
Calvin's Covenant Theology in Light of Contemporary Discussion

Copyright © 2009 Jeong Koo Jeon. All rights reserved. Except for brief quotations in critical publications or reviews, no part of this book may be reproduced in any manner without prior written permission from the publisher. Write: Permissions, Wipf and Stock Publishers, 199 W. 8th Ave., Suite 3, Eugene, OR 97401.

Resource Publishing
A Division of Wipf and Stock Publishers
199 W. 8th Ave., Suite 3
Eugene, OR 97401
www.wipfandstock.com

ISBN 13: 978-1-60608-172-3

Manufactured in the U.S.A.

Contents

Preface

ᴵᵀ ᴵˢ ᴹʸ ˢᴾᴱᶜᴵᴬᴸ honor to publish this monograph to celebrate Calvin's Quincentennial. It is the fruit of my labor during my Visiting Fellowship at Yale University Divinity School from September 2007 to December 2008. I give my special thanks to the library staffs, especially to Mrs. Susan P. Brady, Dr. Suzanne Estelle-Holmer and Mrs. Amy Limpitlaw for their tireless help, providing me a friendly environment, and Dr. Paul Stuhrenberg, the librarian of Yale Divinity School, for his constant encouragement and friendship. The hermeneutical, historical, and theological discussions with Dr. Harold Attridge, Dr. Adela Collins, Dr. John J. Collins, Dr. John Hare, Dr. Serene Jones, Dr. Harry Stout, Dr. Denys Turner, Dr. Judith Gundry-Volf and Dr. Miroslav Volf have broadened and sharpened my scope of the understandings of early Christianity, Pauline theology, Second Temple Judaism, religious history, philosophy, and theology although the subjects are not directly related to my monograph.

I am especially thankful to my former seminary professors of Westminster Seminary California and Westminster Theological Seminary in Pennsylvania, who have molded my spiritual life and expansive visions of hermeneutics, theology, and practice. I express gratitude to the members of the Korean Capital Presbytery in Presbyterian Church in America where I am serving as a teaching elder. They have supported my Visiting Fellowship with prayer, encouraging remarks, and financial support. In addition, the faculty, board members, and students of Chesapeake Reformed Theological Seminary have always supported my teaching and writing ministry since 1999. Dr. and Mrs. Sahng Yeon Kim, Mr. Matthew Park, Mr. David Shin, Mrs. Jung Won Yoon, and others have supported my research and writing project with wholehearted prayer, financial help, constant encouragement, and friendship in Christ. Without their prayer and support the current book would not exist.

My beloved wife, Mi Sun, has always been patient as a godly soul mate and companion even in my absence due to my research. My two daughters, Helen and Hester, have been a constant joy of my life and pilgrimage in the

States. May the Lord use the monograph for His own glory and to expand His kingdom.

Introduction[1]

JOHN CALVIN WAS THE apex of the sixteenth-century Protestant
Reformation in Europe. His life and theology are still influential on the
global scale as we live in the Global Mission Age through the development of science and technology.[2] As we celebrate Calvin's Quincentennial,
it is worth exploring Calvin's covenant theology as one of the best ap-
proaches to read and to view his theological outlook and other related
hermeneutical, theological, and practical visions. Considering the latter
part of the twentieth century, which was a period marked with the rise of
different forms of monocovenantalism,[3] rejecting the antithesis between
law and gospel even in conservative Reformed and evangelical community, although its hermeneutics and theology have had close attachment
and identification to Calvin, it is imperative to explore and to reexamine
Calvin's covenant theology in light of contemporary debates.

For the past several decades, neoorthodox theologians after the
pattern of Karl Barth have argued the "'Calvin against the Calvinists' ap-

1. The Introduction and Chapters One and Two are a reworking and expansion of
the section on John Calvin of chapter one of my book, *Covenant Theology: John Murray's
and Meredith G. Kline's Response to the Historical Development of Federal Theology in
Reformed Thought* (Lanham: University Press of America, 1999 and 2004), which was
originally submitted as a PhD dissertation at Westminster Theological Seminary in
Pennsylvania.

2. For the biographical sketches of Calvin's life and theology and its continuing
impact and legacy, see William J. Bouwsma, *John Calvin: A Sixteenth-Century Portrait*
(New York: Oxford University Press, 1988); David W. Hall, *The Legacy of John Calvin: His
Influence on the Modern World*, in *The Calvin 500 Series* (Phillipsburg: Presbyterian and
Reformed Publishing, 2008); Alister McGrath, *A Life of John Calvin* (Cambridge: Basil
Blackwell Ltd., 1990); T.H.L. Parker, *A Biography of Calvin* (Philadelphia: Westminster
John Knox, 2007).

3. I identify monocovenantalism as any hermeneutical and theological system,
which denies or ignores the importance of the evangelical distinction between law and
gospel, which was a common denominator for the Protestant Reformation, especially
shared by both Martin Luther and John Calvin as the hermeneutical lynchpin of *sola
fide* and *sola gratia*.

proach" concerning the development of federal theology.[4] They see Calvin "as a theologian of grace to be distinguished from the legalism of later 'Calvinists' covenantal or federal theology."[5] This critique of the Reformed development of federal theology by Barthians is an attempt to infuse their theological reference point into Calvin's theology and thus separating Calvinists from Calvin. Muller adequately summarizes the problem of the neoorthodox interpretation of Calvin *against* Calvinists: "Typical here is the attempt to identify Calvin as the direct ancestor of neoorthodox Christocentrism and to discredit theologically the Reformed orthodox teaching as incompatible both with Calvin and with Barth."[6] Therefore, neoorthodox proponents harshly criticize the antithesis between the covenants of works and grace within Reformed orthodoxy, as well as the antithesis between law and gospel as it relates to justification by faith alone excluding good works. Thus they create an erroneous contrast between Calvin and the Calvinists. These critics contend that federal theology changed the biblical order of *grace and law* into *law and grace*. Thus, in their historical theological point of view, they stress the priority of *grace over law* and identify themselves with Calvin, for whom the distinction between the covenants of works and grace and the antithesis between law and gospel are allegedly unknown.[7]

4. I use and define federal theology as a hermeneutical and theological system, well summarized in the distinction between the covenant of works and the covenant of grace, developed and adapted in the Reformed orthodox tradition after the pattern of Calvin's theology though Calvin did not use the term, the covenant of works (*foedus operum*) in respect to the prelapsarian Adamic status.

5. Richard A. Muller, "Calvin and the 'Calvinists': Assessing Continuities and Discontinuities Between the Reformation and Orthodoxy," *Calvin Theological Journal* 30 (1995): 349.

6. Ibid., 353.

7. Paul Althaus, *Die Prinzipien der deutschen reformierten Dogmatik im Zeitalter der aristotelischen Scholastik* (Leipzig, 1914; reprint, Darmstadt: Wissenschaftliche Buchgesellschaft, 1967), 148–52; Barth, *Church Dogmatics*, 4/1:54–66; Donald J. Bruggink, "Calvin and Federal Theology," *The Reformed Review* 13 (1959–1960): 15–22; August Lang, *Der Heidelberger Katechismus und vier verwandte Katechismen* (reprint, Darmstadt: Wissenschaftliche Buchgesellschaft, 1967), LXIV–LXVII; Jürgen Moltmann, "*Föederaltheologie*," in *Lexikon für Theologie und Kirche*, 1960; Otto Ritschl, *Dogmengeschichte des Protestantismus* (Göttingen: Vandenhoeck & Ruprecht, 1926), 3:416–18; Holmes Rolston, III, "Responsible Man in Reformed Theology: Calvin Versus the Westminster Confession," *Scottish Journal of Theology* 23 (1970): 129–56; idem, *John Calvin versus the Westminster Confession* (Richmond: John Knox, 1972); Gottlob Schrenk, *Gotesreich und Bund im älteren Protestantismus vornehmlich bei Johannes Cocceius* (Gutersloh: Bertelsmann,

Rolston, for example, asserts "Indeed, it has seldom been realized by persons otherwise well versed in the Reformed tradition that the twin covenant tectonics which dominate the substructure of all later Reformed dogmatics is totally absent from Calvin. Worse than that, its fundamental incompatibility with Calvin's thought has gone all but unnoticed."[8] In a similar manner, James B. Torrance asserts that "this distinction between a Covenant of Works and a Covenant of Grace was unknown to Calvin and the Reformers–nor indeed would Calvin ever have taught it."[9] Supporting this contention, Bruggink maintains "Nevertheless, even in this brief glimpse of the system, it becomes evident that despite its popularity, federal theology was not a logical development of Calvin's theology. Rather it was a perversion of great seriousness, for it introduced a covenant of works as a valid relationship between man and God, and then carried works into the very covenant of grace."[10] The underlying idea is to reject the antithesis between law and gospel, which was a common theological denominator used by all the major Reformers in their focus on justification by faith alone (*sola fide*) and salvation by grace alone (*sola gratia*). This was set in opposition to the medieval schoolmen's legalistic and moralistic notions of justification and salvation. Ironically, neoorthodox theologians condemn the orthodox Reformed distinction between the covenants of works and grace, and in so doing, create the key problem that leads to a moralistic and legalistic religion.

After Karl Barth faded away from the theological world, a new champion of monocovenantalism arose: E.P. Sanders who is a famous Pauline scholar. He published his landmark research book, *Paul and Palestine Judaism*, in 1977 in which he radically redefined the soteriol-

---

1923), 48–49; James B. Torrance, "Covenant or Contract ? A Study of the Theological Background or Worship in Seventeenth-Century Scotland," *Scottish Journal of Theology* 23 (1970): 51–76 ; idem, "The Covenant Concept in Scottish Theology and Politics and Its Legacy," *Scottish Journal of Theology* 34 (1981): 225–43; idem, "Calvin and Puritanism in England and Scotland—Some Basic Concepts in the Development of 'Federal Theology,'" in *Calvinus Reformator* (Potchefstroom: Potchefstroom University for Christian Higher Education, 1982), 264–77; idem, "Strengths and Weaknesses of the Westminster Theology," in *The Westminster Confession*, ed. Alisdair Heron (Edinburgh: St. Andrews, 1982), 40–53; David N. J. Poole, *The History of the Covenant Concept from the Bible to Johannes Cloppenburg "De Foedere Dei"* (San Francisco: Mellen Research University Press, 1992).

8. Rolston, *Calvin versus the Westminster Confession*, 11.

9. James B. Torrance, *Covenant or Contract*, 61–62.

10. Bruggink, *Calvin and Federal Theology*, 22.

ogy of the Judaism of the Second Temple period as covenantal nomism,
not legalism. This contradicted the typical definition of the Protestant
Reformation by both Luther and Calvin.[11] Covenantal nomism has been
known as "New Perspective on Paul" after James Dunn's definition of it
in his 1983 article.[12] The heart of New Perspectivists, however, is also to
deny the Pauline antithesis between law and gospel in their analysis of the
Pauline soteriology.

Meanwhile, for the past several years, there has been a new theological movement, known as the Auburn Avenue Theology or Federal
Vision, within the conservative Reformed and evangelical circles in
North America. The characteristics of their theology are also monocovenantalism after the pattern of Norman Shepherd and others whereby the
promoters of Federal Vision deny the antithesis between the covenant of
works and the covenant of grace, as well as the distinction between law
and gospel while they identify their new theology with Calvin and the
Westminster Standards.[13] The hermeneutical, theological, and practical
concerns and visions of the Federal Vision have been comprehensively
summarized by Sandlin as one of the active proponents of the Federal
Vision as follows:

11. Cf. E. P. Sanders, *Paul and Palestine Judaism* (Philadelphia: Fortress Press, 1977).

12. Cf. James D.G. Dunn, "The New Perspective on Paul," *Bulletin of the John Rylands
University of Manchester* 65 (1983): 95–122. For my brief and critical interaction with
the New Perspectives on Paul, see Jeon, *Covenant Theology*, 314–18; idem, *Covenant
Theology and Justification by Faith: The Shepherd Controversy and Its Impacts* (Eugene:
Wipf and Stock Publishers, 2006), 26–37. There are great amounts of secondary literature, engaging with the New Perspectives on Paul. However, it is difficult to find sound
literature that deals with the central problem of the New Perspectives on Paul, which is
the rejection of the Pauline evangelical distinction between law and gospel. I would like
to mention a few writings engaging with the New Perspectives on Paul in light of the
Protestant Reformation Perspective. See S. M. Baugh, "The New Perspective, Mediation,
and Justification," in *Covenant, Justification, and Pastoral Ministry: Essays by the Faculty
of Westminster Seminary California*, ed. R. Scott Clark (Phillipsburg: Presbyterian and
Reformed Publishing, 2007), 137–63; Cornelis P. Venema, *The Gospel of Free Acceptance
in Christ: An Assessment of the Reformation and the New Perspectives on Paul* (Edinburgh /
Carlisle: The Banner of Truth Trust, 2006); Guy Prentiss Waters, *Justification and the New
Perspectives on Paul: A Review and Response* (Phillipsburg: Presbyterian and Reformed
Publishing, 2004).

13. For my comprehensive and critical analysis on monocovenantalism of Norman
Shepherd, the Federal Vision, and the New Perspectives on Paul including covenant and the
doctrine of justification, see Jeon, *Covenant Theology and Justification by Faith*, 1–107.

Though the Federal Vision (FV) is a legitimate theological paradigm, it is driven more by pastoral concerns than theology proper. The FV has posited a covenantal conception of the Trinity and God's relation with humanity that emphasizes a more intimate unity between the visible church and the Trinity than has often been suggested by Protestants. A covenant is not merely a means of entering a relation with God but is the relationship itself. In ecclesial terms, this means that union with the church at baptism (and continuing union at the Lord's Table) constitutes union with Jesus Christ. The FV is intent to recover the "objectivity" of the covenant that had been lost in modern evangelicalism, in the latter's preoccupation with individual religious experience. We do not judge who is and is not a Christian by religious experience but by who stands in a visible covenant relationship to God by means of baptism and the Lord's Supper in the church. Though the FV claims precedent in the Reformed tradition, as, for example, in the Mercersburg Theology of John W. Nevin and Phillip Schaff, and all the way back to Calvin himself, its proponents are not averse to all innovation.[14]

Against the backdrop of contemporary challenge and confusion, in his theology, which we shall later discuss in detail, Calvin used three theological reference points as the background for the later development and adaptation of the twofold covenants. They are: (1) an absolute antithesis between law and gospel in expounding the doctrine of justification by faith alone; (2) one covenant of grace in God's redemptive history in the postlapsarian state; (3) and the governing principle of the law in the prelapsarian state, along with identifying the *foedus legale* under the Mosaic Covenant as the *contrast* between the Old Covenant and New Covenant, in which the principle of the law was implied in the former with regard to earthly blessings and curses in the promised nation of Israel. This earthly national administration of the law ultimately pointed to the everlasting heavenly blessing for believers in Christ Jesus and the eternal curse for unbelievers, while believers under the Sinaitic Covenant were justified and saved by the principle of the covenant of grace in Christ Jesus, who would come later. I will seek to endeavor that Calvin's concept of "the covenant of the law" (*foedus legale*) in respect to the Mosaic or Old Covenant provided the hermeneutical and theological background for

14. P. Andrew Sandlin, "The Polemics of Articulated Rationality," in *A Faith That Is Never Alone: a Response to Westminster Seminary California*, ed. P. Andrew Sandlin (La Grange: Kerygma Press, 2008), xiv.

the concept of "the republication of the covenant of works," applied not to the level of personal salvation but to the earthly blessings or curse with redemptive adjustment for the latter-Reformed orthodox theologians.

These hermeneutical tools decisively contributed to and gradually permeated in the thinking that led to the development of the antithesis between the covenants of works and grace hermeneutics and theology in Reformed orthodoxy.

In this connection, I will pay special attention to several scholars' suggestion that even though Calvin did not use the term *foedus operum*, referring to Adam's original situation, his biblical theological concept is fully congruous with the later developed doctrine of the covenant of works. The Reformed orthodox formulation of the prelapsarian covenant of works was gradually developed from Calvin's federal notion of the prelapsarian Adamic administration of law. Therefore, there is a covenantal theological continuity between Calvin and the later Reformed orthodox covenant theologians, in respect to the antithesis between the covenant of works and grace.[15] Upon careful historical theological analysis, I will show that the antithesis between the covenants of works and grace is an important hermeneutical principle that is fully compatible with Calvin's covenantal theological concept, one that has been progressively developed by Reformed orthodox theologians. Meanwhile, the Federal Visionists are very critical to the antithesis between the covenant of works and the

15. Mark W. Karlberg, "The Mosaic Covenant and the Concept of Works in Reformed Hermeneutics: A Historical-Critical Analysis with Particular Attention to Early Covenant Eschatology" (PhD diss., Westminster Theological Seminary, 1980), 74–85; idem, "Reformed Interpretation of the Mosaic Covenant" *Westminster Theological Journal* 43 (Fall, 1980): 13; Peter A. Lillback, "Ursinus' Development of the Covenant of Creation: A Debt to Melanchthon or Calvin," *Westminster Theological Journal* 43 (1981): 247–88; idem, "The Binding of God: Calvin's Role in the Development of Covenant Theology" (PhD diss., Westminster Theological Seminary, 1985), 7–11, 446–97; Richard A. Muller, "The Covenant of Works and the Stability of Divine Law in Seventeenth-Century Reformed Orthodoxy: A Study in the Theology of Herman Witsius and Wilhelmus À Brakel," *Calvin Theological Journal* 29 (1994): 88–89. The precise nature and importance of the bipolar covenants have been addressed by Mark Karlberg: "Chapters three and four develop the importance of the law-gospel distinction and its application to the doctrine of the two covenants, the covenant of works and the covenant of grace. The biblical concept of works (law) is crucial to the Reformed theological system, especially with regard to the doctrine of the atonement of Christ and of justification by faith. Communion with God is possible only on the ground of faithful (sinless) covenant obedience, for God cannot look upon sin. This demand was met exclusively by Christ on behalf of the sinner redeemed by grace. Justification is by faith, not works." Karlberg, *Mosaic Covenant and Works*, 7.

covenant of grace, which was the hallmark of the Reformed orthodox theology in the arena of hermeneutics and theology. I would suggest that it is consistent to the monocovenantalism of the Federal Vision because the antithesis between the covenant of works and the covenant of grace stand or fall together with the antithesis between law and gospel.

In addition, I will demonstrate that Calvin's concept of the antithesis between law and gospel was a controlling hermeneutical and theological motif to penetrate the biblical idea upon the doctrine of double predestination. Meanwhile, the Federal Visionists radically reinterpret the doctrine of double predestination in light of monocovenantalism in which they reject the antithesis between law and gospel. In that sense, I will seek to demonstrate that the idea of double predestination by the Federal Visionists is not compatible to Calvin, as well as the Westminster Standards.

Finally, I will explore Calvin's sacramental theology, particularly on Baptism and Eucharist. The finding will be that Calvin never affirmed the concept of baptismal regeneration because regeneration, according to Calvin, is a sovereign work of the Holy Spirit in God's sovereign time for those who are elected. However, the Federal Visionists insist that Calvin, as well as the Westminster Standards, affirmed baptismal regeneration, injecting their idea of covenantal sacerdotalism into Calvin's baptismal theology while they go against the meritorious sacerdotalism of Roman Catholicism.

In exploring Calvin's Eucharistic theology, we will find out that Calvin did not approve paedocommunion because there is a clear exegetical and theological evidence presented in 1 Corinthians 11 against paedocommunion while he affirmed paedobaptism in light of covenantal continuity between the Old and New Covenants in relation to infant circumcision and baptism. However, Federal Visionists seek to affirm paedocommunion, arguing that children under the Old Covenant participated in the Passover meal with other family members under the Old Covenant. In that sense, I will seek to demonstrate that the Federal Visionists fail to do justice by not giving biblical and theological evidence as clearly presented in 1 Corinthians 11 where Paul goes against paedocommunion as Calvin correctly read it.

It is neither an exhaustive study on Calvin's covenant theology nor the Federal Vision. Rather, it is a comprehensive exploration of Calvin's covenant theology in light of contemporary discussion, especially on the Federal Vision. I will conclude that the theology of the Federal Vision is not compatible to Calvin's covenant theology, as well as the Westminster Standards because the Federal Visionists radically reinterpret the Protestant Reformation, Calvin, and the Westminster Standards with monocovenantal vision in which they deny the antithesis between law and gospel as well as the distinction between the covenant of works and the covenant of grace. In that sense, I will identify the Federal Vision as a consistent monocovenantalism because the exponents of the Federal Vision reinterpret the different aspects of hermeneutics, theology, and practice, self consciously denying the antithesis between law and gospel, which was the foundational backbone of hermeneutics and theology for the Protestant Reformation and Calvin.

Covenant and Justification by Faith

B Y EXPLORING CALVIN'S THEOLOGY, I will demonstrate that Calvin made a concrete balance between the concept of covenantal obedience and justification by faith alone (*sola fide*). He was careful to state that believers' covenantal obedience has a definite role, not in the doctrine of justification, but in the process of sanctification while he embraced all the soteriological blessings within the category of the union with Christ (*unio cum Christo*). Calvin's genius lies in the fact that he applied the law and gospel distinction in his understanding of justification by faith alone. In that sense, the distinction between law and gospel is a concrete hermeneutical and theological background in Calvin's hermeneutics and theology.

However, the Federal Visionists deny applying the law and gospel distinction in their interpretation of justification by faith alone (*sola fide*), although they unanimously appear to affirm the Reformation principle of the *sola gratia* and *sola fide*. In doing so, they identify their new theology and monocovenantalism with Calvin and the Westminster Standards, though their theology is far from a fair representation of these views.[1]

---

1. For the critical discussion against the Federal Visionists' views on covenant and justification by faith, see The Orthodox Presbyterian Church, *Justification: Report of the Committee to Study the Doctrine of Justification* (Willow Grove: The Committee on Christian Education of the Orthodox Presbyterian Church, 2007), 133–53; David VanDrunen, "Where We Are: Justification under Fire in the Contemporary Scene," in *Covenant, Justification, and Pastoral Ministry: Essays by the Faculty of Westminster Seminary California*, ed. R. Scott Clark (Phillipsburg: Presbyterian and Reformed Publishing, 2007), 48–57; Guy Prentiss Waters, *The Federal Vision and Covenant Theology: A Comparative Analysis* (Phillipsburg: Presbyterian and Reformed Publishing, 2006), 59–95.

THE LAW/GOSPEL CONTRAST
AND JUSTIFICATION BY FAITH

In contemporary discussion about Calvin's soteriology and the doctrine of justification by faith, there has been a general tendency to ignore, by-pass, and reject the law and gospel antithesis. In general, scholars have a tendency to focus on the union with Christ in their discussion on Calvin's view on salvation and the doctrine of justification by faith. This exclusive emphasis on the union with Christ without referring to the law and gospel distinction has opened a floodgate of theological confusion in the exposition of Calvin's doctrine of soteriology and justification by faith.[2]

Rich Lusk, an exponent of the Federal Vision, falsely argues that Calvin just paid "mere lip service to Luther's law and gospel antithesis":

> Calvin paid lip service to Luther's law/gospel antithesis, but it never became a controlling feature of his theology (and certainly not of his exegesis) as it was for Luther. In fact, Calvin took a much more positive view of the law's role in redemptive history. According to Calvin the law does indeed show up sin, but that is accidental to its real purpose, which is to serve as a moral guide.
>
> The law/gospel antithesis simply doesn't work as a hermeneutic for a number of reasons. We will focus on two, first showing that law and gospel actually perform the same (rather than contradictory) functions, and then showing that they are simply two phases in the same redemptive program.[3]

2. Cf. Craig B. Carpenter, "A Question of Union with Christ? Calvin and Trent on Justification," *Westminster Theological Journal* 64 (Fall, 2002): 363–86.

Injecting their monocovenantalism into Calvin's soteriology, the proponents of the Federal Vision exclusively emphasize the concept of the union with Christ, rejecting to apply the distinction between law and gospel. Inevitably, they view Calvin as a covenantal legalist after the pattern of Norman Shepherd's monocovenantal injection into Calvin's theology. See Mark Horn, "What's for Dinner?: Calvin's Continuity with the Bible's and the Ancient Church's Eucharistic Faith," in *The Federal Vision*, eds. Steve Wilkins & Duane Garner (Monroe: Athanasius Press, 2004), 127–49; Rich Lusk, "A Response to 'the Biblical Plan of Salvation,'" in *The Auburn Avenue Theology: Pros & Cons: Debating the Federal Vision*, ed. E. Calvin Beisner (Fort Lauderdale: Knox Theological Seminary, 2004), 118–48; Steve Wilkins, "Covenant, Baptism and Salvation," in *The Federal* Vision, eds. Steve Wilkins and Duane Garner (Monroe: Athanasius Press, 2004), 47–69; Douglas Wilson, "Union with Christ: An Overview of the Federal Vision," in *The Auburn Avenue Theology: Pros & Cons: Debating the Federal Vision*, ed. E. Calvin Beisner (Fort Lauderdale: Knox Theological Seminary, 2004), 1–8.

3. Lusk, "A Response to 'the Biblical Plan of Salvation,'" 131. For my critique against Rich Lusk's argument that Calvin did not utilize the law and gospel distinction in his theol-

However, my thesis is that we cannot discuss and exposit Calvin's soteriology and his doctrine of justification by faith without referring to the law and gospel antithesis, on the one hand, and union with Christ, on the other. Calvin used the law and gospel antithesis to exposit Pauline soteriology, especially salvation by grace alone (*sola gratia*) and justification by faith alone (*sola fide*). And at the same time, he used the concept of the mystical or spiritual union with Christ to put together all the soteriological blessings, including justification and sanctification.

From the perspective of Reformation theology, the central problem of the New Perspective on Paul is the denial of the distinction between law and gospel. Critically endorsing monocovenantalism of the New Perspective on Paul, Lusk falsely argues that the New Perspectivists never deny Luther's and Calvin's "*sola gratia* and *sola fide*":

> To the extent that Reformed Protestantism has individualized the message of salvation, and to the extent that N.T. Wright, J.D.G. Dunn, and others call us back to a corporate view of salvation, it does indeed look like a 'different gospel' is being proclaimed. But these 'different gospels' are not really at odds, any more than eggs

ogy and hermeneutics, see Jeon, *Covenant Theology and Justification by Faith*, 37–41. One of the best defense and analysis of the distinction between law and gospel, as well as letter and spirit in Reformed hermeneutics and homiletics, including Calvin, see R. Scott Clark, "Letter and Spirit: Law and Gospel in Reformed Preaching," in *Covenant, Justification, and Pastoral Ministry: Essays by the Faculty of Westminster Seminary California,* ed. R. Scott Clark (Phillipsburg: Presbyterian and Reformed Publishing, 2007), 331–63.

Against the contemporary Reformed theologians' challenge, including the Federal Visionists who argued that Calvin did not maintain the distinction between law and gospel in his hermeneutics and theology, Clark persuasively argues that Calvin brilliantly maintained law and gospel distinction, as well as letter and spirit in his hermeneutics and theology: "As a matter of history, the assertion that the law/gospel distinction is really Lutheran and not Reformed flies in the face of the overwhelming testimony of the Reformed tradition and confessions. Yet Peter A. Lillback juxtaposes Calvin's 'covenantal hermeneutic' with the Lutheran law/gospel hermeneutic. He claims that Calvin replaced Luther's law/gospel hermeneutic with a *spirit/letter* hermeneutic ... Calvin's account of the law/gospel distinction in 2 Corinthians 3 was actually clearer and more pointed than Luther's. It is evident from this passage and others that Calvin adopted the hermeneutical program of distinguishing between law and gospel. This is evident also in *Institutes* 3.11.14 where he attacked the Roman theologians of the Sorbonne (the *sophistae*) because they 'have fun and perverse delights' with Scripture, chiefly by failing to observe the law/gospel 'antithesis.' 'Legal righteousness' (*iustitiam legis*) is obtained by law keeping, whereas gospel righteousness, that is 'the righteousness of faith' (*iustitiam fidei*), is obtained 'if we believe that Christ was dead and raised.' This was his argument also in 3.11.17: The 'distinction' (*discrimen*) between the law and the gospel is that the law 'attributes justification to works,' whereas the gospel 'grants it gratuitously, without [our] works.'" Ibid., 340–42.

and omelets are at odds (to steal another of Wilson's illustrations). Wright's view gives the gospel a broader sweep (since he makes it clear the corporate includes the individual), but compared to our truncated version of the gospel it looks *really* different. The problem is our myopia. We've looked at the gospel from about two inches away for four centuries, and our long-distance vision is dysfunctional. Wright and others, meanwhile, are asking us to look at the gospel from 30,000 feet up. Or, to use an alternative illustration that Peter Leithart has used in his Eucharistic studies, we have gotten used to looking at the gospel through a narrow zoom lens; the 'New Perspective' gives us the wide angle view. Sure, it looks different, but that's to be expected. The 'New Perspective' never denies that Paul actually taught what Luther and Calvin claimed-namely, *sola gratia* and *sola fide*.[4]

Certainly, Calvin's *sola gratia* and *sola fide* are also mere lip service if Calvin made "mere lip service to Luther's law/gospel antithesis," as Lusk claims. In fact, Calvin's *sola gratia* and *sola fide* are deeply rooted in the Pauline antithesis between law and gospel. In short, there is no *sola gratia* and *sola fide* if there is no antithesis between law and gospel in Calvin's theology.

Calvin's careful analysis of the doctrine of justification by faith alone demonstrates his application of the hermeneutical principle of the antithesis between law and gospel. Luther's struggle to discover the Gospel finally concluded when he used this important hermeneutical tool, the antithesis between law and gospel. In his treatise, 'Sermon on the Twofold Righteousness,' on April 13, 1519, Luther articulated justification by faith alone, stating that "alien righteousness" (*iustitia aliena*) excludes the moralistic and ethical concepts of justification for "through faith in Christ," the righteousness of Christ which is "infinite righteousness" becomes "our righteousness."[5] Calvin used and applied this motif throughout his

4. Lusk, "A Response to 'the Biblical Plan of Salvation,'" 135–36. It is interesting to note that Lusk and the other exponents of the Federal Vision critically adapt the New Perspectives on Paul. I think that it is because both schools deny the Pauline distinction between law and gospel, which is foundational for the *sola gratia* and *sola fide*.

5. Martin Luther, *Luther's Works*, vol. 31. ed. Harold J. Grimm (Philadelphia: Muhlenberg Press, 1957), 297–306. We adopt the thesis that despite the theological difference and disagreement between Lutherans and Reformed, both agree on the doctrine of justification by faith alone. It is because both adopt a hermeneutical principle which assumes the antithesis between the principle of law and gospel in relation to justification. Cf. Louis Berkhof, *The History of Christian Doctrines* (Grand Rapids: Baker, 1995),

217-21 ; idem, *Systematic Theology* (Grand Rapids: Eerdmans, 1938; reprint, 1988), 510–26; D. Clair Davis, "A Challenge to Theonomy," in *Theonomy: A Reformed Critique*, eds. William S. Barker and W. Robert Godfrey (Grand Rapids,: Zondervan Publishing House, 1990), 398–402; idem, "How Did the Church in Rome Become Roman Catholicism," in *Roman Catholicism: Evangelical Protestants Analyze What Divides and Unites Us*, ed. John Armstrong (Chicago: Moody Press, 1994), 45–62; idem, "Inerrancy and Westminster Calvinism," in *Inerrancy and Hermeneutic: A Tradition, A Challenge, A Debate*, ed. Harvie M. Conn (Grand Rapids: Baker, 1990), 35–46; W. R. Godfrey, "Law and Gospel," in *New Dictionary of Theology*, eds. Sinclair B. Ferguson and David F. Wright (Downers Grove/ Leicester: InterVarsity Press, 1988), 379–80; idem, "What Really Caused the Great Divide," in *Roman Catholicism: Evangelical Protestants Analyze What Divides and Unites Us*, ed. John Armstrong (Chicago: Moody Press, 1994), 65–82; Charles Hodge, *Systematic Theology* (reprint, Grand Rapids: Eerdmans, 1995), 3: 114–212; Michael Horton, "What Still Keeps Us Apart?" in *Roman Catholicism: Evangelical Protestants Analyze What Divides and Unites Us*, ed. John Armstrong (Chicago: Moody Press, 1994), 245–66; J. Gresham Machen, *What Is Faith* (New York: The Macmillan Company, 1925); Thomas R. Schreiner, *The Law and Its Fulfillment: A Pauline Theology of Law* (Grand Rapids: Baker, 1993), 14–16; R. C. Sproul, *Faith Alone: The Evangelical Doctrine of Justification* (Grand Rapids: Baker; reprint, 1996); Robert B. Strimple, "Roman Catholic Theology Today," in *Roman Catholicism: Evangelical Protestants Analyze What Divides and Unites Us*, ed. John Armstrong (Chicago: Moody Press, 1994), 85–117; Cornelius Van Til, *The Sovereignty of Grace: An Appraisal of G. C. Berkouwer's View of Dordt* (Phillipsburg: Presbyterian and Reformed Publishing, 1969), 8–9, 12.

Louis Berkhof, for example, rightly states that Luther and Calvin agreed on the important doctrine of justification which was a common denominator of evangelical consensus of the Protestant Reformation although they had many different aspects of theological disagreement: "But however Calvin may have differed from Luther as to the order of salvation, he quite agreed with him on the nature and importance of the doctrine of justification by faith. In their common opposition to Rome they both describe it as an act of free grace, and as a forensic act which does not change the inner life of man but only the judicial relationship in which he stands to God. They do not find the ground for it in the inherent righteousness of the believer, but only in the imputed righteousness of Jesus Christ, which the sinner appropriates by faith. Moreover, they deny that it is a progressive work of God, asserting that it is instantaneous and at once complete, and hold that the believer can be absolutely sure that he is forever translated from a state of wrath and condemnation to one of favour and acceptance." Berkhof, *Christian Doctrines*, 220. The Protestant Reformation consensus on the *articulus stantis et cadentis ecclesiae* is summarized in the acute pen of Michael Horton: "It is the *articulus ecclesiae stantis et cadentis*, the 'article by which the church stands and falls,' the Reformers declared of the doctrine of justification. 'As long as a person is unaware of this doctrine' and the distinction between the law and the gospel, Luther insisted, 'he is no different than a Jew, a Turk [Moslem] or a Heathen.' . . . It was not enough for the Reformers to say that we were saved by grace. Nor, indeed, was it even enough to say that we were saved by grace alone. Thus far they would not have said anything that a typical Augustinian would not have affirmed in his day. What Luther and the other Reformers insisted on was grace alone through faith alone. In medieval doctrine, justification was considered what evangelicals call 'regeneration' or the new birth. In baptism, the child received his or her 'first

theological system. Calvin, in his final edition of *Institutes of the Christian Religion* of 1559 and in his commentaries, clearly expounded justification by faith alone, employing the law and gospel hermeneutical principle that Luther developed and applied.

Man is justified by faith, Calvin pointed out, excluding "the righteousness of works." Man embraces "the righteousness of Christ through faith, and clothed in it, appears in God's sight not as a sinner but as a righteous man. Therefore, justification is the acceptance by which God receives us into his favor as righteous men. It consists in the remission of sins *and* the imputation of Christ's righteousness."[6] Contrary to this, the medieval Sophists held that man is justified by *fide et operibus*, by "both faith and works." Their major theological problem, according to Calvin, was a failure to admit a radical antithesis between the principle of law and gospel, elaborated by Paul in Romans 10:5–9 and Galatians 3:11–12:

> Still they do not observe that in the contrast between the righteousness of the law and of the gospel, which Paul elsewhere introduces, all works are excluded, whatever title may grace them [Gal. 3:11–12]. For he teaches that this is the righteousness of the law, that he who has fulfilled what the law commands should obtain salvation; but this is the righteousness of faith, to believe that Christ died and rose again [Rom. 10:5, 9].[7]

To be sure, Calvin applied the Pauline antithesis between law and gospel as an absolutely essential hermeneutical and theological background for the doctrine of justification by faith alone in Jesus Christ who died and rose again in his exposition of Galatians 3:11–12 and Romans 10:5–9. The distinction between law and gospel (*Legis et Evangelii discrimen*) excludes

---

justification,' and this began the process of sanctification. Thus, justification was seen as the beginning of moral change, and only at the end of the process—assuming one made proper use of the sacraments, confessed one's sins verbally to a priest, and died without having committed a mortal sin—could one hope to be justified. In fact, the process actually continued beyond the grave, in purgatory, where the remaining corruptions and transgressions were purged. The whole process may indeed be ascribed to 'grace alone,' and yet the way one received this 'grace' was, in effect, by meriting." Horton, "What Still Keeps Us Apart?" 254–55.

6. John Calvin, *Institutes of the Christian Religion*, ed. John T. McNeill, trans. Ford Lewis Battles, in *Library of Christian Classics*, vols. 20–21 (Philadelphia: The Westminster Press, 1975), 3.9.2.

7. Ibid., 3.11.14. In Calvin's hermeneutics, it is pertinent to notice that the principles of the promises of the law and the gospel are antithetical, which is manifested in Leviticus 18:5, Romans 10:5–9 and Galatians 3:11–12. Ibid., 3.17.3.

all concepts of works in Calvin's doctrine of justification by faith alone, for *faith* embraces the righteousness of God. Calvin emphatically explained how Paul clearly analyzes this in his Epistles:

> For faith is said to justify because it receives and embraces the righteousness offered in the gospel. Moreover, because righteousness is said to be offered through the gospel. For in comparing the law and the gospel in the letter to the Romans he says: "the righteousness that is of the law" is such that "the man who practices these things will live by them" [Rom. 10:5]. But the "righteousness that is of faith" [Rom. 10:6] announces salvation "if you believe in your heart and confess with your mouth that Jesus is Lord and that the Father raised him from the dead" [Rom. 10:9 p.]. *Do you see how he makes this the distinction between law and gospel: that the former attributes righteousness to works, the latter bestows free righteousness apart from the help of works* [Emphasis added]? This is an important passage, and one that can extricate us from many difficulties if we understand that that righteousness which is given us through the gospel has been freed of all conditions of the law. Here is the reason why he so often opposes the promise to the law, as things mutually contradictory: "If the inheritance is by the law, it is no longer by promise" [Gal. 3:18]; and passages in the same chapter that express this idea. Now, to be sure, the law itself has its own promises. Therefore, in the promises of the gospel there must be something distinct and different unless we would admit that the comparison is inept. But what sort of difference will this be, other than that the gospel promises are free and dependent solely upon God's mercy, while the promises of the law depend upon the condition of works?[8]

Likewise, Calvin interpreted Romans 10:5–9 in light of the antithesis between law and gospel. Moreover, he emphasized that Romans 10:5–9 is "an important passage" to make a distinction between "law righteousness" and "faith righteousness," which is the concrete biblical and hermeneutical background of justification by faith alone (*sola fide*). Thus, the antithesis between law and gospel is a biblical theological reference point upon which Calvin drew justification by faith alone, excluding human merit and obedience in this arena. This point is contrasted with the background of the medieval Schoolmen's concept of meritorious salvation, which was embraced in *meritum de congruo et meritum de condigno*.

8. Ibid., 3.11.17.

After Calvin discussed Romans 10:5–9 as "an important passage" to denote the antithesis between law and gospel, he began to pay close attention to another important Pauline passage to discuss the same subject matter, namely Galatians 3:11–12. Commenting on Galatians 3:11–12, Calvin separated the two opposing principles of works and faith. It is important to grasp Calvin's emphasis that "law righteousness" is distinguished from "faith righteousness" in light of the antithesis between law and gospel:

> The second passage is this: 'It is evident that no man is justified before God by the law. For the righteous shall live by faith [cf. Hab. 2:4]. But the law is not of faith; rather, the man who does these things shall live in them' [Gal 3:11–12, Comm., cf. Vg.]. How would this argument be maintained otherwise than by agreeing that works do not enter the account of faith but must be utterly separated. The law, he says, is different from faith. Why? Because works are required for law righteousness. Therefore it follows that they are not required for faith righteousness. From this relation it is clear that those who are justified by faith are justified apart from the merit of works—in fact, without the merit of works. For faith receives that righteousness which the gospel bestows. Now the gospel differs from the law in that it does not link righteousness to works but lodges it solely in God's mercy.[9]

In other words, "law righteousness" seeks to be justified by the merit of works in opposition to "faith righteousness." Works righteousness, emphasized Calvin, is only possible "in perfect and complete observance of the law." From this biblical logic, Calvin argued that man cannot be justified by the merit of works, unless one reaches "to the highest peak of perfection":

> Now we have disposed of the main issue in this discussion: If righteousness is supported by works, in God's sight it must entirely collapse; and it is confined solely to God's mercy, solely to communion with Christ, and therefore solely to faith. But let us carefully note that this is the chief turning point of the matter in order to avoid becoming entangled in the common delusion, not of the common folk only, but also of the learned. For as soon as there is a question concerning justification of faith or of works, they rush off to those passages which seem to attribute to works

9. Ibid., 3.11.18.

some merit in God's sight. As if justification of works would be fully proved by showing that they have some value with God.

To be sure, we have clearly shown above that works righteousness consists solely in perfect and complete observance of the law. From this it follows that no man is justified by works unless, having been raised to the highest peak of perfection.[10]

After making a careful distinction between "law righteousness" and "faith righteousness," Calvin drew a biblical and theological conclusion that indeed "man is justified by faith alone" (*hominem sola fide iustificari*) in his interpretation of Romans 3:28, agreeing with Luther's *sola fide*. In that respect, it is obvious in Calvin's soteriology that *sola gratia* and *sola fide* are not mere lip service or an empty slogan from the Protestant Reformation. Calvin's ideas about *sola gratia* and *sola fide* are deeply rooted in his comprehensive understanding of the Pauline soteriology, guided by the antithesis between law and gospel:

> Now the readers see how fairly the Sophists today cavil against our doctrine when we say that *man is justified by faith alone* [Emphasis added] [Rom. 3:28]. They dare not deny that man is justified by faith because it recurs so often in Scripture. But since the word 'alone' is nowhere expressed, they do not allow this addition to be made. Is it so? But what will they reply to these words of Paul where he contends that righteousness cannot be of faith unless it be free [Rom. 4:2 ff.]? How will a free gift agree with works? With what chicaneries will they elude what he says in another passage, that God's righteousness is revealed in the gospel, surely no mutilated or half righteousness but a full and perfect righteousness is contained there. The law therefore has no place in it.[11]

While Calvin rejected the meritorious concept of works and salvation in the postlapsarian state, he nevertheless affirmed the merit of works in the prelapsarian Adamic state, quoting Augustine's *On the Predestination of the Saints*, 15:31: "For in one place Augustine speaks thus: 'Let *human merits, which perished through Adam* [Emphasis added], here keep silence, and let God's grace reign through Jesus Christ.' Again: 'The saints attribute nothing to their merits; they will attribute all to thy mercy alone, O God.'"[12]

---

10. Ibid., 3.15.1

11. Ibid., 3.11.19

12. Ibid., 3.15.2. Thus, Calvin's point in respect to the law is that if man fulfills the requirement of the law, then it is *meritorious* in relation to salvation and justification, which

In Calvin's theology, the antithesis between Adam and Christ, necessarily entails the meritorious obedience to God's given law, which requires nothing but perfect obedience to obtain the eschatological heavenly blessings. In that respect, Calvin adequately limited meritorious obedience to the prelapsarian Adam as a representative head of all human beings, and the last Adam, who is the perfect and sinless mediator of the New Covenant.

Meanwhile, Calvin, analyzing justification by faith alone in the proper hermeneutical context of the distinction between law and gospel, was not an antinomian. So, he put good works in *the proper place*, which is not justification but sanctification. Likewise, he emphasized that good works in the Christian life are necessary, as Paul demonstrates in 2 Timothy 3:16–17. They, however, are not meritorious, since salvation is based on the principle of *sola gratia*, excluding human merits. In other words, the principle of *soli Deo gloria* of Matthew 5:16 is the ultimate point of reference of believers' good works against the Schoolmen's anthropocentric notion of salvation culminating from the merit of human works. Again, Calvin highly emphasized that "Christ's merit alone" (*Solo Christi merito*) is the only foundation for believers' justification, and it is the concrete reason why justification by faith alone, excluding the merit of human works, is valid: "Finally, I say that it is of no value unless we give prior place to the doctrine that we are justified by Christ's merit alone, which is grasped

---

is not possible in the fallen state: "So also ought we to recognize that God's benevolence has been set forth for us in the law, if we could merit it by works, but it never comes to us by this merit." Ibid., 3.17.2; "We assuredly do not question that the righteousness of the law consists in works, and not even that righteousness consists in the worth and merits of works. But it has not yet been proved that we are justified by works unless they produce some one man who has fulfilled the law." Ibid., 3.17.13.

As observed in the quotation, we may draw a legitimate conclusion from Calvin's analysis that works in the *foedus legale* are meritorious in an ideal situation. Merit can be identified as "the value or worth of a good or obedient act or the act itself." In this respect, the problem of the medieval concept of merit is that human works contribute to salvation in the notion of *meritum de congruo et meritum de condigno*. In opposition to this, the Protestant scholastics suggest that human acts or acts of obedience are not meritorious in the fallen world. As such, good works, flowing from the divine grace, are God's acts in us and cannot do anything for man's salvation. According to this view, "only perfect righteousness can be meritorious, only Christ merits life in and of himself, not for himself, but vicariously for us." Thus, *meritum Christi* is the fundamental ground of salvation. Richard A. Muller, *Dictionary of Latin and Greek Theological Terms: Drawn Principally from Protestant Scholastic Theology* (Grand Rapids: Baker, 1985), 190–92. In that respect, if the absolute distinction between the covenants of works and grace is a legitimate principle in the light of biblical and systematic theology, then Adam's perfect obedience in the original covenant of works would have been *merited*.

through faith, but by no merits of our own works, because no men can be fit for the pursuit of holiness save those who have first imbibed this doctrine."[13] In this sense, it is proper to state that there are no *sola gratia* and *sola fide* without "Christ's merit." In other words, *sola gratia* and *sola fide*, in Calvin's theology, stand and fall together with "Christ's merit."

Following Norman Shepherd's "covenantal paradigm" in which he rejects "works/merit principle" in the background of soteriology, Rich Lusk, as a Federal Viosionist, misrepresents Calvin's concept of the meritorious obedience of Christ:

> Both Rome and the covenant of works proponents agree that at root salvation is a meritorious program. They agree that justice in the abstract, rather than grace and sonship, is at the bottom of everything. Unfortunately, the Reformers did not quite go the whole way in their rejection of a merit/works paradigm. Instead, they tended to relocate merit, removing it from the sinner's works

13. Calvin, *Institutes*, 3.16.3. The problem of *meritum de congruo et meritum de condigno* in the medieval scholastics lies in the fact that it fails to distinguish between law and gospel or grace in the discussion of justification and salvation. In this respect, Calvin properly denoted that merit is only possible based on perfect obedience and can be predicated only by Christ's obedience and Adam's prefall obedience, although this did not happen in the latter case. Thus, there is a logical connection from the distinction between law and grace to the antithesis between merit and grace. In other words, the Schoolmen failed to grasp justification by faith alone apart from good works since they do not make a legitimate distinction between law and grace along with the antithesis between merit and grace. For an incisive discussion on the problem of merit in Roman Catholic theology and the Reformers' reaction to it, see Sproul, *Faith Alone*, 135–51. Here, Sproul properly argues that merit and grace are antithetical in the Reformers' discussion on the doctrine of justification and salvation; and this is set over against the Schoolmen's concept of *gracious merit*: "Rome's view of merit and grace contains an unresolved paradox. On the one hand Rome insists on speaking of merit, while on the other she insists that this merit is rooted in grace. The Germans expressed this paradox by coining the term *Gnadenlohn*, 'gracious merit.' . . . In common language *merit* is usually understood in distinction from grace. The two are polar opposites. To conjoin them paradoxically in certain contexts into a concept of 'gracious merit' sounds like an oxymoron. The New Testament sharply distinguishes between grace and debt. The Reformers made every effort to keep this distinction clean . . . For Rome grace makes human merit possible. For the Reformers grace makes such merit impossible. If we do what we do by grace, then it is seriously misleading to speak of merit at all." Ibid., 148–49. For a further discussion on the concept of merit, its diverse development from the early Church to the Reformation, and its adaptation and refutation, see: Alister McGrath, *Iustitia Dei: A History of the Christian Doctrine of Justification* (Cambridge: Cambridge University Press, 1986), 1:109–18; Heiko A. Oberman, "The Tridentine Decree on Justification in the Light of Late Medieval Theology," in *Journal for Theology and the Church 3: Distinctive Protestant and Catholic Themes Revisited*, ed. Robert W. Funk (New York: Harper and Row, 1967), 28–54.

and placing it in Christ's works. But even Rome can affirm that all merit is found in Christ. A more drastic reworking of the medieval soteriological model is called for.

Calvin nearly accomplished such a paradigm shift. While the debate over whether or not Calvin believed the prelapsarian relationship with Adam was a covenant of works has not been settled, he clearly repudiated the notion that Christ merited God's favor in any strict sense. If Jesus attained merit by his work it was simply because the Father chose to receive as such.[14]

Unlike Lusk's claim, Calvin never sought to make a paradigm shift to soften the importance of the meritorious obedience of Christ as the background for sinners' salvation *sola gratia* and justification *sola fide*. In fact, there is no salvation without the meritorious obedience of Christ in Calvin's theology. In addition, the development and adaptation of distinction between the covenant of works and the covenant of grace in the Reformed orthodoxy are simply covenantal and redemptive historical implications of the distinction between law and gospel while Calvin carefully maintained the captivating drama of redemptive history, inaugurated in Genesis 3:15 under the rubric of the one covenant of grace.

Again, Lusk misrepresents Calvin in regards to the concept of "Christ's merit" in his analysis of *Institutes*, 2.17.1:

> To be sure, in *Institutes*, 2.17.1, Calvin retains usage of the word *merit*. But he also virtually refines it out of existence by subordinating merit to mercy. He rooted the 'merit' of Christ in the deeper grace of the Father rather than strict justice:
>
>> God solely of his own good pleasure appointed him Mediator to obtain salvation for us. Hence it is absurd to set Christ's merit against God's mercy.... *Apart from God's good pleasure Christ could not merit anything.* To sum up: inasmuch as Christ's merit depends upon God's grace alone, which has ordained this manner of salvation for us, it is just as properly opposed to all human righteousness as God's grace is. [italic mine]
>
> Note the nature of this argument: if everything Jesus received from the Father was of grace, how much more is this is the case for sinners? But if that's so, then speaking of sinners-or even sinless creatures-meriting something from God is absurd.[15]

14. Lusk, "A Response to 'The Biblical Plan of Salvation,'" 144.
15. Ibid., 144–45.

Lusk misinterprets Calvin's remarks about "Christ's merit, subordinate to God's mercy." Here, Calvin viewed a broader picture that God had a sovereign plan to save his elected people by his grace alone (*sola gratia*). In doing so, God ordained to save the elected sinners, not through imperfect "human righteousness," but, through "Christ's merit" alone. In that sense, if we understand the relationship between merit and grace properly in Calvin's theology, then merit and grace are antithetical as law and gospel are antithetical in the milieu of the forensic understanding of justification and the gracious aspect of salvation.

Calvin's unambiguous affirmation of "Christ's merit" (*meritum Christi*) is not an unfortunate reality as Lusk mistakenly argues. Rather, in doing so, Calvin laid out a concrete theological foundation of *sola gratia* and *sola fide*. In light of this, in discussing justification by faith alone in Calvin's theology, the principles of law and faith are contrasted, without any mixing between law and gospel. Calvin, in his commentary, stated this issue clearly: "The major is proved by the difference in the methods of justification. The law justifies him who fulfills all its precepts, while faith justifies those who are destitute of the merit of works, and who rely on Christ alone. To be justified by our own merit, and to be justified by the grace of another, are two schemes which cannot be reconciled: one of them must be overturned by the other."[16] Calvin went on to say that "the contradiction between the law and faith lies in the matter of justification."[17]

Good works, in this sense, are only the *fruit* of faith.[18] Indeed, although believers are justified by faith alone in respect to the principle of the covenant of grace, God requires "uprightness and sanctity of life" for believers admitted to "the fellowship of the covenant."[19] A justified believer is "clothed with Christ's righteousness." Accordingly, believers' good works are acceptable to God although they are imperfect, since they are covered by the perfection of Christ.[20] Moreover, good works by believers will be applied to their heavenly reward by the principle of the adopted

16. John Calvin, *Commentaries on the Epistles of Paul to the Galatians,* trans. William Pringle (Edinburgh: Calvin Translation Society, 1843; reprint, Grand Rapids: Baker, 1996), 3:11.

17. Ibid., 3:12

18. Cf. W. Stanford Reid, "Justification by Faith According to John Calvin," *Westminster Theological Journal* 42 (1980): 296–307; Calvin, *Institutes,* 3.11.5–20

19. Ibid., 3.17.5.

20. Ibid., 3.17.8.

sons' right of inheritance as written in Matthew 25:35–37, but their heavenly reward is not by "the merit of works" as the Sophists argue because it is the outworking of the free covenant of God's mercy. It is the divine promise in respect to good works.[21] Thus, Calvin's understanding of good works, produced in progressive sanctification as the law is applied, provides a concrete biblical theological answer to *antinomianism*. On the other hand, the antithesis between law and gospel or grace is a definite hermeneutical principle of justification by faith alone, apart from good works, and provides an answer to *legalism* or *neonomianism*.

LAW / GOSPEL ANTITHESIS AND THE IMPUTATION OF THE RIGHTEOUSNESS OF CHRIST

In contemporary discussion about the doctrine of justification by faith, the imputation of the active obedience of Christ has been the primary object of heated debate. From the perspective of traditional Calvin scholarship, it has been known as one of the twin blessings of the forensic nature of justification with the forgiveness of sins in Calvin's theology. In the analysis of Calvin's doctrine of justification by faith, Norman Shepherd and the exponents of Federal Vision argue that Calvin did not embrace the concept of the imputation of the active obedience of Christ.[22]

---

21. Ibid., 3.18.1–8.

22. For my critical analysis about Norman Shepherd's monocovenantal injection into Calvin's theology, denying the imputation of the righteousness of Christ in believers' justification, see Jeon, *Covenant Theology and Justification by Faith*, 54–67. For a comprehensive discussion about the theological history of the imputation of the righteousness of Christ in believers' justification, as well as the two aspects of one obedience of Christ such as active and passive obedience of Christ, including Calvin's theological affirmation of it, see R. Scott Clark, "Do This and Live: Christ's Active Obedience as the Ground of Justification," in *Covenant, Justification, and Pastoral Ministry: Essays by the Faculty of Westminster Seminary California*, ed. R. Scott Clark (Phillipsburg: Presbyterian and Reformed Publishing, 2007), 229–65. Clark rightly argues that Luther and Calvin alike held "the imputation of active obedience" in sinners' justification. Although the theological terminology of the distinction between the active and passive obedience of Christ surfaced in the 1570s, the essence of the two aspects of one obedience of Christ was already fully present in Calvin's thought: "The essence of the doctrine of the imputation of active obedience is the view that Christ's obedience and our justification have two parts: the remission of sins and the imputation to sinners of Christ's obedience to the law for believers. From the moment Luther became a Protestant he taught that Christ's merits, which was nothing more than shorthand for 'Christ's obedience to the law for me,' are imputed to the believer. Calvin was heartily one with Luther on the doctrine of justification and from him inherited the foundation of what came to be articulated as the doctrine of the imputation of active obedience. The mere

Norman Shepherd, as one of the most influential theologian to the Federal Vision, argues that there is no "imputation of active obedience in Calvin, Ursinus, or the Heidelberg Catechism":

> We do not find a belief in the imputation of active obedience in Calvin, Ursinus, or the Heidelberg Catechism for the reason that their understanding of justification as the remission of sins did not require it and they did not find it in the Bible. The very few Bible texts quoted by later theologians in support of this doctrine are understood by earlier theologians to refer to the imputation of the righteousness Christ wrought out in his suffering and death for his people in obedience to the will of his heavenly father.[23]

It is interesting to see how Norman Shepherd denies "the imputation of the active obedience" of Christ in the doctrine of justification in Calvin, as well as other early Reformed theologians, such as Ursinus. It is true that Calvin did not make an explicit statement in respect to the two aspects of the meritorious obedience of Christ, namely, the active and passive obedience of Christ as the latter Reformed orthodox theologians defined them. However, I would suggest that Calvin's distinction between law and gospel in relation to *sola gratia* and *sola fide* necessarily entails and embraces

---

absence of the later technical terms *obedientia active et passive* [which did not come into use until the 1570s] should not deter us from observing the substance of the doctrine in Calvin. It should also be remembered that the Karg controversy did not begin until 1563, just one year before his death and after he had finished the final revisions to the *Institutes of the Christian Religion*.

In fact, Calvin wrote repeatedly of Christ's entire obedience, under which discussion he included Christ's obedient life before his passion and by which he says Christ earned our redemption. This is evident in his 1539 commentary on Romans [at 5:19] and in the 1559 edition of *Institutes of the Christian Religion*, where he argued that it is not sanctity that forms faith [makes it efficacious] but rather Christ's obedience to the law [*Institutes* 3.11.23]. God accepts sinners only because the *obedientia Christi* is imputed to us. Against Osiander's doctrine of justification by 'essential justice' [the infusion of Christ's person into the Christian], Calvin argued that the righteousness that is 'reputed' [*reputari*] is the obedience and sacrificial death of Christ." Ibid., 230–31.

23. Shepherd, "Justification by Works in Reformed Theology," 115. Rich Lusk, following the monocovenantal pattern of Norman Shepherd, has made a similar argument, injecting monocovenantalism into the theologies of Calvin and early Reformed theology, see Lusk, "A Response to 'the Biblical Plan of Salvation,'" 140: "To be more specific, the freight often carried by the doctrine of Christ's active obedience in Reformed dogmatics ought to more properly be placed on the resurrection. Many earlier Reformed theologians were able to construct a thoroughly evangelical doctrine of justification without reference to the imputation of Christ's active obedience (e.g., William Twisse, Richard Vines, and Thomas Gataker)."

two aspects of the one meritorious obedience of Christ, namely the active and passive obedience of Christ through his entire life and death.

Norman Shepherd, rejecting the distinction between law and gospel in Calvin's soteriology, also rejects the imputation of the active obedience of Christ, as well. In Shepherd's radical monocovenantal reinterpretation of Calvin's doctrine of justification, justification is virtually synonymous with "the forgiveness of sin":

> My point in taking up Ursinus and the Heidelberg Catechism is simply to demonstrate that in the early phase of the Reformation our Reformed theologians accurately reflected the teaching of Paul. I could have demonstrated the same point from Calvin and other early confessions. *Justification is simply the forgiveness of sin grounded in the death and resurrection of Christ* [Emphasis added]. This fact explains the concurrence between Luther and Calvin on the doctrine of justification.[24]

Norman Shepherd and the Federal Visionists deny the distinction between law and gospel as a common denominator between Luther and Calvin in the doctrine of justification by faith alone (*sola fide*). However, we need to be reminded that Calvin interpreted justification by faith alone in light of the distinction between law and gospel as already discussed. It is the reason why Calvin viewed the doctrine of justification in terms of twin pillars by which he understood twin blessings of justification as "the remission of sins and the imputation of Christ's righteousness" as Calvin powerfully demonstrated in his *Institutes of the Christian Religion* 3.11.2. In Calvin, "the remission of sins" has direct bearings with the passive obedience of Christ while "the imputation of Christ's righteousness" has a close connection to the imputation of active obedience of Christ.

However, Shepherd, in his response to Clark's criticism about the denial of the imputation of the active obedience of Christ in sinners' justification among the Federal Visionists and others, including himself, is very skeptical about whether there is theological ground to be found in Calvin about the imputation of the active obedience of Christ: "It is undoubtedly true that for Calvin the justification of sinners is grounded in the imputation of the obedience of Christ, but it is not all clear that Calvin means by this the imputation of the *active* obedience of Christ."[25]

---

24. Shepherd, "Justification by Works in Reformed Theology," 111.

25. Norman Shepherd, "The Imputation of Active Obedience," in *A Faith That Is Never Alone: a Response to Westminster Seminary California*, ed. P. Andrew Sandlin (La

I have already suggested that we may interpret Calvin's *Institutes* 3.11.2 as a classical understanding of the twin pillars of the spiritual blessings of forensic justification, namely "the remission of sins" in relation to the passive obedience of Christ and "the imputation of Christ's righteousness," which has a direct bearing on the active obedience of Christ. However, Shepherd reinterprets Calvin's understanding of "the imputation of Christ's righteousness" in sinners' justification, based upon his monocovenantalism where he denies the antithesis between law and gospel, injecting it into Calvin's theology. In doing so, he denies the imputation of active obedience of Christ in Calvin as he denies the antithesis between law and gospel in Calvin's theology, which is the theological background of the imputation of the active obedience of Christ. So, Shepherd falsely identifies justification with "the remission of sins," grounded on "the *passive* obedience of Christ, specifically his death on the cross for us and in our place," taking away the imputation of the active obedience of Christ in Calvin's theology:

> Calvin begins his discussion of justification in the *Institutes* in Book 3, Chapter 11. At the end of section 2 Calvin writes, "Therefore, we explain justification simply as the acceptance with which God receives us into his favor as righteous men. And we say that it consists in the remission of sins and the imputation of Christ's righteousness.
>
> The key to understanding Calvin is his point that justification consists in the remission of sins. Because our sins are forgiven, we are accepted as righteous men and received into God's favor. This forgiveness is obtained by the imputation of Christ's righteousness, and (as will be discussed below) for Calvin the righteousness of Christ that obtains forgiveness of sin is the *passive* obedience of Christ, specifically his death on the cross for us and in our place. As Calvin goes on to explain his teaching in section 3, there is no mention of or reference to the imputation of active obedience because justification is the remission of sins, and this forgiveness is not grounded in the imputation of active obedience.[26]

Undoubtedly, Calvin discussed the two-fold spiritual blessings of justification as "the remission of sins and the imputation of Christ's righteousness" in light of the distinction between justification by works

---

Grange: Kerygma Press, 2007), 251.

26. Ibid.

and faith, which is the natural theological outworking of the distinction between law and gospel. In that sense, Shepherd's denial of the imputation of the active obedience of Christ in Calvin's doctrine of justification is another good example of how he and the Federal Visionists, as his theological followers, misrepresent Calvin's theology from their own monocovenantal perspective:

> But that we may not stumble on the very threshold—and this would happen if we should enter upon a discussion of a thing unknown—first let us explain what these expressions mean: that man is justified in God's sight, and that he is justified by faith or works. He is said to be justified in God's sight who is both reckoned righteous in God's judgment and has been accepted on account of his righteousness . . . Accordingly, wherever there is sin, there also the wrath and vengeance of God show themselves. Now he is justified who is reckoned in the condition not of a sinner, but of a righteous man; and for that reason, he stands firm before God's judgment seat while all sinners fall. If an innocent accused person be summoned before the judgment seat of a fair judge, where he will be judged according to his innocence, he is said to be 'justified' before the judge. Thus, justified before God is the man who, freed from the company of sinners, has God to witness and affirm his righteousness. In the same way, therefore, he in whose life that purity and holiness will be found which deserves a testimony of righteousness before God's throne will be said to be justified by works, or else he who, by the wholeness of his works, can meet and satisfy God's judgment. On the contrary, justified by faith is he who, excluded from the righteousness of works, grasps the righteousness of Christ through faith, and clothed in it, appears in God's sight not as a sinner but as a righteous man.
>
> Therefore, we explain justification simply as the acceptance with which God receives us into his favor as righteous man. And we say that it consists in the remission of sins and the imputation of Christ's righteousness.[27]

As such, Calvin never defined justification as coterminous with "the forgiveness of sin" as Shepherd falsely argues. Rather, Calvin unambiguously emphasized that believers in the forensic justification receive "forgiveness of sins, and clothed with Christ's righteousness." In other words, for Calvin, "forgiveness of sins" is closely tied to the passive obedience of Christ while the gift of being "clothed with Christ's righteousness" is

27. Calvin, *Institutes*, 3.11.2.

directly related to the imputation of the active obedience of Christ, although he did not use those terminologies:

> If we are to determine a price for works according to their worth, we say that they are unworthy to come before God's sight; that man, accordingly, has no works in which to glory before God; that hence, stripped of all help from works, he is justified by faith alone. But we define justification as follows: the sinner, receive into communion with Christ, is reconciled to God by his grace, while cleansed by Christ's blood, *he obtains forgiveness of sins, and clothed with Christ's righteousness* [Emphasis added] as if it were his own, he stands confident before the heavenly judgment seat.[28]

In his exegesis of Romans 5:19 and 8:3–4, Calvin beautifully portrayed the imputation of the righteousness of Christ as a result of Christ's fulfillment of all the requirements of the law in his life and death. Moreover, it is important to notice that Calvin made the antithesis between Adam and Christ in the milieu of Romans 5:19 in which he expounded a classical expression of the imputation of "the obedience of Christ" in believers' justification. In Calvin, there is no other way to receive the righteousness of Christ except that "we obtain through imputation" (*imputatione consequimur*):

> You see that our righteousness is not in us but in Christ, that we possess it only because we are partakers in Christ; indeed, with him we possess all its riches. And this does not contradict what he teaches elsewhere, that sin has been condemned for sin in Christ's flesh that the righteousness of the law might be fulfilled in us [Rom. 8:3–4]. The only fulfillment he alludes to is that which we obtain through imputation. For in such a way does the Lord Christ share his righteousness with us that, in some wonderful manner, he pours into us enough of his power to meet the judgment of God. It is quite clear that Paul means exactly the same thing in another statement, which he had put a little before: "As we were made sinners by one man's disobedience, so we have been justified by one man's obedience" [Rom. 5:19 p.]. To declare that by him alone we are accounted righteous, what else is this but to lodge our righteousness in Christ's obedience, because the obedience of Christ is reckoned to us as if it were our own.[29]

---

28. Ibid., 3.17.8.
29. Ibid., 3.11.23.

In Calvin's theology, the presupposition of justification by faith alone, through the imputation of Christ's righteousness, is that there is no mixture between law and gospel. In other words, we cannot talk about the imputed righteousness of Christ in justification without a theological point of reference, namely, the antithesis between law and gospel.

Because of Christ's perfect obedience to the law, his righteousness is imputed to us through faith apart from good works. So, Calvin properly argued that the imputation of Christ's righteousness is the ultimate basis of our justification, since Christ was once and for all the "atoning sacrifice of sin." Therefore, our righteousness is an alien righteousness which is only in Christ.[30] In that sense, faith is "merely passive" and the "instrumental cause" in our justification because it is a free gift of God whereby Christ's righteousness is imputed to us.[31] No one, however, is justified by works because "works righteousness" is possible only in "perfect and complete observance of the law."[32]

Shepherd and the Federal Visionists identify their theology not only with Calvin but also with John Murray. Interestingly, denying the imputation of the active obedience of Christ in Calvin and the early Reformed theology, including the Heidelberg Catechism and the Belgic Confession, Shepherd quotes Murray's writing to justify his rejection to the active obedience of Christ:

> My third objection to the imputation of active obedience is that it is not the view of the original Reformation. In a formal sense this is not a valid objection because we ought to be making progress in our understanding of the word of God, and progress will mean moving beyond and perhaps even moving away from the original Reformers in some ways. In the words of John Murray,
>
> > However epochal have been the advances made at certain periods and however great the contributions of particular men we may not suppose that theological construction ever reaches definite finality. There is the danger of a stagnant traditionalism and we must be alert to this danger, on the one hand, as to that of discarding our historical moorings, on the other.
>
> The problem is that Reformed theology took a wrong turn toward the end of the sixteenth century with the introduction

30. Ibid., 3.11.19–21; 3.14.10.
31. Ibid., 3.13.5; 3.14.17.
32. Ibid., 3.15.1.

of an unbiblical works principle into soteriology. We need the humility now to go back to the point where we took the wrong turn in order to get out our bearings from the word of God and to move on from there.[33]

Thus, Shepherd blames the covenant of works, developed and adopted by the latter Reformed orthodox theologians during the latter part of the sixteenth century, on the imputation of the active obedience of Christ for believers' forensic justification. Again, he misinterprets historical theology. The imputation of the active obedience of Christ is not only related to the covenant of works but also to the distinction between law and gospel. It is a well known fact that Murray did not like the terminology, the covenant of works as a means for the eschatological justification and heavenly inheritance for the prelapsarian Adamic status, although his theology is fully compatible to the distinction between the covenant of works and the covenant of grace. Moreover, Murray, following Calvin's footsteps, correctly viewed that the distinction between law and gospel is foundational for the doctrine of justification *sola fide* and salvation *sola gratia*. In relation to this, Murray maintained that the active and passive obedience of Christ is essential biblical doctrine for the doctrine of justification by faith alone. Murray wrote a brief article about the importance of the active obedience of Christ, introducing Machen's final words before his death to his readers:

> "I'M SO thankful for active obedience of Christ: no hope without it." This was the last message of our beloved friend Dr. Machen to the present writer. It was apparently dictated to his nurse on the day of his decease January 1st. The subject of the active obedience of Christ formed the topic of one of the last conversations we were privileged to have with him, and by the message quoted above he wanted us to know how much that precious truth meant to him as he was passing through the valley of the shadow of death. He was then about to pass into the immediate presence of his Lord. Why should he have suspended the issues of eternal hope upon this truth? Why did he dare to say: "*No hope without it*"? WE hang on to the last words of our friends, but particularly should we do so when they are pregnant with the issues of eternal life or death. It surely interests us to know what precisely he meant by that expression.[34]

33. Shepherd, "A Faith That Is Never Alone," 277–78.

34. John Murray, "Dr. Machen's Hope and the Active Obedience of Christ," *The*

Murray comprehensively interpreted "two distinct aspects of the substitutionary work of Christ," namely "the active and passive obedience of Christ." He correctly viewed that "the passive obedience of Christ" is to fulfill all the requirements of the law "as the substitute of His people, to satisfy all the claims of law and justice against their sins." Murray continued to argue that "the passive obedience of Christ" becomes "the ground of full remission of sin and exemption from its condemnation." Representatively, Murray found the biblical concept of "the passive obedience of Christ" from the Pauline passage, Romans 3:26:

> In Reformed Theology the formula of the "active and passive obedience of Christ" has been used to set forth and guard two distinct aspects of the substitutionary work of Christ. The passive obedience of Christ is the term that has been used to denote all that Christ did, as the substitute of His people, to satisfy all the claims of law and justice against their sins. It denotes the satisfaction on the part of Christ of all the penal demands of the divine law. The sins of His people were imputed to Christ, and that imputation became the ground of the penalty-bearing that He endured in their room and stead. That satisfaction rendered by Christ is in turn imputed to His people, and becomes the ground of full remission of sin and exemption from its condemnation. So by the grace of God complete remission of sin and of its penalty is grounded in real satisfaction to law and justice. God is just and the justifier of him who hath faith in Jesus (Cf. Rom. 3:26).[35]

After a comprehensive discussion on the passive obedience of Christ, Murray noted the active obedience of Christ as the *sole ground* of believers' forensic justification and everlasting life. Murray carefully argued that the ground of forensic or declarative justification lies in "not only satisfaction for sin and guilt," related to the passive obedience of Christ "but also obedience to the law in all the extent and detail of its demands," which is directly related to the active obedience of Christ. According to Murray, the righteousness of Christ became possible by him as "our representative and substitute in virtue of His perfect obedience to the divine law." Therefore, God imputes the righteousness of Christ "to the believer that justifies the sentence of justification, and is the proper ground of reception into the divine favor and of the title to everlasting life." In that sense,

---

Presbyterian Guardian 3 (1937): 163.

35. Ibid.

in Murray's biblico-systematic theology, the active obedience of Christ and justification *sola fide* and salvation *sola gratia* stand and fall together. Likewise, Murray comprehensively summarized and explained the biblical concept of the active obedience of Christ in relation to the forensic understanding of justification by faith alone in the milieu of the antithesis between Adam and Christ, exemplified in Romans 5:18–19:

> But the law of God demands more than penalty for sin. It requires of us also perfect obedience to its precept. Justification is a reckoning of us in the divine judgment as not only free from guilt and condemnation but also as having fulfilled all the requirements of His law. It is a declaration that we are, in His sight, righteous. In other words it involves not only remission of sin but also acceptance with God as righteous and therefore reception into the divine favor. There must, then, be positive righteousness placed to the account of the justified person. What is that righteousness? Or, to put it otherwise, what is the ground of this actual justification? It is surely the substitutionary work of Christ, and therefore that substitutionary work must, in order to supply the ground of a real justification, include not only satisfaction for sin and guilt but also obedience to the law in all the extent and detail of its demands. It is this latter that the term "active obedience" denotes. It refers to that undefiled and undefilable righteousness of Christ that is His as our representative and substitute in virtue of His perfect obedience to the divine law. It is that righteousness imputed to the believer that justifies the sentence of justification, and is the proper ground of reception into the divine favor and of the title to everlasting life. Eternal life is a gift of divine grace, but this grace reigns through *righteousness* unto eternal life by Jesus Christ our Lord. "Therefore as by the offence of one *judgment came* upon all men to condemnation; even so by the righteousness of one *the free gift came* upon all men unto justification of life. For as by one man's disobedience many were made sinners, so by the obedience of one shall many be made righteous" (Rom. 5:18, 19).[36]

Murray is one of the representative theologians, who maintained two aspects of Christ's perfect and meritorious obedience to the law, namely the active and passive obedience, although he did not accept the classical Reformed understanding of the covenant of works. This is because Murray carefully maintained the antithesis between law and gospel in his depiction of justification *sola fide* and salvation *sola gratia* after the pattern

---

36. Ibid.

of Calvin. One of Shepherd's objections to the doctrine of the imputation of the active obedience of Christ is he thinks that it was the theological outcome of "a covenant of works" without biblical warrant: "My basic objection to the doctrine is simply that it has no biblical warrant. It arose out of a need created by the imposition of a covenant of works on the text of Scripture and is actually defended as a "good and necessary consequence" flowing from that doctrine."[37]

In response to Clark's biblical affirmation of the imputation of the active obedience of Christ in light of Romans 5:18–19, Shepherd notes that the passage is not about the active obedience but the passive obedience of Christ, which is the foundation of "the forgiveness of sins." In doing so, he reduces that justification *is* "the forgiveness of sins (Rom. 3:25; 4:7, 8) grounded in the righteousness of Christ as revealed in the gospel." This is another example revealing that Shepherd and the Federal Visionists destroy the antithesis between Adam and Christ, as well as the antithesis between law and gospel, which is foundational, not only justification *sola fide* but also the imputation of the active obedience of Christ:

> I dealt at length with Romans 5:18, 19 in its surrounding Biblical context in *Backbone of the Bible* (87–9). I showed that justification in this passage is the forgiveness of sins (Rom. 3:25; 4:7, 8) grounded in the righteousness of Christ as revealed in the gospel. This righteousness is his sacrifice of atonement, his death on the cross, such that we are justified in the blood of Christ (3:25; 4:25; 5:9, 10). His death on the cross is the one act of righteousness that brings justification and life according to verse 18. It corresponds to the one trespass of Adam that brought condemnation and death. Just as the one trespass of Adam is the disobedience of the one man that made many to be sinners in verse 19, so also Christ's death on the cross, his one act of righteousness, is the obedience that made many to be righteous according to this same verse.[38]

As such, Shepherd and the Federal Visionists interpret Romans 5:18–19 in light of monocovenantalism by which they deny the antithesis between law and gospel. Murray, as a biblico-systematic theologian, was one of the representative theologians, who interpreted the Pauline passage as a classical example of the biblical doctrine of the active obedience of Christ, although he did not maintain the classical concept of the covenant

---

37. Shepherd, "The Imputation of Active Obedience," 275.
38. Ibid., 265.

of works. This is because Murray read Romans 8:18–19 not only from the perspective of the Pauline antithesis between Adam and Christ but also from the perspective of the antithesis between law and gospel. Therefore, we must reject the notion that the imputation of the active obedience of Christ was neither present in Calvin nor in the early Reformed theology, blaming it on the covenant of works.

UNION WITH CHRIST AND THE *DUPLEX GRATIA*

Undoubtedly, Calvin was the champion of "the union with Christ" (*unio cum Christo*) in the exposition of the Pauline soteriology during the sixteenth-century Protestant Reformation. All the soteriological blessings, including divine election, are embraced within the biblical and theological category and concept of union with Christ as Calvin brilliantly laid out in his *Institutes*, commentaries, and other writings. It is the controlling motif of all redemptive blessings, including the doctrine of justification in Calvin's soteriology.

However, in contemporary discussion on Calvin's soteriology and the doctrine of justification, there is a growing tendency to emphasize *exclusively* the concept of the union with Christ without mentioning or implying the antithesis between law and gospel. As a result, some scholars postulate Calvin as a neonomian or a covenantal legalist, perhaps against their own will and most importantly Calvin's own will.

In her recent writings from the perspective of neoorthodox interpretation on Calvin's doctrine of justification, Karla Wübbenhorst suggests that Calvin in contrast to Luther headed towards "more a neonomian and realistic direction":

> Calvin's doctrine of justification corrects the Lutheran doctrine or, rather, protects it in the face of certain Catholic objections and, in doing so, develops that doctrine in a more neonomian and realistic direction. The neonomian emphasis is shared by reformed thinkers before Calvin and becomes characteristic of later Calvinism. Calvin's realism is also shared by the Calvinists to the extent that they, too, complement the evangelical perspective with a more scholastic one and place justification within the context of an *ordo salutis*.[39]

---

39. Karla Wübbenhorst, "Calvin's Doctrine of Justification: Variations on a Lutheran Theme," in *Justification in Perspective*, ed. Bruce L. McCormack (Grand Rapids: Baker, 2006), 100.

Wübbenhorst's reading of Calvin as a neonomian is the result of not recognizing the importance of the antithesis between law and gospel in Calvin's soteriology and the doctrine of justification by faith alone, exclusively emphasizing the concept of union with Christ. Analyzing the final edition of Calvin's *Institutes* of 1559, she does not notice the *proper places* of justification, on the one hand, and sanctification, on the other:

> Calvin speaks here of a mystical union with Christ, wrought by the Holy Spirit, the Author of faith, the Creator of this community of righteousness, and from this union arises double grace: justification and sanctification. They are simultaneous, and although they can be distinguished, they cannot be separated. The death and resurrection of Christ, which we saw provided the basis for a distinction within justification itself, effect a similar distinction within sanctification.[40]

To be sure, Calvin closely connected and integrated together the soteric twin blessings of justification and sanctification under the umbrella of the mystical union with Christ as "double grace" (*duplex gratia*). Indeed, Calvin's brilliance lies in the fact that he used the soteriological benefits of double grace, namely justification and sanctification under the umbrella of the union with Christ, not only to emphasize their interconnectedness but also to safeguard against antinomianism. In Calvin's theology, we need to remember that the antithesis between law and gospel in the doctrine of justification by faith alone was a concrete hermeneutical and theological background to safeguard the principle of *sola gratia / sola fide* against the background of neonomianism or legalism. In Calvin's theological mind, however, there is no exclusiveness between the antithesis between law and gospel *and* union with Christ. In short, Calvin never used the concept of union with Christ and *duplex gratia* to direct himself into neonomianism as Wübbenhorst falsely argues.

Meanwhile, Shepherd makes Calvin a covenantal legalist, denying the antithesis between law and gospel in Calvin's theology while he exclusively emphasizes the union with Christ:

> Justification and sanctification in union with Christ summarize what belongs to the essence of my salvation. Justification and sanctification are what Calvin called the "double grace" that we receive through union with Christ (*Institutes,* 3/11/1). United to Christ I

---

40. Ibid., 115.

am justified and sanctified. Jesus saves us by destroying both the guilt and the corruption of sin. That is to say he saves us by forgiving our sins and by transforming us so that we become righteous persons. Those who are forgiven and who are transformed into covenant keepers are the righteous who will inherit eternal life.[41]

Shepherd's monocovenantal concept of union with Christ is vastly different from Calvin's; Calvin's union with Christ does not eliminate the antithesis between law and gospel. Calvin's presupposition of believers' rich soteriological blessings, including justification and sanctification as "double grace," lies in the fact that Jesus Christ, as the mediator of the New Covenant, fulfilled all the requirements of the law through his entire life and atoning death whereby no sinners may accomplish them. In other words, in Calvin's theology, there are no spiritual blessings of union with Christ for the believers without his precedent perfect obedience to the law. Therefore, it is not fair to Calvin's concretely balanced concept of the union with Christ to inject the monocovenantal idea of the union with Christ in which Shepherd, as a monocovenantalist, denies the distinction between law and gospel, which was Calvin's profound hermeneutical and theological background to embrace the rich spiritual blessings of the union with Christ.[42]

Calvin laid out "the contrast between the righteousness of the law and of the gospel" in his exposition of the Pauline passages such as Romans 10:5–9 and Galatians 3:11–12 as a hermeneutical and theological background of justification by faith alone. Immediately following that, Calvin pointed out the importance of "its proper place" (*postea suo loco*) of double grace, namely justification and sanctification: "Moreover, we shall see afterward, in its proper place, that the benefits of Christ—sanctification and righteousness—are different. From this it follows that not even spiritual works come into account when the power of justifying is ascribed to faith."[43]

41. Shepherd, "Justification by Works in Reformed Theology, 110.

42. Following Shepherd's monocovenantal understanding of union with Christ, the Federal Vision promoters, including Rich Lusk, identify their monocovenantal reinterpretation of union with Christ with Calvin's balanced concept of union with Christ. In their monocovenantal interpretation of union with Christ, justification and sanctification are virtually indistinguishable and confused. For critical engagement against Lusk's misrepresentation about Calvin's union with Christ in relation to the doctrines of justification and sanctification, see Jeon, *Covenant Theology and Justification by Faith*, 39–41.

43. Calvin, *Institutes*, 3.11.14. Calvin affirmed the imputation of the righteousness of

Meanwhile, Osiander represented the Reformation period as a person who distorted the biblical understanding of the union with Christ (*unio cum Christo*) in relation to the doctrines of justification and sanctification. That is the reason why Calvin extensively discussed the problem of Osiander's concept of union with Christ in relation to the doctrine of justification and sanctification. Calvin argued that God unites believers through the powerful work of the Holy Spirit with Christ, who is the Head of the Church, bestowing all the promised spiritual blessings. The mystical union (*mystica unio*) depicts "indwelling of Christ in our hearts" (*habitation Christi in cordibus nostris*). However, Osiander's concept of "essential righteousness" (*essentialis iustitiae*) destroys the biblical notion of spiritual union, which is expressed by Calvin as "spiritual bond" (*spirituali coniunctione*) between believers and Christ because it forces "a gross mingling of Christ with believers," confusing not only the Creator and creature distinction but also the distinction between justification and sanctification. Thus, Calvin provided his critique against Osiander as follows:

> Now, lest Osiander deceive the unlearned by his cavils, I confess that we are deprived of this utterly incomparable good until Christ is made ours. Therefore, that joining together of Head and members, that indwelling of Christ in our hearts-in short, that mystical union—are accorded by us the highest degree of importance, so that Christ, having been made ours, makes us sharers with him in the gifts with which he has been endowed. We do not, therefore, contemplate him outside ourselves from afar in order that his righteousness may be imputed to us but because we put on Christ and are engrafted into his body—in short, because he deigns to make us one with him. For this reason, we glory that we have fellowship of righteousness with him. Thus is Osiander's slander refuted, that by us faith is reckoned righteousness. As if we were to deprive Christ of his right when we say that by faith we come empty to him to make room for his grace in order that he alone may fill us! But Osiander, by spurning this spiritual bond, forces a

---

Christ in light of the antithesis between law and gospel in the forensic declaration of the doctrine of *sola fide*. In addition, he safeguarded the concept of the union with Christ as "the mystical union" over against Osiander's unbiblical notion of "essential righteousness" (*essentialis iustitiae*), which destroys not only the biblical doctrine of *sola fide* but also the Creator and creature distinction. That is the major reason why Calvin provided a comprehensive critique against Osiander's "essential righteousness." We see Calvin's comprehensive analysis and critique against Osiander's concept of "essential righteousness" in his *Institutes* 3.11.5–12.

gross mingling with believers. And for this reason, he maliciously calls "Zwinglian" all those who do not subscribe to his mad error of "essential righteousness" because they do not hold the view that Christ is eaten in substance in the Lord's Supper.[44]

Calvin noticed that by introducing the concept of "essential righteousness," Osiander did not intend to obscure God's "freely given righteousness" in the doctrine of justification. However, the consequence of Osiander's "essential righteousness" in light of union with Christ demolished the biblical notion of believer's spiritual union with Christ as Calvin succinctly provided his critique against Osiander:

> But Osiander has introduced some strange monster of 'essential' righteousness by which, although not intending to abolish freely given righteousness, he has still enveloped it in such a fog as to darken pious minds and deprive them of a lively experience of Christ's grace. Consequently, before I pass on to other matters, it behooves me to refute this wild dream.
>
> First, this speculation arises out of mere feeble curiosity. Indeed, he accumulates many testimonies of Scripture by which to prove that Christ is one with us, and we in turn, with him—a fact that needs no proof. But because he does not observe the bond of this unity, he deceives himself. Now it is easy for us to resolve all his difficulties. For we hold ourselves to be united with Christ by the secret power of his Spirit.[45]

Calvin continued to argue that Osiander, following the footsteps of Manichaeism, promotes the unbiblical notion "to transfuse the essence of God into men" (*essentiam Dei in hominess transfundere*), which is a clear denial of the distinction between the Creator and creature. Advocating the concept of union with Christ, Osiander falsely argued that "Christ's essence is mixed with our own" (*misceri Christi essentiam cum nostra*). In doing so, Osiander cast aside "Christ's obedience and sacrificial death" that he offered as the mediator of the New Covenant:

> That gentleman had conceived something bordering on Manichaeism, in his desire to transfuse the essence of God into men . . . He says that we are one with Christ. We agree. But we deny that Christ's essence is mixed with our own. Then we say that this principle is wrongly applied to these deceptions of his: that

44. Ibid., 3.11.10.
45. Ibid., 3.11.5.

> Christ is our righteousness because he is God eternal, the source of righteousness, and the very righteousness of God. My readers will pardon me if I now only touch upon what my teaching plan demands that I defer to another place. Although he may make the excuse that by the term 'essential righteousness' he means nothing else but to meet the opinion that we are considered righteous for Christ's sake, yet he has clearly expressed himself as not content with that righteousness which has been acquired for us by Christ's obedience and sacrificial death, but pretends that we are substantially righteous in God by the infusion both of his essence and of his quality.[46]

Osiander confused "righteousness and sanctification" (*iustitiam et sanctificationem*) in his affirmation of the unbiblical concept of essential righteousness. Responding to Osiander's confusion between justification and sanctification, Calvin properly argued that spiritual blessings of "righteousness and sanctification" as "double grace" (*duplex gratia*) are distinct although the two are inseparable in light of the mystical union with Christ "as a mutual and indivisible connection":

> To prove the first point—that God justifies not only by pardoning but by regenerating—he asks whether God leaves as they were by nature those whom he justifies, changing none of their vices. This is exceedingly easy to answer: as Christ cannot be torn into parts, so these two which we perceive in him together and conjointly are inseparable—namely, righteousness and sanctification. Whomever, therefore, God receives into grace, on them he at the same time bestows the spirit of adoption [Rom. 8:15], by whose power he remakes them to his own image. But if the brightness of the sun cannot be separated from its heat, shall we therefore say that the earth is warmed by its light, or lighted by its heat? Is there anything more applicable to the present matter than this comparison? The sun, by its heat, quickens and fructifies the earth, by its beams brightens and illumines it. Here is a mutual and indivisible connection. Yet reason itself forbids us to transfer the peculiar qualities of the one to the other. In this confusion of the two kinds of grace that Osiander forces upon us there is a like absurdity. For since God, for the preservation of righteousness, renews those whom he freely reckons as righteous, Osiander mixes that gift of regeneration with this free acceptance and contends that they are one and the same. Yet Scripture, even though it joins them, still lists them separately in order that God's manifold grace may better appear to us. For

---

46. Ibid.

Paul's statement is not redundant: that Christ was given to us for our righteousness and sanctification [1 Cor. 1:30]. And whenever he reasons—from the salvation purchased for us, from God's fatherly love, and from Christ's grace—that we are called to holiness and cleanness, he clearly indicates that to be justified means something different from being made new creatures.[47]

Calvin further argued that Osiander's "essential righteousness" wrongly results in "essential indwelling of Christ in us" (*essentialem in nobis Christi habitationem*), which is directly against the biblical concept of the mystical union with Christ. As a result, Osiander denies the forensic or legal concept of once for all nature of *sola fide*, confusing justification and sanctification:

The fact, then, that he insists so violently upon essential righteousness and essential indwelling of Christ in us has this result: first, he holds that God pours himself into us as a gross mixture, just as he fancies a physical eating in the Lord's Supper; secondly, that he breathes his righteousness upon us, by which we may be really righteous with him, since according to Osiander this righteousness is both God himself and the goodness or holiness or integrity of God.[48]

Interpreting the doctrine of justification in light of "essential righteousness," Osiander denied "a legal term" in the depiction of justification, as well as the imputation of the righteousness of Christ, which may be defined as "free imputation." Against Osiander, Calvin understood justification with the concept of twin spiritual blessings such as "acquittal and pardon," which is another way to express the imputation of the righteousness of Christ and the forgiveness of sins:

Osiander laughs at those men who teach that 'to be justified' is a legal term; because we must actually be righteous. Also, he despises nothing more than that we are justified by free imputation. Well then, if God does not justify us by acquittal and pardon, what does Paul's statement mean: 'God was in Christ, reconciling the world to himself, not imputing men's trespasses against them' [2 Cor. 5:19]? 'For our sake he made him to be sin who made done no sin so that we might be the righteousness of God in him.' [V. 21 p.] First, I conclude that they are accounted righteous who are reconciled to

47. Ibid., 3.11.6.
48. Ibid., 3.11.10.

God. Included is the means: that God justifies by pardoning, just as in another passage justification is contrasted with accusation. This antithesis clearly shows that the expression was taken from legal usage.[49]

In light of the mystical union with Christ, Calvin argued that believers receive the grace of justification, as well as regeneration or sanctification. And the twin spiritual blessings of justification and sanctification may not be separated "although they are things distinct." However, Calvin rightly argued that Osiander's concept of "essential righteousness" confuses justification and sanctification. In doing so, Osiander stole "the assurance of salvation" (*fiducia salutis*) from believers' hearts because his concept of righteousness relies on intrinsic righteousness instead of righteousness through free imputation:

> Osiander objects that it would be insulting to God and contrary to his nature that he should justify those who actually remain wicked. Yet we must bear in mind what I have already said, that the grace of justification is not separated from regeneration, although they are things distinct. But because it is very well known by experience that the traces of sin always remain in the righteous, their justification must be very different from reformation into newness of life [cf. Rom. 6:4]. For God so begins this second point in his elect, and progresses in it gradually, and sometimes slowly, throughout life, that they are always liable to the judgment of death before his tribunal. But he does not justify in part but liberally, so that they may appear in heaven as if endowed with the purity of Christ. No portion of righteousness sets our consciences at peace until it has been determined that we are pleasing to God, because we are entirely righteous before him. From this it follows that the doctrine of justification is perverted and utterly overthrown when doubt is thrust into men's minds, when the assurance of salvation is shaken and the free and fearless calling upon God suffers hindrance—nay, when peace and tranquility with spiritual joy are not established.[50]

As such, Osiander confused "justification and regeneration" (*iustificandi et regenerandi*) or sanctification under the idea of "double righteousness" (*duplicem iustitiam*), which is carefully analyzed by Paul. Countering Osiander's confusion of justification and sanctification, Calvin rightly argued that Paul announces his ongoing struggle through his own spiritual

49. Ibid., 3.11.11.
50. Ibid.

experience in the process of sanctification, reflecting "his own real righteousness" (*reali sua iustitia*) in Romans 7:24. However, Calvin carefully noticed that Paul boldly proclaims that there is an assurance of salvation and true peace in a believer's heart when we meditate on justification by faith alone, "founded solely upon God's mercy"(*in sola Dei misericordia fundata*) in his reflection on Romans 8:33–39:

> This distinction between justification and regeneration, which two things confuses under the term 'double righteousness,' is beautifully expressed by Paul. Speaking of his own real righteousness, or of the uprighteous that had been given him, which Osiander labels 'essential righteousness,' he mournfully exclaims: 'Wretched man that I am! Who will deliver me from the body of this death?' [Rom. 7:24]. But fleeing to that righteousness which is founded solely upon God's mercy he gloriously triumphs over both life and death, reproaches and hunger, the sword and all other adverse things. 'Who will make accusation against God's elect,' whom he justifies [Rom. 8:33 p.]? For I am surely convinced that nothing 'will separate us from his love in Christ' [Rom. 8:38–39 p.]. He clearly proclaims that he has a righteousness which alone entirely suffices for salvation before God, so that he does not diminish his confidence in glorying, and no hindrance arises from the miserable bondage, consciousness of which had a moment before caused him to bemoan his lot.[51]

Recently, A. T. B. McGowan, a historical theologian, wrote an interesting and very important article about 'Justification and the *ordo salutis*.' In examining the development of the *ordo salutis* in Reformed soteriology, including that of Calvin, McGowan pays special attention to the concept of union with Christ in relation to "the order of salvation" (*ordo salutis*). Afterwards, he makes a distinction between "Union with Christ in Neoorthodoxy" and "Union with Christ in Westminster Calvinism" in contemporary development. In his analysis on "Union with Christ in Westminster Calvinism," McGowan identifies contemporary Westminster Calvinism, represented by Gaffin, Ferguson, and others as placing exclusive emphasis on the union with Christ and eschatology in the discussion on Pauline soteriology with the theologies of Vos and Murray:

> We now turn to the second group of theologians who have focused attention on union with Christ rather than on the traditional *ordo*

51. Ibid.

salutis method. We must keep in mind the trenchant criticism that McCormack applied to the Barthian scholars who did likewise. We must ask whether, in taking this position, these Westminster Seminary theologians have somehow managed to maintain forensic justification including the nonimputation of sin and the imputation of the righteousness of Christ.

From the influence of Geerhardus Vos and John Murray, there gradually developed within Westminster Theological Seminary (WTS) an approach to the application of redemption that seeks to draw together strands of the two positions considered so far. There is indeed an emphasis upon the union-with-Christ method, but there is also a commitment to forensic justification including the imputation of Christ's righteousness.[52]

After a brief historical connection and analysis about the background of "Union with Christ in Westminster Calvinism," McGowan summarizes its essentials, which are exemplified and represented by Gaffin's monumental work, "Resurrection and Redemption: A Study in Pauline Soteriology," submitted to Westminster Theological Seminary as a doctoral dissertation in 1969, and published in 1978 with a minor revision as *The Centrality of the Resurrection*.[53] McGowan writes the importance of Gaffin's view for the shaping of 'Union with Christ in Westminster Calvinism'":

> Gaffin's view has been very influential at WTS, and others have followed his line of reasoning, including Sinclair Ferguson, who writes, "Union with Christ must therefore be the dominant motif in any formulation of the application of redemption and the dominant feature of any 'order' of salvation."
>
> There is, however, a marked difference between the understanding of union with Christ as developed by Gaffin, Ferguson, and others developed by the neoorthodox theologians. As we saw in the previous section, particularly in Torrance and Hart, neoorthodoxy views union with Christ as an alternative to a forensic understanding of atonement with its key component of imputation. In Gaffin, Ferguson, and the WTS theologians, the forensic element is retained. The imputation of the righteousness of Christ to believers remains a key element in their theology; it

---

52. A. T. B. McGowan, "Justification and the *ordo salutis*," in *Justification in Perspective*, ed. Bruce L. McCormack (Grand Rapids: Baker, 2006), 160.

53. For the most recent thought of Gaffin's Pauline soteriology in light of contemporary discussion on the New Perspectives on Paul, see Richard B. Gaffin Jr., *By Faith Not by Sight: Paul and the Order of Salvation* (Waynesboro: Paternoster Press, 2006).

is simply that the means by which this imputation is effected is located in the prior doctrine of union with Christ.[54]

In general, I agree with McGowan's distinction between "Union with Christ in Neoorthodoxy" and "Union with Christ in Westminster Calvinism." It is very encouraging to read that the scholars in "Union with Christ in Westminster Calvinism" maintain "a forensic understanding of atonement" and "the imputation of the righteousness of Christ to believers" "in the prior doctrine of union with Christ" against neoorthodox theologians' denial of them, making "union with Christ as an alternative" to them. However, McGowan mistakenly argues when he sets union with Christ against "a clear law/grace antithesis" in Reformed theology:

> This position has not gone unchallenged, related as it is to the development of John Murray's modified covenant theology, in which he argued against a legal "covenant of works" in favor of a gracious "Adamic administration." Meredith Kline and others,

---

54. McGowan, "Justification and the *ordo salutis*," 161–62. I classify Gaffin, Ferguson, and others as "Union with Christ School" while McGowan designates them as "Union with Christ in Westminster Calvinism" as a means to make a distinction of their conservative Reformed theology from neoorthodox theology. Cf. Jeon, *Covenant Theology and Justification by Faith*, 1–53. For the most recent and representative writings about the doctrine of justification by faith in relation with union with Christ within "Union with Christ in Westminster Calvinism," see Richard B. Gaffin Jr., "Justification and Union with Christ," in *Theological Guide to Calvin's Institutes: Essays and* Analysis, eds. David W. Hall & Peter A. Lillback (Phillipsburg, Presbyterian and Reformed Publishing, 2008), 248–69; Mark A. Garcia, "Christ and the Spirit: The Meaning and Promise of a Reformed Idea," in *Resurrection and Eschatology: Theology in Service of the Church*, eds. Land G. Tipton & Jeffrey C. Waddington (Phillipsburg: Presbyterian and Reformed Publishing, 2008), 424–42; idem, "Imputation and the Christology of Union with Christ: Calvin, Osiander, and the Contemporary Quest for a Reformed Model," *Westminster Theological Journal* 68 (2006): 219–51; idem, *Life in Christ: Union with Christ and Twofold Grace in Calvin's Theology* (Milton Keynes: Paternoster, 2008). Thomas Wenger identifies the interpretation of Calvin's soteriology, especially in respect to the doctrines of justification and sanctification in relation to union with Christ by the exponents of "Union with Christ School" as "the New Perspective on Calvin." See Thomas L. Wenger, "The New Perspective on Calvin: Responding to Recent Calvin Interpretations," *Journal of Evangelical Theological Society* 50 (2007): 311–28. Meanwhile, VanDrunen provides a very interesting critique on the Union with Christ School scholars' interpretation of justification and sanctification in light of union with Christ from "the two kingdoms" perspective. In doing so, he defends a logical priority of justification over sanctification in the *ordo salutis* while he comprehensively embraces the doctrines of justification and sanctification under the rubric of union with Christ. See David VanDrunen, "Inaugural Lecture: The Two Kingdoms and the *Ordo Salutis*: Life Beyond Judgment and the Question of a Dual Ethic," *Westminster Theological Journal* 70 (2008): 207–24.

particularly Mark Karlberg, have argued that this failure to pursue a clear law/grace antithesis is a departure from Reformed theology and endangers the doctrine of justification, which they believe to be dependent upon this antithesis.[55]

However, it is important to remember that Murray, a predecessor of "Union with Christ in Westminster Calvinism," never set the concept of union with Christ against the distinction between law and gospel or grace. Certainly, Murray highly emphasized the Pauline union with Christ in his analysis on soteriology. Nevertheless, he never thought that the antithesis between law and gospel or grace is incompatible to the concept of union with Christ. At least, in Murray's biblico-systematic theology, the rejection of the distinction between law and gospel in the milieu of union with Christ is an alien idea as it was with Calvin.

In fact, Murray displayed the masterful analysis of soteriology in relation to the union with Christ, including the doctrine of election.[56] Murray analyzed the *ordo salutis* as the application of redemption, accomplished through Christ's life, death, resurrection, and exaltation to heaven. And he categorized the blessings of the *ordo salutis* as "calling, regeneration, faith and repentance, justification, adoption, sanctification, perseverance, glorification."[57] In doing so, Murray connected all the soteriological blessings, including election under the realm of union with Christ, which was already richly envisioned in Calvin's theology:

> We thus see that union with Christ has its source in the election of God the Father before the foundation of the world and it has its fruition in the glorification of the sons of God. The perspective of God's people is not narrow; it is broad and it is long. It is not confined to space and time; it has the expanse of eternity. Its orbit has two foci, one the electing love of God the Father in the counsels of eternity, the other glorification with Christ in the manifestation of his glory. The former has no beginning, the latter has no end. Glorification with Christ at his coming will be but the beginning of a consummation that will encompass the ages of the ages. 'So shall we ever be with the Lord' (1 Thess. 4:17). It is a perspective with a past and with a future, but neither the past nor the future is bounded by what we

---

55 McGowan, "Justification and the *ordo salutis*," 162.

56. Cf. John Murray, *Redemption Accomplished and Applied* (Grand Rapids: Eerdmans, 1989).

57. Ibid., 87.

know as our temporal history. And because temporal history falls within such a perspective it has meaning and hope.[58]

Murray persuasively argued that the biblical concept of union with Christ in his death and resurrection is a definitive hermeneutical framework to grasp all the soteriological blessings from election to the heavenly glorification for all the believers who are in Christ. In short, in Murray, the idea of union with Christ is a hermeneutical key for profound biblical soteriology:

> It is union with Christ now in the virtue of his death and the power of his resurrection that certifies to him the reality of his election in Christ before the foundation of the world—he is blessed by the Father with all spiritual blessings in the heavenlies in Christ just as he was chosen in Christ from eternal ages (cf. Eph. 1:3,4). And he has the seal of an eternal inheritance because it is in Christ that he is sealed with the Holy Spirit of promise as the earnest of his inheritance unto the redemption of the purchased possession (cf. Eph. 1:13,14). Apart from union with Christ we cannot view past, present, or future with anything but dismay and Christless dread. By union with Christ the whole complexion of time and eternity is changed and the people of God may rejoice with joy unspeakable and full of glory.
>
> Union with Christ is a very inclusive subject. It embraces the wide span of salvation from its ultimate source in the eternal election of God to its final fruition in the glorification of the elect. It is not simply a phase of the application of redemption; it underlies every aspect of redemption both in its accomplishment and in its application. Union with Christ binds all together and insures that to all for whom Christ has purchased redemption he effectively applies and communicates the same.[59]

58. Ibid., 164.

59. Ibid., 164–65. When Murray discussed the idea of union with Christ, it is true that he highlighted Christ's death and resurrection which are the culmination of his redemptive accomplishment. However, Murray self consciously viewed and embraced not only Christ's death and resurrection but also *the whole Christ*, embracing his life, death, resurrection, and exaltation to heaven in relation to union with Christ: "It is also because the people of God were in Christ when he gave his life a ransom and redeemed by his blood that salvation has been secured for them; they are represented as united to Christ in his death, resurrection, and exaltation to heaven (Rom. 6:2–11; Eph. 2:4–6; Col. 3:3,4). 'In the beloved,' Paul says, 'We have redemption through his blood' (Eph. 1:7). Hence we may never think of the work of redemption wrought once for all by Christ apart from the union with his people which was effected in the election of the Father before the foundation of the world. In other words, we may never think of redemption in abstraction from the

Although Murray faithfully applied the idea of union with Christ to the comprehensive understanding of biblical soteriology, embracing the doctrine of election under the realm of union with Christ, he did not use it as a means to deny the antithesis between law and gospel or grace like Shepherd and the Federal Visionists. Contrastingly, as a good historical theologian, as well as a biblico-systematic theologian, Murray warned the danger of the denial of the antithesis between law and grace in the understanding of the heart of the gospel, as well as the danger of the denial of the implication of the law in believers' lives in the process of sanctification. In doing so, Murray emphasized the balanced understanding of the relationship between law and gospel or grace:

> No subject is more intimately bound up with the nature of the gospel than that of law and grace. In the degree to which error is entertained at this point, in the same degree is our conception of the gospel perverted. An erroneous conception of the function of law can be of such a character that it completely vitiates our view of the gospel; and an erroneous conception of the antithesis between law and grace can be of such a character that it demolishes the substructure and the superstructure.[60]

In Murray's mind, it was very clear that the antithesis between law and gospel or grace is a non-negotiatiable component of the doctrine of justification by faith alone, avoiding legalism or neonomianism. And believers' practical application to the law is foundational for Christian life in progressive sanctification. We find a remarkable hermeneutical and theological balance in Murray when he described the relationship between law and gospel with the implication of justification, on the one hand, and progressive sanctification, on the other hand:

> In a word it was the relation of law and gospel. 'I do not make void the grace of God: for if righteousness is through the law, then Christ died in vain' (Galatians 2:21). 'For if a law had been given which could make alive, verily from the law righteousness would have been' (Galatians 3:21). 'By the works of the law shall no flesh be justified in his sight' (Romans 3:20).

---

mysterious arrangements of God's love and wisdom and grace by which Christ was united to his people and his people were united to him when he died upon the accursed tree and rose again from the dead. This is but another way of saying that the church is the body of Christ and 'Christ loved the church and gave himself for it' (Eph. 5:25)." Ibid., 162–63.

60. John Murray, *Principles of Conduct: Aspects of Biblical Ethics* (Grand Rapids: Eerdmans, 1991), 181.

The simple truth is that if law is conceived of as contributing in the least degree towards our acceptance with God and our justification by him, then the gospel of grace is a nullity. And the issue is so sharply and incisively drawn that, if we rely in any respect upon compliance with law for our acceptance with God, then Christ will profit us nothing. 'Ye have been discharged from Christ whosoever of you are justified by law; ye have fallen away from grace' (Galatians 5:4). But lest we should think that the whole question of the relation of law and grace is thereby resolved, we must be reminded that Paul says also in this polemic, 'Do we then make void the law through faith? God forbid, yea we establish the law' (Romans 3:31). We are compelled therefore to recognize that the subject of law and grace is not simply concerned with the antithesis that there is between law and grace, but also with law as that which makes grace necessary and with grace as establishing and confirming law. It is not only the doctrine of grace that must be jealously guarded against distortion by the works of law, but it is also the doctrine of law that must be preserved against that must be preserved against the distortions of a spurious concept of grace. This is just saying that we are but echoing the total witness of the apostle of the Gentiles as the champion of the gospel of grace when we say that we must guard grace from the adulteration of legalism and we must guard law from the depredations of antinomianism.[61]

Murray argued that believers' spiritual blessings may be effectively applied "through union with Christ in the efficacy of his death and the power of his resurrection life" after the pattern of Calvin's concept of union with Christ; however, Murray did not use the concept of union with Christ as a hermeneutical and theological tool to deny the antithesis between law and gospel or grace. In the milieu of Romans 6:14, Murray viewed the antithesis between law and gospel as he understood *the proper place* of the doctrine of justification and salvation. Murray continued to argue that the Pauline concept of justification and salvation, represented by the notion of 'under grace,' must be understood by "an absolute antithesis between the potency of law and the potency of grace, between the provisions of law and the provisions of grace." Although Murray was a champion of union with Christ in his depiction of the *ordo slutis* and soteriology in the twentieth-century Reformed theology, he did not mature the theology of union with Christ at the expense of the antithesis between law and gospel or grace:

61. Ibid., 181–82.

It is in this light that the apostle's antithetical expression 'under grace' becomes significant. The word 'grace' sums up everything that by way of contrast with law is embraced in the provisions of redemption. In terms of Paul's teaching in this context the redemptive provision consists in our having become dead to the law by the body of Christ (Romans 7:4). They have, therefore, come *under* all the resources of redeeming and renewing grace which find their epitome in the death and resurrection of Christ and find their permanent embodiment in him who was dead and is alive again. The virtue which ever continues to emanate from the death and resurrection of Christ is operative in them through union with Christ in the efficacy of his death and the power of his resurrection life. All of this Paul's brief expression 'under grace' implies. And in respect of the subject with which Paul is dealing there is an absolute antithesis between the potency of law and the potency of grace, between the provisions of law and the provisions of grace. Grace is the sovereign will and power of God coming to expression, not for the regulation of thought and conduct consonant with God's holiness, but for the deliverance of men from thought and conduct that bind them to the servitude of unholiness. Grace is deliverance from the dominion of sin and therefore deliverance from that which consists in transgression of the law.[62]

Murray went on to argue that "the purity and integrity of the gospel" are closely tied to "the absoluteness of the antithesis between the function and potency of law" and "the function and potency of grace." In other words, the good news of the gospel itself stands or falls with the absolute antithesis between law and gospel or grace in Murray's biblico-systematic theology, which is following the genuine theological pattern of Calvin's thought. Moreover, Murray made a concrete balance, insisting that the antithesis between law and gospel in relation to the doctrine of justification and salvation, does not eliminate the necessity of obedience "to the law to the believer as a believer" in the process of progressive sanctification. Likewise, Murray articulated the antithesis between law and gospel in the milieu of Romans 6:14 while he viewed 1 Corinthians 9:21 as one of the classical Pauline passages that God demands believers' obedience to the law in their Christian life:

The purity and integrity of the gospel stand or fall with the absoluteness of the antithesis between the function and potency of law, on

62. Ibid., 186.

the one hand, and the function and potency of grace, on the other. But while all this is true it does not by any means follow that the antithesis eliminates all relevance of the law to the believer as a believer. The facile slogan of many a professed evangelical, when confronted with the claims of the law of God, to the effect that he is not under law but under grace, should at least be somewhat disturbed when it is remembered that the same apostle upon whose formula he relies said also that he was not without law to God but under law to Christ (1 Corinthians 9:21). This statement of the apostle demands careful examination because it bears the implication that Paul was under law to God and he expressly states that he was under law to Christ. It would seem as if he said the opposite of what he says in Romans 6:14. But in any case what Paul says to the Corinthians prohibits us from taking the formula 'not under law' as the complete account of the relation of the believer to the law of God.[63]

As such, Murray, after the pattern of Calvin's union with Christ, embraced all the soteriological blessings under the umbrella of union with Christ. In doing so, Murray did not fall into neither legalism nor neonomianism in his understanding of justification by faith alone (*sola fide*). Certainly, Murray understood justification and sanctification in light of the double grace (*duplex gratia*) in the milieu of union with Christ. However, Murray correctly argued that there is *a proper place* for each facet of the *ordo salutis*, including the doctrines of justification and sanctification. We have to remember that the antithesis between law and gospel or grace is the hermeneutical and theological tool for the proper understanding of the *sola fide* not only in Calvin's soteriology but also in Murray's soteriology. In that sense, no one can properly interpret Murray's understanding of the doctrine of justification without referring to union with Christ, on the one hand, and the antithesis between law and gospel or grace, on the other hand.

The similar principle can be applied to Geerhardus Vos. Vos, as a biblical theologian, was highly devoted to the exposition of the Pauline eschatological concept of the Kingdom of God in light of the already but not yet. In doing so, he never jeopardized the principle of *sola gratia* and *sola fide* in his exposition of Pauline soteriology and eschatology. This is because Vos carefully maintained the distinction between law and gospel, as well as the distinction between the covenant of works and the covenant of grace in his understanding of *sola gratia* and *sola fide*.[64] If that is the

63. Ibid., 186–87.

64. Cf. Jeon, *Covenant Theology*, 79–190.

case, we wonder how McGowan, as a historical theologian, will interpret the theologies of Calvin, Reformed orthodoxy, and Murray exclusively emphasizing union with Christ without referring to or denying the distinction between law and gospel.

It is very obvious that in McGowan's analysis and endorsement of "Union with Christ in Westminster Calvinism," there is immense historical theological confusion and distortion taking place. McGowan observes that scholars in "Union with Christ in Westminster Calvinism" against "Union with Christ in Neoorthodoxy" maintain the priority of union with Christ in soteriology while they affirm "a forensic understanding of atonement with its key component of imputation" and "the imputation of the righteousness of Christ to believers." If we accept McGowan's analysis, then there is a common denominator between Neoorthodoxy and Westminster Calvinism, namely a rejection of the distinction between law and gospel, although there is a great theological gulf between the two schools. However, from the perspective of Calvin's theology and the Reformed orthodoxy, a forensic understanding of justification, the imputation of the righteousness of Christ to believers, and the antithesis between law and gospel along with union with Christ are not competing ideas. Rather, they are necessary and essential corollaries as we already observed.

SUMMARY

We have explored Calvin's covenant theology and the doctrine of justification by faith in light of contemporary debate. In doing so, we found out that the most important hermeneutical and theological background for the comprehensive understanding of Calvin's *sola gratia* and *sola fide* is the antithesis between law and gospel and the concretely balanced concept of the union with Christ. I have proposed that no matter how well theologians adorn Calvin's soteriology with the idea of union with Christ, we cannot adequately expound Calvin's concrete and yet balanced understanding of justification by faith alone (*sola fide*) without referring to Calvin's evangelical distinction between law and gospel. In the process of interacting with neoorthodox theologians, Norman Shepherd, and the exponents of the Federal Vision, we identified that they inject their monocovenantalism to Calvin's theology while claiming to base their view on his work. Denial of the distinction between law and gospel with an exclusive emphasis on the union with Christ, in the portrayal of Calvin's soteriology, leads to depicting Calvin as a neonomian or covenantal legalist.

2

Covenant and Redemptive History

THE FORERUNNER OF THE DISTINCTION BETWEEN THE COVENANT OF WORKS AND THE COVENANT OF GRACE: LAW AND GOSPEL AS THE HISTORICAL ORDER

CALVIN DID NOT REGARD the prelapsarian Adamic state as the *foedus naturale, foedus legalis* or *foedus operum* as latter orthodox Reformed theologians did. Nevertheless, he laid out the concrete hermeneutical and theological grounds for the development of the distinction between the covenant of works and the covenant of grace. For example, Calvin attached the motif of natural law to it, which was an important step toward the *foedus operum* as developed by Reformed scholastic orthodoxy.[1]

It is remarkable to find out that Calvin read the Bible from the beginning in light of the *eschatology*. Adam in the Garden of Eden did not mean to stay there although it was earthly paradise. Adam in his original state was always waiting for the eschaton. The means of eschatological heavenly blessing was not grace or gospel but the law. In this regard, the principle of law informs "the order of creation" in Calvin's thought.[2]

At this point, Rolston, after the pattern of Karl Barth, fails to see the law as the road or means to eschatological consummation before the Fall in Calvin, making a polar distinction between Calvin and the Calvinists:

1. Muller, "The Covenant of Works and the Stability of Divine Law," 88–89.

2. Karlberg, "Reformed Interpretation of the Mosaic Covenant," 13. For the comprehensive exploration on Calvin's view on eschatology in terms of its traditional concept, see Cornelis P. Venema, "Calvin's Doctrine of the Last Things: The Resurrection of the Body and the Life Everlasting," in *Theological Guide to Calvin's Institutes: Essays and Analysis*, eds. David W. Hall and Peter A. Lillback (Phillipsburg: Presbyterian and Reformed Publishing, 2008), 441–67.

"Calvinism failed to understand and retain Calvin's concept of the grace of God as primary even in this primal and general relation between God and man; very soon the principle of it was no longer grace, but law."[3] James B. Torrance, who championed monocovenantal injection into Calvin's theology, reinterprets Calvin the same way Rolston does: "For Calvin, all God's dealings with men are those of grace, both in Creation and in Redemption. They flow from the loving heart of the Father. The two poles of his thought are grace and glory—from grace to glory."[4]

The promoters of the Federal Vision after Norman Shepherd vehemently reject the concept of the covenant of works, though they identify their monocovenantalism with the theology of Calvin. However, I would like to suggest that their rejection of the covenant of works is not better than neoorthodox theologians' rejection of it. Certainly, there is no room for the distinction between the covenant of works and the covenant of grace when they reject the Pauline evangelical distinction between law and gospel. In their theology, then, the historical and logical order of the law and gospel, which is the foundational order for Calvin's understanding of redemptive history and soteriology, is eclipsed.[5]

Calvin did not see the means to attain the blessings of "eternal life" in the prelapsarian Garden of Eden as grace or gospel but law contrary to what neoorthodox theologians claim. Neoorthodox theologians ignore and reject the importance of historical order as law and grace, which became the means to safeguard creation, fall, redemption, and consummation in Calvin's theology:

> In this integrity man by free will had the power, if he so willed, to attain eternal life. Here it would be out of place to raise the question of God's secret predestination because our present subject is not what happen or not, but what man's nature was like. Therefore

---

3. Rolston, *Calvin versus the Westminster Confession*, 36.

4. James B. Torrance, *Covenant or Contract?*, 62.

5. For critical interaction against the Federal Visionists' denial of the distinction between the covenant of works and the covenant of grace, see Michael S. Horton, "Which Covenant Theology," in *Covenant, Justification, and Pastoral Ministry: Essays by the Faculty of Westminster Seminary California*, ed. R. Scott Clark (Phillipsburg: Presbyterian and Reformed Publishing, 2007), 197–227; Morton H. Smith, "The Biblical Plan of Salvation with Reference to The Covenant of Works, Imputation, and Justification by Faith", in *The Auburn Avenue Theology, Pros and Cons: Debating the Federal Vision*, ed. E. Calvin Beisner (Fort Lauderdale: Knox Theological Seminary, 2004), 96–117; Waters, *The Federal Vision and Covenant Theology*, 30–58.

Adam could have stood if he wished, seeing that he fell solely by his own will. But it was because his will was capable of being bent to one side or the other, and was not given the constancy to persevere, that he fell so easily.[6]

Calvin unambiguously stated that Adam would have passed into eschatological life, had he obeyed God's law.[7] Thus, the principle of law or obedience was a principle of eschatological heavenly glorification in the prelapsarian state. Commenting on Genesis 2:16, Calvin observed that Adam underwent a probationary test period: "a law is imposed upon him in token of his subjection; for it would have made no difference to God, if he had eaten indiscriminately of any fruit he pleased. Therefore, the prohibition of one tree was a test of obedience."[8]

In addition, the law written in man's heart was a rule of life in the Garden of Eden. Calvin wrote "Therefore, abstinence from the fruit of one tree was a kind of first lesson in obedience, that man might know he had a Director and Lord of his life, on whose will he ought to depend, and in whose commands he ought to acquiesce."[9] Furthermore, Calvin closely correlated the law, which governed the Adamic prelapsarian state, as the law written in men's hearts and the moral law, written on the two stone Tablets.[10]

In short, Calvin believed that the eschatological heavenly vision in the prelapsarian Garden of Eden was expressed by means of obedience to the law. Calvin explained that if Adam confirmed "the authority of the law" by not eating the forbidden fruit in the Garden of Eden, then "he would have passed into heaven without death, and without injury":

> To the end that Adam might the more willingly comply, God commends his own liberality. 'Behold,' he says, 'I deliver into thy hand whatever fruits the earth may produce, whatever fruits every kind of tree may yield: from this immense profusion and variety I except only one tree.'... He was, in every respect, happy; his life, therefore, had alike respect to his body and his soul, since in his soul a right judgment and a proper government of the affections

6. Calvin, *Institutes*, 1.15.8.

7. Calvin, *Genesis*, 3:19.

8. Ibid., 2:16.

9. Ibid.

10. Calvin, *Institutes*, 2.8.1, 4.20.16.; Cf., Karlberg, "Reformed Interpretation of the Mosaic Covenant," 13.

prevailed, there also life reigned; in his body there was no defect, wherefore he was wholly free from death. His earthly life truly would have been temporal; yet he would have passed into heaven without death, and without injury . . . Wherefore the question is superfluous, how it was that God threatened death to Adam on the day in which he should touch the fruit, when he long deferred the punishment? For then was Adam consigned to death, and death began its reign in him, until supervening grace should bring a remedy.[11]

It is remarkable that Calvin envisioned the eschatological outlook of the original creation through the antithesis between Adam and Christ. For example, Calvin, in the context of explaining the meaning of Genesis 3:19, developed and applied the *creation eschatology* in his exegesis of 1 Corinthians 15:22, which is one of the classical Pauline passages of the antithesis between Adam and Christ along with Romans 5:12–21:

And therefore some understand what was before said, 'Thou shalt die,' in a spiritual sense; thinking that, even if Adam had not sinned, his body must still have been separated from his soul. But since the declaration of Paul is clear, that 'all die in Adam, as they shall rise again in Christ,' (1 Cor. Xv. 22,) this wound also was inflicted by sin. Nor truly is the solution of the question difficult,—'Why should God pronounce, that he who was taken from the dust should return to it.' For as soon as he had been raised to a dignity so great, that the glory of the Divine Image shone in him, the ter-restrial origin of his body was almost obliterated. Now, however, after he had been despoiled of his divine and heavenly excellence, what remains but that by his very departure out of life, he should recognize himself to be earth? Hence it is that we dread death, because dissolution, which is contrary to nature, cannot naturally be desired. Truly the first man would have passed to a better life, had he remained upright; but there would have been no separation of the soul from the body, no corruption, no kind of destruction, and, in short, no violent change.[12]

Calvin's eschatological heavenly vision for the prelapsarian Adam in respect to the obedience or conformity to the law, indeed, laid out the con-crete hermeneutical and theological foundation for the Calvinists' develop-ment and adaptation of the distinction between the covenant of works and

11. Calvin, *Genesis*, 2:16–17.
12. Ibid., 3:19.

the covenant of grace. In this respect, Calvin's redemptive historical order of creation, fall, redemption, and consummation was safely guarded by the historical and logical order of *law and gospel or grace not vice versa.*

Meanwhile, the Federal Visionists take an entirely different route compared to Calvin. As we have already explored, Calvin had a concrete consciousness of the distinction between law and gospel in his understanding of soteriology, and he applied its principle not only to the doctrine of justification by faith alone (*sola fide*) but also to the understanding of the redemptive history. In that sense, Calvin envisioned that the law was a governing principle for the prelapsarian Edenic community to view the eschatological heavenly blessings, not the gospel. However, the Federal Visionists have lost the consciousness of the distinction between law and gospel not only in their systematic theology but also in their understanding of redemptive history. Thus, they read the prelapsarian Edenic eschatological vision without the distinction between law and gospel, which is a vital hermeneutical tool in Calvin's eschatological outlook for the prelapsarian Edenic community. As the promoter of the Fedeal Vision, Sandlin puts himself "at odds with both traditional dispensationalism and traditional covenant theology." In doing so, he argues that the Bible presents the unity between law and gospel, which is an Achilles' heel for the theology of the Federal Vision. Emphatically speaking, then, he continues to argue that "there is no fundamental Gospel-Law distinction." As such, the presupposition of the understanding of both systematic theology and redemptive history for the Federal Visionists is to deny the distinction between law and gospel as we witness it in Sandlin's analysis:

> I hold that the Bible presents at root one Gospel, one Law, one salvation, one ethic, one hope, one Faith, all ensconced in one message. This view puts me at odds with both traditional dispensationalism and traditional covenant theology. Properly understood, *there is no fundamental Gospel-Law distinction.* I do not, of course, hold that the Bible's message is a flat revelation without any internal progress, and I do not advocate that dreaded "wooden hermeneutic," insensitivity to the historical and theological context. I believe that the beginning of the Biblical revelation is a seed, out of which the entire plant flowers with the arrival of Jesus. However, I do not believe that this progress of revelation entails two or more basic, conflicting messages.[13]

---

13. Sandlin, "Covenant in Redemptive History," 66–67.

Confusingly, Sandlin argues that he affirms "a totally gracious soteriology," which can be summarized as "salvation by grace alone through faith alone in Christ alone" while he denies "a Gospel-Law distinction." Moreover, he falsely argues that "a Gospel-Law distinction may actually *threaten* salvation by grace." We know that Sandlin's affirmation of "a totally gracious soteriology" while he denies the distinction between law and gospel, which is foundational for the *sola fide* and the sovereign grace of God in personal salvation and redemptive history is, at best, confusing and misleading:

> The immediate countering response is that this notion may threaten a totally gracious soteriology, which I enthusiastically affirm—salvation by grace alone through faith alone in Christ alone. In fact, however, I dispute the charge. I hold fervently to individual (and communal) salvation accomplished and applied wholly by God in Christ in redemptive history; but I am quite convinced that a Gospel-Law distinction does not serve this gracious soteriology very well. Indeed, I posit (and will attempt to show) that, in some cases, a Gospel-Law distinction may actually *threaten* salvation by grace.[14]

The rejection of the distinction between law and gospel in the theology of the Federal Vision leads to the denial of the distinction between the covenant of works and the covenant of grace, which is a logical outcome of the monocovenantalism of the Federal Vision.[15] However, here, we have to remember that the development of the distinction between the covenant of works and the covenant of grace in the Reformed orthodoxy is compatible to Calvin's theology as we have already explored because Calvin already laid out the concrete hermeneutical and theological ingredients for the bipolar covenant distinction, namely the covenant of works and the covenant of grace. The Federal Visionists deny the covenant of works in their interpretation of the prelapsarian Adamic status as the means of eschatological heavenly blessings as they deny the distinction between law and gospel. For example, Sandlin is very critical about the concept of the covenant of works, critiquing Charles Hodge's classical understanding of the covenant of works, which presents "two ways of gaining eternal life,

---

14. Ibid., 67.

15. Cf. Mark Horne, "Reformed Covenant Theology and Its Discontents," in *A Faith That Is Never Alone: a Response to Westminster Seminary California*, ed. P. Andrew Sandlin (La Grange: Kerygma Press, 2007), 73–107.

one by works and one by faith." This is another theological expression of two opposite ways of obtaining everlasting heavenly blessings, one by law and another by gospel:

> In the Garden of Eden, God told Adam and Eve that they could eat of all the trees except one—the tree of the knowledge of good and evil (Gen. 2:16–17). We also know that if they are of the tree of life, they would have lived forever—or gained eternal life (Gen. 3:22). I do not believe this has anything to do with what is traditionally termed a prelapsarian (or pre-Fall) "covenant of works": that eternal life was something man was rewarded as merit for his obedience. Before the Fall, this view alleges, man was to merit eternal life and afterwards Christ must merit it for us. I disagree with Charles Hodge when he asserts that the Bible presents *two* ways of gaining eternal life, one by works and one by faith, just as I disagree with C.I. Scofield's statement: "As a dispensation, grace begins with the death and resurrection of Christ . . . The point of testing is no longer *legal obedience as the condition of salvation*, but acceptance or rejection of Christ, with good works as a fruit of salvation."[16]

16. Sandlin, "Covenant in Redemptive History," 67–68. John Murray, as a Reformed biblico-systematic theologian, was very critical to the classical dispensationalism, represented in *Scofield Reference Bible*, as Sandlin quotes a part of it as the means of a critique. But, Sandlin's critique of the classical dispensationalism is not sound because his criticism is based upon monocovenantalism with the rejection to the antithesis between law and gospel, which is foundational for the principle of the gospel and *sola fide*. However, it is very important to remember that Murray's critique of the classical dispensationalism did not lie in the antithesis between law and gospel itself. Rather, his critique properly lied in the two different ways of individual salvation under the Old and New Covenants, one as obedience to the law and the other as grace or gospel where the classical dispensationalists viewed the two opposite principles of salvation under the Old and New Covenants, denying the redemptive historical continuity in both periods: "In modern dispensationalism a sharp antithesis in respect of governing principle is set up between the dispensation of law (Sinai to Calvary) and the dispensation of grace (Calvary to Christ's second coming), as also, perhaps to a lesser extent, between the kingdom dispensation (millennial reign of Christ) and the dispensation of grace. A great many of the statements of dispensationalists are perfectly correct insofar as they express the antithesis that does exist, and on which Scripture lays the greatest emphasis, between obedience to law as the way of justification and acceptance with God and the way of grace. Every evangelical must recognize and appreciate this absolute antithesis. The error of dispensationalism in this connection is twofold. First of all, it applies this sharp antithesis to the successive dispensations and interprets the Mosaic as exemplifying law in contrast with grace, and the gospel dispensation as exemplifying grace in contrast with law. Secondly, this antithesis which is applied to the successive dispensations in respect of governing principle leads dispensationalism into a false view of the place of law within the sphere of grace. This bias of dispensationalism appears, for example, in the Scofield Reference Bible

Sandlin and the Federal Visionists do not understand that "two methods of attaining eternal life" described by the Old Princeton theologian Charles Hodge was just a reiteration of the Protestant Reformation principle of the distinction between law and gospel as two opposite ways of eternal life, one as the law and the other as the gospel. So, the denial of the distinction between law and gospel among the Federal Visionists not only radically reinterprets the theology of Calvin but also Reformed orthodoxy, represented by Charles Hodge. Charles Hodge unambiguously noticed two opposite ways of eternal life because it is a biblically warranted way of hermeneutics and theology, especially in respect to soteriology. In doing so, Charles Hodge affirmed the classical biblical doctrine of the covenant of works. It is necessary to unpack what Charles Hodge actually describes:

> This statement does not rest upon any express declaration of the Scriptures. It is, however, a concise and correct mode of asserting a plain Scriptural fact, namely, that God made to Adam a promise suspended upon a condition, and attached to disobedience a certain penalty. This is what in Scriptural language is meant by a covenant, and this is all that is meant by the term as here used. Although the word covenant is not used in Genesis, and does not elsewhere, in any clear passage, occur in reference to the transaction there recorded, yet inasmuch as the plan of salvation is constantly represented as a New Covenant, new, not merely in antithesis to that made at Sinai, but new in reference to all legal covenants whatever, it is plain that the Bible does represent the arrangement made with Adam as a truly federal transaction. The Scriptures know nothing of any other than two methods of attaining eternal life: the one that which demands perfect obedience, and the other that which demands faith. If the latter is called a covenant, the former is declared to be of the same nature....
>
> God then did enter into a covenant with Adam. That covenant is sometimes called a covenant of life, because life was promised as the reward of obedience. Sometimes it is called the covenant of works, because works were the condition on which that promise

---

in its comments on the sermon on the mount (pp. 999f., 1002). In the literature of dispensationalism perhaps no one sets forth the position more insistently than Lewis Sperry Chafer (*cf. Systematic Theology*, Dallas, 1948, Vol. IV, pages 180–251). One or two examples will illustrate. 'The very nature of grace precepts precludes them from being reduced to a Decalogue. They are free in character in the sense that they are not required for acceptance with God' (p. 184)." Murray, *Principles of Conduct*, 264.

was suspended, and because it is thus distinguished from the new covenant which promises life on condition of faith.[17]

Reflecting on Sandlin's critique against Charles Hodge's two opposite ways of eternal life, here, we have to be reminded that Sandlin's failure to recognize the distinction between the covenant of works and the covenant of grace is a covenantal implication of the distinction between law and gospel in which Calvin carefully applied not only in the arena of soteriology but also in the historical order as law and gospel, not vice versa, covering creation, fall, and redemption as the means of the escha- tological heavenly blessings and eternal life. In that sense, Sandlin fails to recognize the importance of the distinction between law and gospel as the two opposite means of salvation to denote the concept of salvation by grace alone and justification by faith alone in the postlapsarian era. The denial of the distinction between law and gospel in the theology of the Federal Vision has led them to deny two ways of obtaining eternal life between the prelapsarian and postlapsarian eras. In that manner, Sandlin argues the monocovenantal way understanding of the means of eternal life, falsely arguing "only one way of obtaining eternal life," rejecting the distinction between the prelapsarian and postlapsarian eras of the two opposite ways of obtaining eternal life, one by law and another by gospel:

> (One is reminded of John Gerstner's quip that dispensationalists are legalists in the Old Testament and antinomians in the New Testament.) There are not *two* ways of gaining of eternal life, one in the prelapsarian era and one in the postlapsarian era, or one in the Mosaic era and one in the resurrection era. There is only one way of obtaining eternal life, *and there has always been only one way.*[18]

In Calvin's soteriology, the concept of merit is foundational, as well as the distinction between law and gospel. However, the monocovenantalism of the Federal Vision does not allow the concept of *merit* to be played out in their theology along with the distinction between law and gospel. So, the Federal Visionists are not only critical to the concept of the covenant of works in respect to the prelapsarian Adamic status but also to the

---

17. Charles Hodge, *Systematic Theology*, 3 vols. (reprint, Grand Rapids: Eerdmans, 1995), 2:117–18. For the brief sketch on Charles Hodge's covenant theology and the doc- trine of justification by faith, see Jeon, *Covenant Theology*, 69–79.

18. Sandlin, "Covenant in Redemptive History," 68.

concept of merit, which is closely attached to the biblical idea of the covenant of works.

James B. Jordan, as he endorses the Federal Vision, typically denies the distinction between law and gospel, as well as the distinction between the covenant of works and the covenant of grace. In doing so, he replaces the classical understanding of the two Adams' obedience to the law not as merit but maturity. He is critical to the concept of the covenant of works, identifying his rejection to Murray's apparent rejection of it. Moreover, he labels the concept of the covenant of works as a Pelagian idea, which is a clear reflection of his poor historical theological understanding and orientation:

> Moreover, the phrase "covenant of works" was seen as problematic. What did it mean? Better, what did this phrase quickly communicate to people not rigorously schooled in systematic theology? It might mean that God had a Plan A, and by which people could "earn their way to eternal life by doing good works." Since Adam had not earned eternal life, Jesus came to do so, and now it is given to us by grace and received by faith. It almost seems as if that is the view. Murray summarizes Robert Rollock's opinions, delivered in 1596 and 1597, as follows: "The *promise* [of the Adamic covenant] is eternal life accruing to man, not on the basis of his original righteousness or integrity, but on the basis of good works performed in the strength of this integrity."[19]

Jordan argues that the idea of the covenant of works must be rejected whether we conceive it meritoriously or graciously because it is "still fundamentally Pelagian in character." In doing so, Jordan denies the meritorious obedience of Jesus Christ as the mediator between God and

19. Jordan, "Merit Versus Maturity," 152–53. Robert Rollock (1555–1599), as a Scottish theologian greatly contributed to the development and adaptation of the distinction between the covenant of works and the covenant of grace. And he properly applied the bi-covenantal distinction to the arena of justification by faith alone and salvation by grace alone, which is very harmonious with Calvin's theology. For the comprehensive exploration of Robert Rollock's covenant theology and its implication to hermeneutics and theology, see Jeon, *Covenant Theology*, 33–40.

James B. Jordan has promoted the hermeneutical, theological and practical ideals of theonomy, represented by Greg Bahnsen, R. J. Rushdoony, and others. Although there are some hermeneutical and theological variations within theonomy, it is my assessment that there is a common denominator among the theonomists, which is a rejection of the antithesis between law and gospel. In that respect, I think that there is a point of contact between the Federal Vision and theonomy as we witness it through James Jordan's participation in the Federal Vision.

His people, which is foundational for biblical soteriology and for proper understanding of the progressive development of redemptive history. So, the hermeneutical and theological foundations of *sola fide* and *sola gratia* are abandoned. Logically, then, Jordan denies that Jesus Christ earned our eternal life as the representative covenantal head through his perfect obedience to the law, and he denies that we receive our salvation "as a gift by faith alone":

> Despite Turretin's strictures, this scheme is still fundamentally Pelagian in character: God graciously set up a system by which Adam would earn eternal life, though the reward earned was out of all proportion to the merits acquired through Adam's work.
>
> If this be what the Bible reaches, then so be it. Simply charging it with "Pelagianism" or work-salvation is not enough. After all no one was suggesting that we as sinners are capable of working out our own eternal life. The thought was that Jesus has earned it for us, and we receive it as a gift by faith alone.
>
> There are, however, several problems with this theological scheme, despite the fact that what it seeks to affirm is quite true (to wit: the two-stage nature of human life). One problem is the notion of earning glorified eternal life through meritorious works. As I intend to show in this paper, nothing in the Bible teaches that Adam was supposed to earn glory. He was, rather, called to remain faithful and mature to the point of awareness that he needed a fuller kind of life from God, which God would freely give him at the proper time.[20]

Similarly, denying the biblical doctrine of the covenant of works, Sandlin also denies the meritorious obedience of the two Adams as the representative covenantal heads. In doing so, he blames Meredith G. Kline's affirmation of meritorious obedience of the two Adams for the classical formulation of the covenant of works. Not only does Sandlin reject the covenant of works, but he also rejects the antithesis between Adam and Christ, which is crucial for the biblical understanding of limited atonement, *sola fide*, the sovereign grace of God in personal salvation, and the proper understanding of redemptive history, inaugurated in Genesis 3:15:

> I am especially troubled by the idea that eternal life in the prelapsarian era was something that man could, and must,

20. Jordan, "Merit Versus Maturity," 153.

merit. This is the view, and language, of Old Testament scholar Meredith Kline. But I do not encounter "merit theology" in the Bible—except perhaps as espoused by Judaizers and Pharisees, but there, of course, it is fervently condemned.

God threatened judgment if Adam and Eve disobeyed, but he did not promise eternal life as the *reward* for obedience. I infer from this omission that they would have been granted eternal life on some *other* ground than their obedience. It seems to me that this ground is the unmerited favor of God. Eternal life, even in the prelapsarian period, was of grace, and not of merit. Obedient faith was the *means* of gaining eternal life, but not the *grounds*.[21]

The Federal Visionists destroy the *distinction* between Adam and Christ in terms of the means of the eschatological heavenly blessings because they read Adam and Christ in light of monocovenantalism as they deny the distinction between law and gospel. However, it was clear to Calvin that Adam could have *merited* the eschatological heavenly blessings as the representative head of his descendents if we apply Calvin's concept of merit to the prelapsarian Adamic status. Certainly, Calvin limited the meritorious obedience to only the two Adams because the perfect obedience to the requirements of the law is only possible to Adam before the Fall and to Christ as the mediator of the New Covenant, according to his concept of merit. As such, the Federal Visionists' understanding of the parallel between Adam and Christ is not compatible to Calvin's *antithesis* of Adam and Christ.

Sandlin denies that Adam's obedience could have "merited eternal life." In that sense, he falsely argues that "the ground of eternal life in the prelapsarian era" is not the meritorious obedience to the law by Adam but "the grace of God." Here, we need to pay close attention to Sandlin's theological logic. There is no problem if Sandlin admits that "the grace of God" as "the ground of eternal life in the prelapsarian era" may be applicable in light of the distinction between the Creator and creature. But, that is not the case here. For the Federal Visionists, as Sandlin argues, God's grace as "the ground of eternal life" before the Fall is simply a theological byproduct of monocovenantalism. Furthermore, Sandlin argues that denying the *antithesis* between Adam and Christ, "faith in the Lord, accompanied by obedience" was the "instrument and means" of eternal life in the prelapsarian era, as well as the subsequent postlapsarian era. As

21. Sandlin, "Covenant in Redemptive History," 68–69.

a result, Sandlin rejects the antithesis between Adam and Christ as well as the historical and logical order of the law and gospel as the means of everlasting life, covering creation, fall, and redemption:

> I realize that before the Fall, Adam and Eve did not need redemption or salvation in the way that they did, and the rest of us do, *after* the Fall. But to assert that they did not need redemption is not to assert that eternal life was not a gift, that it did not require grace. Nor is it to say—worse yet—that they could have merited eternal life. Man before the fall was no sinner, but he was finite he needed God's favor.
>
> So, in theological language, the *ground* of eternal life in the prelapsarian era is the grace of God. What is its instrument and means? I believe that they are really no different that in the subsequent eras—faith in the Lord, accompanied by obedience, and, in fact, a faith that is itself an act of obedience. This faith is a gift of God, and it is not something that can merit eternal life—in any era. If we wish to simplify this arrangement, we may employ the words of the old hymn, "Trust and Obey."[22]

The Federal Visionists' denial of the antithesis between Adam and Christ, rejecting the historical and logical order of law and gospel, directly affects their understanding of soteriology. In doing so, they deny the meritorious obedience of Adam and Christ, which is crucial to a profound biblical soteriology, which the Reformers, including Calvin, safeguarded the principle of sovereign grace in sinner's salvation and *sola gratia*, as well as *sola fide*. Likewise, Sandlin denies the meritorious obedience of the two Adams in his interpretation of Galatians 3:21, as he denies the concept of the covenant of works, which is a logical development by the Reformed orthodox theologians after the hermeneutical and theological pattern of Calvin:

> Now, this conviction relating to the prelapsarian era has specific implications for the redemptive ministry of Jesus Christ. If eternal life is not something that Adam merited, and if it is not something that man could even conceivably merit (Gal. 3:21), it is not, therefore, something that Jesus Christ Himself merited. There is simply no such thing as a meritorious basis of eternal life, and there is no such thing as a meritorious soteriology. It is simply a fiction.[23]

22. Ibid., 69.
23. Ibid., 69–70.

As the Federal Visionists deny the validity of the meritorious obedience of the two Adams as well as the distinction between the covenant of works and the covenant of grace, they view the concept of union with Christ in light of their understanding of monocovenantalism as I have already discussed. In that sense, once again, we should understand that Calvin's profound concept of mystical union with Christ in soteriology and the Federal Visionists' significantly altered concept of mystical union with Christ in light of monocovenantalism are not compatible. For example, Sandlin argues that "union with Christ by faith" is a channel by which Christ's righteousness becomes our righteousness as Paul states in 1 Corinthians 1:30. Because Sandlin denies the meritorious obedience of Jesus Christ, he also denies faith as the sole channel to receive Jesus' "Law-keeping righteousness," mixing faith and obedience in the realm of righteousness:

> Do not misunderstand: in union with Christ by faith, all of His righteousness becomes ours (1 Cor. 1:30). We obtained all of His Law-keeping righteousness, because He has fulfilled all righteousness for us (Mt. 3:15; 2 Cor. 5:14–21). But this righteousness is simple faith in and reliance on His Father and the obedience that constitutes it and flows from it. So, eternal life was not something that Jesus was "rewarded" for being extraordinary virtuous. He was a humble, obedient Son (Jn. 5:30; 8:29); and He was faithful in His humble obedience where Adam failed (Rom. 5:12–21). The righteousness that becomes ours as we are mystically united to Him by faith alone is a love-filled, Law-keeping righteousness: a faithful trust and reliance on the Father that necessarily issues good works.[24]

While the Federal Visionists identify their theology with Calvin, they blame the Roman Catholic theology and Reformed covenant theology for adopting the concept of merit into the arena of soteriology. In doing so, they adopt the misconstrued historical theological analysis, representatively formulated by Norman Shepherd, who makes a serious historical theological mistake. However, we should remember that in Calvin's theology, the idea of merit was *foundational* to reach the grace-oriented soteriology as I have already examined extensively. Unfortunately, Sandlin, as the other Federal Visionists, blindly follows Shepherd's rejection of the idea of merit in relation to the two Adams' obedience:

24. Ibid., 70.

If, however, we insist that eternal life is in its essence something that man merits, as Rome did, we may slowly drift (as, in fact, Rome has) into a synergism that sees man as contributing to his own salvation. In fact, as Norman Shepherd observes, "[I]f we do not reject the idea of merit, we are not really able to challenge the Romanist doctrine of salvation at its very root." Traditional covenant theology tries valiantly to avoid this error by claiming that Christ as man did the meriting, so sinful man need no longer merit as he once had to in the Garden of Eden. So, while all of God's benefits to man today are gracious, eternal life is fundamentally *achieved* by merit and not *bestowed* by grace. It is just that Jesus, not sinful man, now does the meriting.[25]

Following the lead of Karl Barth's idea of Christomonistic grace, Sandlin argues that the concept of merit makes "Christ something of an afterthought in God's plan for man's gaining eternal life." Furthermore, he argues that for Jesus Christ to be "ultimate" in personal salvation the idea of "merit and justice" should be rejected. However, we have to remember that in Calvin's theology, without the meritorious obedience of Jesus Christ, Christ cannot be *ultimate* in our personal salvation and eternal life. Committing to monocovenantalism, Sandlin insists that in the Garden of Eden before the Fall, God would have granted eternal life to Adam and Eve "by the grace (or unmerited favor) of God" through "faith and obedience." In that sense, Sandlin, as one of the members of the Federal Vision, clearly rejects Adam's perfect obedience to the law as the means of receiving eternal life, rejecting the historical and logical order of law and gospel:

> It seems to me that this makes Christ something of an afterthought in God's plan for man's gaining eternal life. Christ is no longer really the Lamb slain from the world's foundation (Rev. 13:8). He is, rather, an instrument to get something more ultimate than Him: merit. Merit and justice, not Jesus, becomes ultimate. This I judge to be a serious error.
>
> In the Garden, the man and woman would be granted eternal life by the grace (or unmerited favor) of God. They were called to faith and obedience—there was no need for redemption (of course), but there was still need for grace and faith and obedience. "Trust and Obey."[26]

25. Ibid., 70–71.
26. Ibid., 71.

It is obvious that although the Federal Visionists try to identify their hermeneutics and theology with Calvin, their hermeneutics and theology are much closer to Barth than Calvin. Interpreting Romans 10:4–9, a classical Pauline passage about the antithesis between law and gospel in Calvin's theology, Sandlin uses the passage to deny the distinction between law and gospel after the hermeneutical and theological pattern of Karl Barth's monocovenantalism:

> It is a Gospel message contained in the revelatory Law of Moses that is near God's covenant people and ready for them to appropriate by faith. It is not the imposition of codified demands apart from a gracious salvation. For this reason Karl Barth writes:
>
>> With regard to the New Testament, must one not draw special attention to the fact that it, like the Old Testament, is law —i.e., ordinance, command and instruction for the new life of the people and children of God—but not therefore—not even in part—an authorization and invitation to self-justification and self-sanctification? It is therefore not a book of religion but rather the consistent proclamation of the justifying and sanctifying grace of God, thereby exposing the faithlessness of all religion . . . One forgets . . . what is so clear and self-evident, that the essence of the benefit of Jesus Christ and therefore of his gospel as experienced in the church of the New Testament is his *Lordship* over human beings. And there can be no purer, or more total *imperative* than the simple invitation directed to man in the New Testament—that he should believe in this Jesus Christ—and no stricter and fuller *obedience* than that which the New Testament describes precisely as faith.
>
> This simplified description of a unified message of Gospel and Law reflects the Biblical data more accurately than the antithetical Gospel-Law paradigm, which tends to surrender the Lordship of Christ in the Gospel on the one hand, and on the other hand, transforms God's commands and requirements ('Law') into a system of works-righteousness. This paradigm breaks apart what God has joined together.[27]

27. P. Andrew Sandlin, "The Gospel of Law and the Law of Gospel: An Assessment of the Antithetical Gospel-Law Paradigm," in *A Faith That Is Never Alone: A Response to Westminster Seminary California*, ed. P. Andrew Sandlin (La Grange: Kerygma Press, 2007), 238–39.

Thus, the denial of the distinction between law and gospel in the theology of the Federal Vision has led the Federal Visionists to reject the distinction between the covenant of works and the covenant of grace, which is a logical outcome of Calvin's hermeneutics and theology, developed by the Reformed orthodox theologians. Logically, they also reject the notion of merit, which was foundational for Calvin in his understanding of the antithesis between Adam and Christ to apply and to develop the grace-oriented soteriology, as well as the Christ-centered redemptive history.

THE INAUGURATION OF THE COVENANT OF GRACE AND REDEMPTIVE HISTORICAL CONTINUITY

As I have demonstrated, Calvin's use of the law and gospel antithesis was a decisive theological reference point to safeguard *sola gratia* and *sola fide* against the background of the medieval Schoolmen's meritorious notion of salvation. In understanding God's redemptive history from a covenantal perspective, this hermeneutical principle was applied under the rubric of one covenant of grace in the postlapsarian state: "The covenant made with all the patriarchs is so much like ours in substance and reality that the two are actually one and the same. Yet they differ in the mode of dispensation. But because no one can gain a clear understanding from such a statement, a fuller explanation is required if we wish to make any progress."[28] This one covenant of grace was also identified as a "spiritual covenant" (*spirituale foedus*), covering all of redemptive history since Adam's Fall, including the Mosaic Covenant. For Calvin, this covenantal continuity was a theological reference point for standing against the Anabaptists and Servetus. It signified the redemptive spiritual covenant continuity between the Old and New Covenants in which believers in the Old Testament as well as those in the New Testament were saved by God's grace alone in Christ. Once again, Calvin wrote:

> But my readers may prefer to have testimonies cited from the Law and the Prophets, to prove to them that, as we have heard from Christ and the apostles, the spiritual covenant was also common to the patriarchs. Well then, I shall comply with their desire, and the more willingly because our adversaries will thus be more surely refuted; and afterward be quite unable to evade the issue[29]

28. Calvin, *Institutes*, 2.10.2.
29. Ibid., 2.10.7. Servetus, as the representative theologian amongst the Anabaptists,

During the period of the Protestant Reformation, the Anabaptists denied that the Old Testament believers received *spiritual blessings*, including the heavenly realm and eternal life like the believers under the New Covenant. In that sense, they viewed the Old Testament believers to be only under the carnal covenant in which the blessings were limited to the earthly and carnal ones. Pondering 1 Peter 1:23–24 and Isaiah 40:6, Calvin insisted that God bound "the Jews to himself by this sacred bond" even in the Old Testament. In that sense, we can be sure that God bestowed the Old Testament Jews "the hope of eternal life" (*spem aeternae vitae*). Thus, Calvin demonstrated that all the patriarchs, starting from Adam, entered into "God's immortal Kingdom" with "the blessing of eternal life":

> I shall then begin with this proof—even though I know the Anabaptists will disdainfully consider it pointless and even ridiculous—yet it will be most valuable for sound and teachable folk. I take it for granted that there is such life energy in God's Word that it quickens the souls of all to whom God grants participation in it. For Peter's saying has always been valid, that it is an imperishable seed, which abides forever [1 Peter 1:23], as he also infers from Isaiah's words [1 Peter 1:24; Isa. 40:6]. Now since God of old bound the Jews to himself by this sacred bond, there is no doubt that he set them apart to the hope of eternal life. When I say they embraced the Word to be united more closely to God, I do not mean that general mode of communication which is diffused through heaven and earth and all the creatures of the world . . . Rather, I mean that special mode which both illumines the souls of the pi-

---

denied the redemptive historical continuity between the Old and New Covenants in terms of soteriological blessings for believers in his famous treatise, *Christianismi restitutio* in 1553. In his writing, Servetus denied that the Old Testament believers received the eschatological heavenly blessings, arguing that "in the Law. . . remission of sins was carnal and earthly." In response to Servetus and other Anabaptists, Calvin emphasized that the Old Testament believers received the same spiritual blessings like us, developing the covenantal continuity and discontinuity which exist between the Old and New Testaments: "Indeed, that wonderful rascal Servetus and certain madmen of the Anabaptists sect, who regard the Israelites as nothing but a herd of swine, make necessary what would in any case have been very profitable for us. For they babble of the Israelites as fattened by the Lord on this earth without any hope of heavenly immortality. So, then, to keep this pestilential error away from godly minds, and at the same time to remove all the difficulties that usually rise up immediately when mention is made of the difference between the Old and New Testament, let us look in passing at the similarities and differences between the covenant that the Lord made of old with the Israelites before Christ's advent, and that which God has now made with us after his manifestation." Ibid., 2.10.1.

ous into the knowledge of God and, in a sense, joins them to him.
Adam, Abel, Noah, Abraham, and the other patriarchs cleaved to
God by such illumination of the Word. Therefore I say that without
any doubt they entered into God's immortal Kingdom. For theirs
was a real participation in God, which cannot be without the blessing of eternal life.[30]

Calvin demonstrated that "the very formula of the covenant" (*ipsam foederis formulam*) in the Old Covenant between the Lord and his servants
is manifested in God's covenantal promise, saying "I will be your God, and
you shall be my people" in Leviticus 26:2. Moreover, the prophetic messages embrace the rich blessings of "life and salvation." Calvin observed
that the manifestation of the shining glory to God's covenant people was
"a very present pledge of salvation," opening to His people "the treasures
of His salvation." As such, Calvin interpreted the Old Covenant in light
of redemptive historical continuity in which God bestowed rich spiritual
blessings, including salvation and heavenly inheritance as believers receive them under the New Covenant:

> Does this still a little unclear? Well, then, let us pass on to the very
> formula of the covenant. This will not only satisfy calm spirits but
> will also abundantly demonstrate the ignorance of those who try
> to contradict it. For the Lord always covenanted with his servants
> thus: "I will be your God, and you shall be my people" [Lev. 26:12].
> The prophets also commonly explained that life and salvation
> and the whole of blessedness are embraced in these words. For
> with good reason David often declares: "Blessed the people whose
> God is the Lord" [Ps. 144:15]; "Blessed . . . the nation whom he
> has chosen as his heritage" [Ps. 33:12]. This is not for the sake of
> earthly happiness, but because he delivers them from death, he
> preserves forever and keeps in his everlasting mercy those whom
> he has chosen as his people . . . But not to belabor superfluous mat-
> ters, this admonition repeatedly occurs in the Prophets: we lack
> nothing for an abundance of all good things and for assurance of
> salvation so long as the Lord is our God. And rightly so! For if his
> face, the moment that it has shone forth, is a very present pledge of
> salvation, how can he manifest himself to a man as his God with-
> out also opening to him the treasures of His salvation? He is our
> God on this condition: that he dwells among us, as he has testified
> through Moses [Lev. 26:11]. But one cannot obtain such a presence
> of him without, at the same time, possessing life. And although

30. Ibid., 2.10.7.

nothing further was expressed, they had a clear enough promise of spiritual life in these words: "I am ... your God" [Ex. 6:7].[31]

In fact, Calvin was a wonderful redemptive historical theologian. He envisioned the grand outlook of redemptive history, which is inaugurated in Genesis 3:15. The progressive nature of redemptive history was well captured and saturated in Calvin's redemptive historical, and theological mind. Calvin demonstrated that the *protevangelium* of Genesis 3:15 is the beginning of God's redemptive covenant of grace by which Adam received "the first promise of salvation" (*prima salutis promissio*) from God. This covenant of grace which Calvin termed as "the covenant of his mercy" (*misericordiae suae foedere*) is progressively revealed in Scripture:

> The Lord held to this orderly plan in administering the covenant of his mercy: as the day of full revelation approached with the passing of time, the more he increased each day the brightness of its manifestation. Accordingly, at the beginning when the first promise of salvation was given to Adam [Gen. 3:15] it glowed like a feeble spark. Then, as it was added to the light grew in fullness, breaking forth increasingly and shedding its radiance more widely. At last—when all the clouds dispersed—Christ, the Son of Righteousness, fully illumined the whole earth [cf. Mal., ch. 4] [32]

In his interpretation of the Old Testament after Adam's Fall, Calvin had eschatological consciousness, and he brilliantly argued that God imparted the pilgrim or the sojourner character to the Old Testament believers while they lived in this world. That is the reason why the prophets emphasized that God's people seek for the ultimate blessing not "in the present life" (*in praesenti vita*) but in "the happiness of the spiritual life to come" (*futurae ac spiritualis vitae felicitatem*):

> Nevertheless, I shall warn my readers beforehand to remember to open up their way with the key that I previously put into their hands. That is, whenever the prophets recount the believing people's blessedness, hardly the least trace of which is discerned in the present life, let them take refuge in this distinction: the better to commend God's goodness, the prophets represented it for the people under the lineaments, so to speak, of temporal benefits. But they painted a portrait such as to lift up the minds of people above the earth, above the elements of this world [cf. Gal. 4:3] and the

31. Ibid., 2.10.8.
32. Ibid., 2.10.20.

perishing age, and that would of necessity arouse them to ponder the happiness of the spiritual life to come.[33]

In his analysis on redemptive historical continuity between the Old and New Testaments, Calvin avoided the nature of a prosperity-centered life whereby the Anabaptists easily fell into this because they interpreted the Old Testament believers' blessings not from a spiritual and eternal perspective but from a carnal and material one. Calvin, exploring "the holy patriarchs" from Adam onward, rightly concluded that the patriarchs "lifted up their hearts to God's sanctuary, in which they found hidden what does not appear in the shadows of the present life." Pondering upon the Psalmist David's confession, Calvin argued that hardships and sufferings during the pilgrimage for the Old Testament believers were "the Last Judgment of God." The Old Testament patriarchs believed that "God's promises" will be fulfilled ultimately not in the present world but in God's eternal Kingdom. Likewise, Calvin carefully avoided the nature of the prosperity Gospel in his interpretation of the Old Testament through the concept of eschatological heavenly blessings, which was conspicuously lacking in the Anabaptistic hermeneutics and theology:

> Let us, therefore, learn from this confession of David's that the holy patriarchs under the Old Testament were aware how rarely or never God fulfills in this world what he promises to his servants; and that they therefore lifted up their hearts to God's sanctuary, in which they found hidden what does not appear in the shadows of the present life. This place was the Last Judgment of God, which, although they could not discern it with their eyes, they were content to understand by faith. Relying upon this assurance, they did not doubt that, whatever might happen in the world, the time would nevertheless come when God's promises would be fulfilled. So these statements witness: "I shall behold thy face in righteousness. . . . I shall be satisfied with thy countenance" [Ps. 17:15p.]. Again, "I am like a green olive tree in the house of the Lord." [Ps. 52:8p.] Again: "The righteous shall flourish like the palm tree, and grow like a cedar in Lebanon. Planted in the house of the Lord, they shall flourish in the courts of our God. They shall still bring forth fruit; in old age they shall be fat and green" [Ps. 92:12–14p.]. A little before, he had said: "How deep are thy thoughts, O Jehovah, . . . While evildoers flourish and sprout like grass, that they may perish forever" [Ps. 92:5, 7p.]. Where does that beauty and grace of

---

33. Ibid.

believers appear save when this world of appearances is overturned by the manifestation of God's Kingdom? When they cast their eyes upon that eternity, they despised the momentary harshness of present calamities and burst forth fearlessly in these words.[34]

Against the Anabaptistic hermeneutics and theology whereby they denied redemptive historical continuity, Calvin had the gospel consciousness in his interpretation of redemptive history and the Old Testament. In that respect, his approach to the Old Testament is profoundly Christocentric, and redemptive historical through and through. Calvin argued that we cannot separate the Old Testament Jews "from Christ, since with them, we hear, was made the covenant of the gospel, the soul foundation of which is Christ." Furthermore, Calvin argued that Jesus himself in John 8:56 confirmed that Abraham rejoiced to see Jesus' day and saw it with gladness, which signifies that Abraham, as the father of faith, enjoyed the soteriological and spiritual blessings in Jesus Christ, which is summed up in "the covenant of gospel" (*Evangelii foedus*). So, with a concrete redemptive historical mindset, Calvin noted that "the Old Testament always had its end in Christ and in eternal life." Likewise, Calvin wrote as follows:

> For the same reason it follows that the Old Testament was established upon the free mercy of God, and was confirmed by Christ's intercession. For the gospel preaching, too, declares nothing else than that sinners are justified apart from their own merit by God's fatherly kindness; and the whole of it is summed up in Christ. Who, then, dares to separate the Jews from Christ, since with them, we hear, was made the covenant of the gospel, the sole foundation of which is Christ? Who dares to estrange from the gift of salvation those to whom we hear the doctrine of the righteousness of faith was imparted? Not to dispute too long about something obvious—we have a notable saying of the Lord: "Abraham rejoiced that he was to see my day; he saw it and was glad" [John 8:56]. And what Christ there testified concerning Abraham, the apostle shows to have been universal among the believing folk when he says: "Christ remains, yesterday and today and forever" [Heb. 13:8]. Paul is not speaking there simply of Christ's everlasting divinity but of his power, a power perpetually available to believers. Therefore, both the blessed Virgin and Zacharias in their songs called the salvation revealed in Christ the manifestation of the promises that

---

34. Ibid., 2.10.17.

the Lord had formerly made to Abraham and the patriarchs [Luke 1:54–55, 72–73]. If the Lord, in manifesting his Christ, discharged his ancient oath, one cannot but say that the Old Testament always had its end in Christ and in eternal life.[35]

As such, Calvin demonstrated that he understood the Old Testament not only from a redemptive historical perspective, which can be identified as Christocentric but also a Christotelic perspective, which always directed "its end in Christ and in eternal life" (*eius finis in Christo et vita aeterna*).[36] Calvin made a great theological point when he demonstrated

---

35. Ibid., 2.10.4.

36. Reflecting on the discussion of theology in light of "christocentrism" by the nineteenth-century liberals, including Schleiermacher and twentieth-century neoorthodox theologians, represented by Karl Barth, Muller proposes not to use the term "christocentrism" in respect to Reformation theology, including Calvin. Muller adds that the neoorthodox theologians inject the christomonistic concept and grace to interpret Calvin's theology. This has created enormous confusion in understanding Calvin's theology. See Richard Muller, "A Note on 'Christocentrism' and the Imprudent Use of Such Terminology," *Westminster Theological Journal* 68 (2006): 253–60. Muller rightly suggests that we must separate Calvin's christocentrism from Barth's christomonism in which Barth and his followers fail to keep the logical and historical orders of law and grace in their interpretation of Calvin's theology in the depiction of redemptive history as creation, Fall, and redemption: "At the wellspring of twentieth-century christocentrism, Karl Barth argued that, in Calvin's theology,

> Christ is that unspoken original presupposition in terms of which we see God *a priori* as the ground and goal, the one who judges us and shows us mercy.... Looking from Christ to God, we have knowledge of God, or, as
> it is put later, knowledge of God the Creator.

Here Christ becomes the focus of all knowledge of God, including knowledge of God as Creator. Redemption is somehow prior to creation, just as, in the Barthian perspective, grace is prior to law, despite the clearly different order and arrangement of Calvin's *Institutes*, and (despite some neo-orthodox argument to the contrary) the very clear statements of Calvin to his theological intentions on the issue. Klooster wisely remarked that 'while Calvin is indeed christocentric—christologically theocentric is more accurate—his christocentrism is certainly not that of neo-orthodoxy.' But even here, in this fundamentally accurate observation, we are confronted with a problem of definition: Calvin's 'christocentrism' is not the 'christocentrism' of Barth and to identify both of these theologians as 'christocentric' is either to create a demand that various christocentrisms be distinguished or to lapse into a muddled equivocation." Ibid., 258. Observing contemporary confusion in the designation of "christocentrisms" to different theological traditions, especially by neoorthodox theologians, Muller suggests avoiding and abolishing the term "christocentrism" in respect to Reformation studies, including Calvin: "We turn to the point that various 'christocentrisms' need to be distinguished and that the term is sorely in need of more careful and discriminating usage. Beyond that, given the highly restricted application of the more meaningful usages of the term, it simply ought not

that there is only one covenant of grace in all of God's redemptive history. For Calvin, it was not anachronistic to apply back the "promise of spiritual and eternal life" (*spiritualis aeternaeque vitae promissionem*) of redemptive grace in Christ to the Old Testament believers. So, even the Old Testament believers were justified by faith alone in Christ, in whom they had everlasting hope and spiritual life, while they enjoyed earthly blessings through obedience to God's law:

> The Old Testament fathers (1) had Christ as pledges of their covenant, and (2) put in him all trust of future blessedness. These I shall not labor to prove because they are less controversial and clearer. Let us, therefore, boldly establish a principle unassailable by any stratagems of the devil: the Old Testament or Covenant that the Lord had made with the Israelites had not been limited to earthly things, but contained a promise of spiritual and eternal life . . . In this he [the Lord] has given a sure pledge that whatever he did or suffered in acquiring eternal salvation pertains to the believers of the Old Testament as much as to our-selves. Truly, as Peter testifies, they were endowed with the same Spirit of faith whereby we are reborn into life [Acts 15:8]. [37]

For several decades, many scholars have argued that there are two traditions of the covenant of grace within the continental Reformation. One was developed by the Rhinelanders such as Zwingli, Bullinger, John Oecolampadius, and Martin Bucer, and the other tradition was forwarded by the Genevan Reformers such as Calvin and Beza. The former has been identified as *bilateral* and the latter as *unilateral*.[38] However, some, such as

---

to be used as a point of reference or of analysis with regard to the Chrisitan theological tradition in general. In the case of Reformation studies, the term 'christocentrism' ought simply to be avoided, indeed, its use abolished. In the past, particularly in the neo-orthodox historiography of the twentieth century, the term has caused nothing but confusion." Ibid., 260. Although I respect Muller's concern about neoorthodox theologians' injection of christomonism into Calvin's theology and the resulting theological confusion, I still prefer using Calvin's depiction of redemptive history, soteriology as concretely christocentric and christotelic with the recognition of the proper places of creation, Fall, and redemption, as well as the historical and logical orders of law and gospel or grace.

37. Calvin, *Institutes*, 2.10.23.

38. Charles S. McCoy and Wayne J. Baker, *Fountainhead of Federalism: Heinrich Bullinger and the Covenant Tradition* (Louisville: Westminster John Knox Press, 1991); Joseph C. McLelland, "Covenant Theology—A Re-Evaluation," *Canadian Journal of Theology* 3 (1957): 182–88; Jens Møller, "The Beginning of Puritan Covenant Theology," *Journal of Ecclesiastical History* 14 (1963): 46–67; Leonard Trinterud, "The Origins of Puritanism," *Church History* 20 (1951): 37–57.

Bierma, Karlberg, and Lillback rightly conclude that there is only one covenant tradition, which is *bilateral,* originating with Zwingli in Zürich and developed by the Rhinelanders, especially Bullinger. It was well received and permeated into Calvin's covenant thinking, harmonizing double predestination and a *bilateral* covenant of grace.[39] In this manner, Lillback concludes:

> There is no basis for the thesis that pits the Rhineland Reformers, Bullinger and Zwingli, against Calvin in terms of the mutuality and conditionality of the covenant of grace. There clearly is a difference of emphasis and difference of rationale for stating the distinctive doctrines of predestination and covenant in each of these Reformed theologians. But foundationally, all three affirm a conditional, mutual covenant of grace that is worked out in the context of a sovereign predestination that includes reprobation.[40]

39. Lyle D. Bierma, "Federal Theology in the Sixteenth Century: Two Traditions?" *Westminster Theological Journal* 45 (1983): 304–21; Peter A. Lillback , "The Continuing Conundrum: Calvin and The Conditionality of the Covenant," *Westminster Theological Journal* (1994): 42–74. However, the Reformed biblical covenant theologian Geerhardus Vos errs when he states that the covenant idea is not dominant in the theology of Calvin because Calvin's theology is deeply rooted in the concept of Trinity rather than that of covenant. In this regard, he argues that the development of the covenant theology of Reformed orthodoxy was influenced by the Rhinelanders instead of Genevan Reformers: "In Calvin, too, mention is frequently made of the covenants. However, his theology was built on the basis of the Trinity, and therefore the covenant concept could not arise as a dominant principle in his case. He is the forerunner of such Reformed theologians who allocate to it subordinate place as a separate locus. Even his *Geneva Catechism,* where one would most expect this idea to be elaborated, bypasses it. The theologians of Zürich, on the other hand, are to be regarded as the forerunners of federal theology in the narrower sense insofar as the covenant for them becomes the dominant idea for the practice of the Christian life. Both Olevianus and Ursinus, the well-known Heidelberg theologians, stood in the closest connection to the Zürich theologians." Geerhardus Vos, *Redemptive History and Biblical Interpretation,* ed. Richard B. Gaffin, Jr. (Phillipsburg: Presbyterian and Reformed Publishing, 1980), 236.

40. Lillback, "The Continuing Conundrum," 73–74. However, Lillback makes a serious theological mistake when he applies Calvin's "mutuality and conditionality of the covenant of grace" to the doctrine of justification and salvation, denying the substantial implication of the distinction between law and gospel in its arena. As a result, he puts Calvin's justification by faith in between Luther and the Medieval Schoolmen, rejecting *sola gratia* and *sola fide* as the Reformation consensus between Luther and Calvin. For a critical analysis on Lillback's monocovenantal injection into Calvin's theology, see Jeon, *Covenant Theology,* 248–50; idem, *Covenant Theology and Justification by Faith,* 22–26, 51–53. Lillback's monocovenatal interpretation of Calvin, denying the validity of the distinction between law and gospel in Calvin's hermeneutics and theology is very influential within conservative Reformed and evangelical circles. As a Calvin scholar, he

Briefly, Calvin's and the Rhinelanders' *bilateral* covenant of grace, the mutuality and conditionality of the covenant, was harmonized splendidly with double predestination, making for a balance between covenant and predestination.[41]

THE DIFFERENCE BETWEEN THE OLD COVENANT AND NEW COVENANT

Calvin made a contrast between the Old and New Covenants, explaining the contrast in terms of redemptive historical significance and eschatology with the vivid implication of *typology*. Calvin carefully argued that the Lord of the Old Covenant desired that the covenant people elevate "their minds to the heavenly heritage" while they taste it "under earthly benefits." However, the believers under the New Covenant have "the grace of the future life" in the gospel "more plainly and clearly," putting aside "the lower mode of training" that God used with the covenant people under the Old Covenant:

> Now this is the first difference: the Lord of old willed that his people direct and elevate their minds to the heavenly heritage; yet, to nourish them better in this hope, he displayed it for them to see and, so to speak, taste, under earthly benefits. But now that the gospel has more plainly and clearly revealed the grace of the future life, the Lord leads our minds to meditate upon it directly, laying aside the lower mode of training that he used with the Israelites.[42]

As the editor of *Institutes*, McNeill correctly points out, Servetus, as the representative spokesman of the Anabaptists in his famous work entitled *De justitia regni Christi* in 1532, insisted that the promises of the Mosaic law are fulfilled spiritually only to Christians under the New Covenant. However, the Old Testament Israelites "obtained the Land

---

has provided a safe haven for the Federal Visionists to deny the validity of the distinction between law and gospel in Calvin. For his most recent discussion about Calvin's understanding of continuity and discontinuity of the covenant from a redemptive historical perspective, see Peter A. Lillback, "Calvin's Interpretation of the History of Salvation: The Continuity and Discontinuity of the Covenant," in *Theological Guide to Calvin's Institutes: Essays and Analysis*, eds. David W. Hall and Peter A. Lillback (Phillipsburg: Presbyterian and Reformed Publishing, 2008), 168–204.

41. Lillback, "The Continuing Conundrum," 58–73; Cf. Calvin, *Genesis*, 17:1–27; idem, *Leviticus*, 26:40–43.

42. Calvin, *Institutes*, 2.11.1.

of Canaan and were satisfied with both milk and honey." Likewise, the Anabaptists interpreted the blessings of the Old Testament Israelites from the perspective of the earthly centered life, ignoring their eschatological and spiritual aspects and significance. So, Calvin countered the Anabaptistic hermeneutics and theology, arguing that God, in bestowing "all these earthly benefits" on the Old Testament Israelites, decided to lead them "to the hope of heavenly things" (*ad spem coelestium*). Thus, Calvin powerfully demonstrated his eschatological and redemptive historical hermeneutics over against the Anabaptistic earthly centered hermeneutics in his interpretation of the Old Covenant as follows:

> Those who do not pay attention to this plan of God think that the ancient people did not transcend those promised to the body. They hear that the Land of Canaan is very often characterized as the excellent and even sole reward for the keepers of God's law. They hear that the Lord threatens the transgressors of his law with nothing harsher than expulsion from possession of this land, and dispersion into foreign regions [cf. Lev. 26:33; Deut 28:36]. They see herein almost the sum total of the blessings and curses uttered by Moses. From such evidence they unhesitatingly conclude that the Jews were set apart from all other peoples not for their own benefit but for that of others, in order that the Christian church might have an outward image in which it might discern proofs of spiritual things. But Scripture sometimes shows that God, in conferring all these earthly benefits on them, determined to lead them by his own hand to the hope of heavenly things. Hence it was the height of ignorance—nay, blockishness—not to consider this sort of dispensation.[43]

Calvin continued to argue that the Anabaptists do not see the redemptive historical continuity between the Old and New Covenants, insisting that the Old Testament Israelites idealized "the possession of the Land of Canaan" as "their highest and ultimate blessedness" (*pro summa atque ultima beatudine*). In that sense, the Anabaptists wrongly argued that "after the revelation of Christ" "the possession of the Land of Canaan" under the Old Covenant typified *only* for New Testament believers "the heavenly inheritance." Calvin, however, properly argued that the Old Testament Israelites enjoyed the earthly blessing in the promised Land,

43. Ibid.

looking toward "the future inheritance," which God prepared for them in the everlasting heaven:

> The point of our quarrel with men of this sort is this: they teach that the Israelites deemed the possession of the Land of Canaan their highest and ultimate blessedness, and that after the revelation of Christ it typified for us the heavenly inheritance. We contend, on the contrary, that, in the earthly possession they enjoyed, they looked, as in a mirror, upon the future inheritance they believed to have been prepared for them in heaven.[44]

Mentioning the Pauline passage Galatians 4:1–2, Calvin conceived Paul as a redemptive historical theologian who interpreted the blessings of the Old Testament Israelites from a redemptive historical perspective and continuity. From a redemptive historical perspective, Calvin argued that "the same church" existed among the Old Testament Israelites in a child form. So, God bestowed them "spiritual promises" "by earthly promises" as a shadow. Likewise, God promised "Abraham, Isaac, Jacob, and their descendants" "the Land of Canaan as an inheritance," giving "the hope of immortality." However, God did not mean the Land of Canaan to be "the final goals of their hopes." So, Abraham's heart was elevated "to the Lord by a greater promise" when he received "the promise of the land." As such, Calvin had redemptive historical consciousness and sensitivity when he interpreted the history of the Old Testament Israelites after the pattern of Paul's redemptive historical reading of the Old Testament:

> This will be more apparent from the comparison that Paul made in the letter to the Galatians. He compares the Jewish nation to a child heir, not yet fit to take care of himself, under the charge of a guardian or tutor to whose care he has been entrusted [Gal. 4:1–2] . . . The same church existed among them, but as yet in its childhood. Therefore, keeping them under this tutelage, the Lord gave, not spiritual promises unadorned and open, but ones foreshadowed, in a measure, by earthly promises. When, therefore, he adopted Abraham, Isaac, Jacob, and their descendants into the hope of immortality, he promised them the Land of Canaan as an inheritance. It was not to be the final goal of their hopes, but was to exercise and confirm them, as they contemplated it, in hope of their true inheritance, an inheritance not yet manifested to them. And that they might not be deceived, a higher promise was given, attesting that the land was not God's supreme benefit. Thus

44. Ibid.

Abraham is not allowed to sit idly by when he receives the promise of the land, but his mind is elevated to the Lord by a greater promise. For he hears: "I am your protector, Abraham; your reward shall be great" [Gen 15:1].[45]

After the pattern of Paul's redemptive historical reading of the Old Testament earthly blessings of the Israelites, Calvin revisited the Psalmist David's recognition of the earthly blessings in the Land of Canaan, and he reinterpreted them in light of redemptive historical continuity and the eschatological heavenly blessings:

Here we see that for Abraham his final reward is put in the Lord alone—so as not to seek a fleeting and elusive reward in the elements of this world [cf. Gal. 4:3], but an imperishable one. Then he adds the promise of the land, solely as a symbol of his benevolence and as a type of the heavenly inheritance. The saints testify in their own words that they have experienced it. David thus mounts up from temporal blessings to that highest and ultimate blessing. "My heart," he says, "and my flesh fail for desire of thee.... God is ... my portion forever." [Ps. 73:26 p.; cf. Ps. 84:2] Again, "The Lord is the portion of my inheritance and of my cup; thou holdest my inheritance." [Ps. 16:5 p.] Again, "I cried to thee, O Lord; I said, Thou art my hope, my portion in the land of the living." [Ps. 142:5.][46]

With eschatological consciousness in his interpretation of the blessings and curses in the Land of Canaan, Calvin argued that the blessings of the Old Testament of the Israelites represented "the blessedness of the age to come through the type." In that sense, *typology* was a great hermeneutical tool for Calvin to exposit the Old Covenant eschatology and redemptive historical continuity. Examining some key passages on blessings and curses, Calvin concluded that the Prophetic messages about the blessings ultimately cannot apply "to the land of our pilgrimage, or to the earthly Jerusalem, but to the true homeland of believers," which will be fulfilled in the heavenly city:

Those who dare speak thus surely profess that in their hope they transcend the world and all present benefits. Yet the prophets more often represent the blessedness of the age to come through the type that they had received from the Lord. In this sense we are to understand these sayings: "The godly will possess the land" by

45. Ibid., 2.11.2.
46. Ibid.

inheritance [Prov. 2:21 p.], but "the wicked will perish from the earth" [Job 18:17 p.; cf. Prov. 2:22; cf. Ecclus. 41:9, Vg.; cf. 41:6, EV]. In many passages of Isaiah we read that Jerusalem will abound with all kinds of riches, and Zion shall overflow with plenty of all things [cf. Isa. 35:10; 52:1 ff.; 60:4 ff.; ch. 62]. We see that all these things cannot properly apply to the land of our pilgrimage, or to the earthly Jerusalem, but to the true homeland of believers, that heavenly city wherein "the Lord has ordained blessing and life forevermore" [Ps. 133:3].[47]

Calvin explained the blessings and curses of the Israelites under the Old Covenant from the perspective of *eschatology*. Certainly, I think that Calvin's eschatological interpretation of the Old Covenant is one of the most important contributions to the Old Testament hermeneutics and theology for the community of church. Calvin argued that "the saints under the Old Testament" eagerly esteemed "mortal life and its blessings." Calvin further noted that the enjoyment of "present good things" under the Old Covenant was a foreshadow of "spiritual happiness" in the everlasting heaven while the physical punishment of covenant people was "proofs of his coming judgment against the wicked" in eternal hell:

> This is why we read that the saints under the Old Testament esteemed mortal life and its blessings more than we ought today. Even though they well knew they were not to stop there as at the end of their race, yet because they recognized what the Lord had imprinted on them to be marks of divine grace to train them according to the measure of their weakness, they were attracted by its sweetness more than if they had contemplated his grace directly. But as the Lord, in testifying his benevolence toward believers by present good things, then foreshadowed spiritual happiness by such types and symbols, so on the other hand he gave, in physical punishments, proof of his coming judgment against the wicked.[48]

In the early church, the Manicheans rejected the God of the Old Testament because in their eyes, the God of the Old Testament is different from the God of the New Testament similar to the Anabaptists during the Protestant Reformation. Calvin answered to the Manichean quest as well as the Anabaptistic quest, interpreting the blessings and curses under the Old Covenant from the perspective of redemptive history and eschatology.

47. Ibid.
48. Ibid., 2.11.3.

Israel's blessings and curses in the Land of Canaan, administered by the Mosaic law, were a mirror and a type of the heavenly blessing and eternal curse whereby Calvin expressed eschatologically as "the grace of future and eternal happiness." On this, Calvin summarized beautifully as follows:

> Thus, as God's benefits were more conspicuous in earthly things, so also were his punishments. The ignorant, not considering this analogy and congruity, to call it that, between punishments and rewards, wonder at such great changeableness in God. He, who once was prompt to mete out stern and terrifying punishments for every human transgression, now seems to have laid aside his former wrathful mood and punishes much more gently and rarely. Why, on that account they even go so far as to imagine different Gods for the Old and New Testaments, like the Manichees! But we shall readily dispose of these misgivings it we turn our attention to this dispensation of God which I have noted. He willed that, for the time during which he gave his covenant to the people of Israel in a veiled form, the grace of future and eternal happiness be signified and figured under earthly benefits, the gravity of spiritual death under physical punishments.[49]

It is remarkable that Calvin not only interpreted the prelapsarian Adamic status from the perspective of eschatology but also the Old Covenant. To be sure, for Calvin, not grace but law was the means to attain eternal heavenly blessings although it was not realized due to Adam's sin in the Garden of Eden. In a similar manner, God blessed the Israelites in the promised land when they obeyed the law under the Old Covenant while he cursed them when they disobeyed the principle of "the covenant of the law" (*foedus legale*). In this manner, according to Calvin, it was God's will to administer "in a veiled form, the grace of future and eternal happiness," "signified and figured under earthly benefits, the gravity of spiritual death under physical punishments."

The earthly nation of Israel, pointing ultimately to eternal heaven, was administered by types and figures, and at last abolished by Christ's eternal priesthood in which the law was fulfilled. In this regard, Calvin contrasted the Old and New Covenants:

> The second difference between the Old and New Testaments consists in figures: that, in the absence of the reality, it showed but an image and shadow in place of the substance; the New Testament

49. Ibid.

reveals the very substance of truth as present. This difference is mentioned almost wherever the New Testament is contrasted with the Old, but a fuller discussion of it is to be found in the Letter to the Hebrews than anywhere else.[50]

While Calvin recognized one bilateral covenant of grace after the Fall, he stipulated that the Mosaic Law was in a sense "the covenant of law" or the *foedus legale*. But, did Calvin use the term *foedus legale* of the Mosaic Covenant accidentally or did he intend for a significant theological meaning? Calvin, in a limited sense, regarded the Mosaic Covenant as a *foedus legale,* contrasting it with the New Covenant. This is because the Mosaic Covenant was an administration of temporary ceremonies and sacrifices which were applied to the earthly nation of Israel. It was called a temporary covenant, whereas the Abrahamic Covenant was an everlasting covenant, finally fulfilled in the New Covenant:

> Here we are to observe how *the covenant of the law compares with the covenant of the gospel, the ministry of Christ with that of Moses* [Emphasis added]. For if the comparison had reference to the substance of the promises, then there would be great disagreement between the Testaments. But since the trend of the argument leads us in another direction, we must follow it to find the truth. Let us then set forth the covenant that he once established as eternal and never-perishing. Its fulfillment, by which it is finally confirmed and ratified, is Christ . . . The Old Testament of the Lord was that covenant wrapped up in the shadowy and ineffectual observance of ceremonies and delivered to the Jews; it was temporary because it remained, as it were, in suspense until it might rest upon a firm and substantial confirmation.[51]

We need to pay a close attention to Calvin's comparison of "the covenant of the law" (*foedus Legale*) "with the covenant of the gospel" (*foedere Evangelico*). It is very important to notice that Calvin, in a sense, understood the Old Covenant as "the covenant of the law" to emphasize the pedagogical function of the law in redemptive history. That is the reason why the author of Hebrews indicates that the Old Covenant as "the

50. Ibid., 2.11.4. Calvin often used the word testament (*testamentum*) and covenant (*foedus*) interchangeably, especially when he made a comparison and contrast between the Old and New Covenants. The editors of *Institutes* properly note this phenomena as follows: "In this section and elsewhere Calvin uses the words *testamentum* and *foedus* interchangeably, as they used in the Vulgate." Ibid. Footnote number 6.

51. Ibid.

covenant of the law" must be "terminated and abrogated, to give place to Christ, the sponsor and Mediator of a better covenant" in Hebrews 7:22. In addition, according to Calvin, it is the reason why the Old Covenant was a temporary covenant while the New Covenant became an eternal covenant, sealed by the blood of the Mediator of a better covenant:

> Because nothing substantial underlies this unless we go beyond it, the apostle contends that it ought to be terminated and abrogated, to give place to Christ, the Sponsor and Mediator of a better covenant [cf. Heb. 7:22]; whereby he imparts eternal sanctifications once and for all to the elect, blotting out their transgressions, which remained under the law. Or, if you prefer, understand it thus: the Old Testament of the Lord was that covenant wrapped up in the shadowy and ineffectual observance of ceremonies and delivered to the Jews; it was temporary because it remained, as it were, in suspense until it might rest upon a firm and substantial confirmation. It became new and eternal only after it was consecrated and established by the blood of Christ. Hence Christ in the Supper calls the cup that he gives to his disciples "the cup of the New Testament in my blood" [Luke 22:20]. By this he means that the Testament of God attained its truth when sealed by his blood, and thereby becomes new and eternal.[52]

Having the consciousness of the contrast between the covenant of the law and the covenant of the gospel in light of the distinction between the Old and the New Covenants, Calvin argued that the Jews under the Old Covenant were guided to "Christ by the tutelage of the law" before his first Coming as Paul describes it in Galatians 3:24; 4:1–2. Again, Calvin pointed out how the pedagogical function of the law was applied to the Jews under the Old Covenant in redemptive history whereby Paul also explains it from the perspective of the progressiveness of redemptive history:

> Hence it is clear in what sense the apostle said that the Jews were led to Christ by the tutelage of the law before he appeared in the flesh [Gal. 3:24; cf. ch. 4:1–2]. He also confesses that they were sons and heirs of God, but because of their youth they had to be under the charge of a tutor. It was fitting that, before the sun of righteousness had arisen, there should be no great and shining revelation, no clear understanding. The Lord, therefore, so meted out the light of his Word to them that they still saw it afar off and darkly. Hence

---

52. Ibid.

Paul expresses this slenderness of understanding by the word "childhood."[53]

Calvin went on to argue that the contrast between the covenant of the law and the covenant of the gospel in light of the Old and New Covenants is not only affirmed by Paul's affirmation of "the tutelage of the law" but also by Christ's teaching to his disciples in Matthew 11:13 and Luke 16:16. Calvin demonstrated that "the Law and the Prophets" provided "a foretaste of that wisdom," which would be clearly revealed in "the good news of the Kingdom of God" under the New Covenant:

> Christ himself implied this distinction when he said: "The Law and the Prophets were until John; since then the good news of the Kingdom of God is preached" [Luke 16:16; cf. Matt. 11:13]. What did the Law and the Prophets teach to the men of their own time? They gave a foretaste of that wisdom which was one day to be clearly disclosed, and pointed to it twinkling afar off. But when Christ could be pointed out with the finger, the Kingdom of God was opened. In him have been revealed "all the treasures of wisdom and understanding" [Col. 2:3], whereby we attain almost to the inmost sanctuary of heaven.[54]

Reflecting on Jeremiah 31 and 32, Calvin contrasted the *foedus legale* and the New Covenant because while the former was temporal, being governed by the principle of works for the Israelites' earthly blessings and curses and signifying the temporal nature of Israel, the latter was a "perpetual covenant." In the Mosaic Covenant, the Israelites tasted exile due to their general corporate disobedience, thus voiding the *foedus legale*. Based upon the Abrahamic Covenant of promise, however, the Israelites returned to the promised land from the curse of exile. It is quite remarkable to observe that Calvin did not fall into legalism or neonomianism in his interpretation of the Old Covenant though he designated it as "the covenant of law" (*foedus legale*). He was able to do this because he carefully applied the principle of "the covenant of law" under the Old Covenant, not to individual salvation, but to the earthly blessings or curses, which were applied in the Israelites' covenant community in the promised land. Here, we see the richness and brilliance of Calvin's redemptive historical hermeneutics. He applied the rich hermeneutical ingredients of *typology*

53. Ibid., 2.11.5.
54. Ibid.

to his interpretation of the Old Covenant as a hermeneutical tool to avoid legalism or neonomianism:

> We must notice *the contrast between the covenant of the Law, and the covenant of which the Prophet now speaks* [Emphasis added]. He called it in the thirty-first chapter a new covenant, and gave the reason for it, because their fathers had soon fallen away after the Law was proclaimed, and because its doctrine was that of the letter, and deadly, and also fatal. But he now calls it a *perpetual covenant.* That the covenant of the Law was not valid, this was accidental to it; for the Law would remain in force, were we only to keep it; but through men's fault it happened that the covenant of the Law became void and immediately vanished ... We must, at the same time, bear in mind that this covenant peculiarly belongs to the kingdom of Christ. For though it was a part of God's grace, which was manifested in delivering his people from captivity, yet the continued stream of his grace ought to be extended to the coming of Christ. The Prophet then, no doubt, brings Christ before us, together with the new covenant; for without him there is not the least hope that God would make another covenant, as it appears evident from the whole Law and the teaching of the Prophets. *Then Christ is here opposed to Moses, and the Gospel to the Law* [Emphasis added]. It hence follows, that the Law was a temporary covenant, for it had no stability, as it was that of the letter; but that the Gospel is a perpetual covenant, for it is inscribed on the heart.[55]

Exploring the contrast between the Old and New Covenants, spoken through the mouth of the Lord in Jeremiah 31:31–34, Calvin drew attention to 2 Corinthians 3:6–11, which is a New Testament parallel of Jeremiah 31:31–34. Calvin observed that Paul made "a comparision between the law and the gospel" (*comparationis huius inter Legem et Evangelium*) in the milieu of Jeremiah 31:31–34, which is a theological and redemptive historical context to make a contrast between the Old and New Covenants, providing several contrasting theological ingredients:

> I come to the third difference, taken from Jeremiah. His words are: "Behold, the days will come, says the Lord, when I will make a new covenant with the house of Israel and the house of Judah, not like the agreement which I made with your fathers, in the day when I took them by the hand to lead them out of the land of Egypt, my covenant which they broke, though I ruled over them. . . . But this

---

55. Calvin, *Jeremiah,* 32:40.

will be the covenant which I will make with the house of Israel.... I will put my law within them, and I will write it upon their hearts .. . and I will forgive their iniquity. And each will not teach his neighbor, each man his brother. For all will know me, from the least to the greatest" [Jer. 31:31–34, ...]. From these words the apostle took occasion to make a comparison between the law and the gospel, calling the former literal, the latter spiritual doctrine; the former he speaks of as carved on tables of stone, the latter as written upon men's hearts; the former is the preaching of death, the latter of life; the former of condemnation, the latter of righteousness; the former to be made void, the latter to abide [2 Cor. 3:6–11].[56]

Calvin made a contrast between the letter and the Spirit in the milieu of the contrast between the Old and New Covenants, as well as the antithesis between law and gospel. Calvin argued that the Old Covenant brings "death, for it can but envelop the whole human race in a curse," which is closely related to the pedagogical function of the law in his interpretation of 2 Corinthians 3:6a. On the other hand, Calvin rightly demonstrated that the New Covenant is "the instrument of life" because it provides men freedom "from the curse and restores them to God's favor" as Paul indicates clearly in 2 Corinthians 3:6b. According to the pattern of Paul's contrast of the Old and New Covenants in 2 Corinthians 3:9, Calvin affirmed that there is a clear antithesis between the Old and New Covenants because the Old Covenant is "the ministry of condemnation," while the New Covenant is "the ministry of righteousness":

Now let us explain the apostle's comparison, item by item. The Old Testament is of the letter, for it was published without the working of the Spirit. The New is spiritual because the Lord has engraved it spiritually upon men's hearts [2 Cor. 3:6a]. The second antithesis is by way of clarification of the first. The Old brings death, for it can but envelop the whole human race in a curse. The New is the instrument of life, for it frees men from the curse and restores them to God's favor [2 Cor. 3:6b]. The Old is the ministry of condemnation, for it accuses all the sons of Adam of unrighteousness. The New is the ministry of righteousness because it reveals God's mercy, through which we are justified [2 Cor. 3:9].[57]

56. Calvin, *Institutes*, 2.11.7.

57. Ibid., 2.11.8. "The Protestant scholastics, both Lutheran and Reformed" analyzed the moral law into three different uses. The first use is "the political or civil use" (the *usus politicus sive civilis*), which is related to the stability of society, restraining sin. The second use is "the elenctical or pedagogical use" (the *usus elenchticus sive paedagogicus*) where

the law serves "for the confrontation and refutation of sin and for the purpose of pointing the way to Christ." And "the third use of the law" (the *tertius usus legis*) is applied to
"believers in Christ who have been saved through faith apart from works." It functions "as
a norm of conduct, freely accepted by those in whom the grace of God works the good."
Muller, *Dictionary of Latin and Greek Theological Terms*, 320–21.

Meanwhile, Calvin located the pedagogical function of the law as the first use instead
of the second use while he put the political or civil function of the law as the second
use. It is important to remember that Calvin's pedagogical function of the law is closely
related to the distinction between law and gospel as the background for *sola fide* and *sola
gratia*. So, the sinners before the law look at nothing but "God's righteousness" (*iustitiam
Dei*), which is "alone acceptable to God" (*sola Deo accepta*). In that sense, in Calvin's theology, *sola fide* and *sola gratia* are organically related to the pedagogical function of the
law on the one hand and the distinction between law and gospel on the other hand: "But
to make the whole matter clearer, let us survey briefly the function and use of what is
called the 'moral law.' Now, so far as I understand it, it consists of three parts.

The first part is this: while it shows God's righteousness, that is, the righteousness
alone acceptable to God, it warns, informs, convicts, and lastly condemns, every man of
his own unrighteousness. For man, blinded and drunk with self-love, must be compelled
to know and to confess his own feebleness and impurity . . .

But after he is compelled to weigh his life in the scales of the law, laying aside all that
presumption of fictitious righteousness, he discovers that he is a long way from holiness,
and is in fact teeming with a multitude of vices, with which he previously thought himself
undefiled. So deep and tortuous are the recesses in which the evils of covetousness lurk
that they easily deceive man's sight. The apostle has good reason to say: "I should not have
known covetousness, if the law had not said, 'You shall not covet'" [Rom. 7:7]. For if by the
law covetousness is not dragged from its lair, it destroys wretched man so secretly that he
does not even feel its fatal stab." Calvin, *Institutes*, 2.7.6.

Calvin's analysis of the civil use of the law reflects that Calvin embraced the comprehensive biblical worldview. Calvin located the civil use of the law as "the second function of the law" (*Secundum Legis officium*), which is not directly related to soteriology.
Rather, it plays as the background for the possibility of the continuity of human history
where people may live together both believers and unbelievers, having a stable society
because the law functions to restrain human sins. Calvin pointed to the Pauline passage,
1 Timothy 1:9–10, as one of the representative biblical passages, supporting the civil use
of the law: "The second function of the law is this: at least by fear of punishment to
restrain certain men who are untouched by any care for what is just and right unless
compelled by hearing the dire threats in the law. But they are restrained, not because their
inner mind is stirred or affected, but because, being bridled, so to speak, they keep their
hands from outward activity, and hold inside the depravity that otherwise they would
wantonly have indulged. Consequently, they are neither better nor more righteous before
God. Hindered by fright or shame, they dare neither execute what they have conceived in
their minds, nor openly breathe forth the rage of their lust. Still, they do not have hearts
disposed to fear and obedience toward God . . .

The apostle seems specially to have alluded to this function of the law when he teaches
'that the law is not laid down for the just but for the unjust and disobedient, for the un-
godly and sinners, for the unholy and profane, for murderers of parents, for manslayers,
fornicators, perverts, kidnapers, liars, perjurers, and whatever else runs counter to sound

Calvin made another contrast between the Old and New Covenants. God instituted "the ceremonial law" to observe under the Old Covenant as "the image of things," which represents the substance of the gospel. However, the ceremonial law is abrogated under the New Covenant because the gospel reveals "the very substance" of things as Paul makes a contrast between the Old and New Covenants:

> The final contrast is to be referred to the ceremonial law. For because the Old bore the image of things absent, it had to die and vanish with time. The gospel, because it reveals the very substance, stands fast forever [2 Cor. 3:10–11]. Indeed, Jeremiah calls even the moral law a weak and fragile covenant [Jer. 31:32]. But that is for another reason: by the sudden defection of an ungrateful people it was soon broken off. However, because the people were to blame for such a violation, it cannot properly be charged against the covenant. Now the ceremonies, because by their own weakness they were abrogated at Christ's advent, had the cause of their weakness within themselves.[58]

Calvin extended his discussion, making a contrast between the Old and New Covenants, indicating the Old Covenant as the covenant of "bondage" while the New Covenant is the covenant of "freedom," alluding to Romans 8:15. Furthermore, Calvin applied a contrast to the Old and New Covenants in his interpretation of Hebrews 12:18–22. Believers

---

doctrine' [1 Tim. 1:9–10]. He shows in this that the law is like a halter to check the raging and otherwise limitlessly ranging lusts of the flesh." Ibid., 2.7.10.

Lastly, Calvin located believers' application of the law in their daily lives as "the third and principal use" (*tertius usus et praecipuus*). In that sense, Calvin made a comprehensive harmony between the pedagogical function of the law, related to the distinction between law and gospel, and *sola fide* and believers' fervent obedience to the law in the process of sanctification: "The third and principal use, which pertains more closely to the proper purpose of the law, finds its place among believers in whose hearts the Spirit of God already lives and reigns. For even though they have the law written and engraved upon their hearts by the finger of God [Jer. 31:33; Heb. 10:16], that is, have been so moved and quickened through the directing of the Spirit that they long to obey God, they still profit by the law in two ways . . . .

For the law is not now acting toward us as a rigorous enforcement officer who is not satisfied unless the requirements are met. But in this perfection to which it exhorts us, the law points out the goal toward which throughout life we are to strive. In this the law is no less profitable than consistent with our duty. If we fail not in this struggle, it is well. Indeed, this whole life is a race [cf. 1 Cor. 9:24–26]; when its course has been run, the Lord will grant us to attain that goal to which our efforts now press forward from afar." Ibid., 2.7.12–13.

58. Ibid., 2.11.8.

under the New Covenant do not come to "a physical mountain, a blazing fire, whirlwind, gloom, and tempest." Rather, they come to "Mt. Zion, and to the city of living God, the heavenly Jerusalem." Likewise, Calvin drew rich theological and redemptive historical ideas from the Bible in light of the contrast between the Old and New Covenants:

> The fourth difference arises out of the third. Scripture calls the Old Testament one of "bondage" because it produces fear in men's minds; by the New Testament, one of "freedom" because it lifts them to trust and assurance. So Paul states in the eighth chapter of Romans: "You did not receive the spirit of slavery again unto fear, but you have received the spirit of sonship, through which we cry, 'Abba! Father!'" [v. 15p.]. The passage in Hebrews is also applicable here: that believers "have not come to a physical mountain, a blazing fire, whirlwind, gloom, and tempest," where nothing is heard or seen that does not strike minds with terror, so that when that terrible voice resounded, which they all begged not to fear, even Moses became terrified. "But they have come to Mt. Zion, and to the city of the living God, the heavenly Jerusalem," etc. [Heb. 12:18–22, cf. Vg.].[59]

Calvin avoided legalism or neonomianism in his interpretation of the Old Covenant when he made a contrast between the Old and New Covenant. This is because he brilliantly applied typological or allegorical interpretation in his contrast between the Old and New Covenants. With typological or allegorical consciousness, Calvin argued that Hagar as "the bondwoman" is "the type of Mt. Sinai" while Sarah as "the free woman" is "the figure of the heavenly Jerusalem" in his interpretation of Galatians 4:22–31. Moreover, Calvin made a contrast between law and gospel in the milieu of the contrast between Hagar and Sarah. Here, we find out a very important hermeneutical and theological concept in Calvin's thinking, namely the contrast between law and gospel, which is coterminous with the contrast between the Old and New Covenants:

> Paul briefly touches on this in the statement that we quoted from the letter to the Romans but explains it more fully in the letter to the Galatians, where he allegorically interprets Abraham's two sons in this way: Hagar, the bondwoman, is the type of Mt. Sinai where the Israelites received the law; Sarah, the free woman, is the figure of the heavenly Jerusalem whence flows the gospel. Hagar's offspring were born in bondage, never to arrive at the inheritance;

59. Ibid., 2.11.9.

Sarah's, free and entitled to it. In like manner, we are subjected to bondage through the law, but are restored to freedom through the gospel alone [Gal. 4:22–31]. To sum up: the Old Testament struck consciences with fear and trembling, but by the benefit of the New they are released into joy. The Old held consciences bound by the yoke of bondage; the New by its spirit of liberality emancipates them into freedom.[60]

Calvin made the fifth contrast between the Old and New Covenants. He argued that the Lord chose only one nation among the nations "to confine the covenant of his grace" (*foedus gratiae suae contineret*), while the gospel of the good news may be applied to all nations under the New Covenant. Therefore, the Lord provided "the knowledge of his name" only upon the Israelites under the Old Covenant. In doing so, he made his covenant with the chosen nation of the Israelites, manifesting "the presence of his majesty." As such, Israel, as a chosen nation, was "the Lord's darling son," whereas all the other nations were strangers. In this manner, Calvin described the contrast between the Old and New Covenants in terms of the chosen nation as follows:

The fifth difference, which may be added, lies in the fact that until the advent of Christ, the Lord set apart one nation within which to confine the covenant of his grace. "When the Most High gave to the nations their inheritance, when he separated the sons of Adam," says Moses, "his people became his possession; Jacob was the cord of his inheritance." [Deut. 32:8–9 p.] Elsewhere he addresses the people as follows: "Behold, to the Lord your God belong heaven and . . . earth with all that is in it. Yet he cleaved only to your fathers, loved them so that he chose their descendants after them, namely, you out of all peoples" [Deut. 10:14, 15 p., cf. Vg.]. He, therefore, bestowed the knowledge of his name solely upon that people as if they alone of all men belonged to him. He lodged his covenant, so to speak, in their bosom; he manifested the presence of his majesty to them; he showered every privilege upon them. But—to pass over the remaining blessing—let us consider the one in question. In communicating his Word to them, he joined them to himself, that he might be called and esteemed their God. In the meantime, "he allowed all other nation to walk" in vanity [Acts 14:16], as if they had nothing whatsoever to do with him. Nor did he give them the sole remedy for their deadly disease—the preaching of his Word. Israel was then the Lord's darling son; the

60. Ibid.

others were strangers . . . Israel was hollowed by God; the others were profaned. Israel was honored with God's presence; the others were excluded from all approach to him.[61]

Calvin informed "the calling of the Gentiles" as an important signature of "the excellence of the New Testament over the Old" (*supra Vetus Testamentum Novi excellentia*). According to Calvin, the mission to the Gentiles had been prophesied by the prophets although its fulfillment was delayed "until the Kingdom of the Messiah" (*in regnum Messiae*). Observing the New Testament passages, Calvin argued that "Christ at the beginning of his preaching" did not command the mission to the Gentiles until he finished "the work of our redemption" and "the time of his humiliation." It is the reason why Christ rejected a Canaanite woman, saying that he had not been sent to just any body but "the lost sheep of the house of Israel" as he proclaimed in Matthew 15:24. In that sense, the Lord commanded the apostles not to go "beyond the boundaries of Israel" on their first mission trip when he called them as the original apostles in Matthew 10:5:

> The calling of the Gentiles, therefore, is a notable mark of the excellence of the New Testament over the Old. Indeed, this had been attested before by many very clear utterances of the prophets, but in such a way that its fulfillment was postponed until the Kingdom of the Messiah. Even Christ at the beginning of his preaching made no immediate progress toward it. He deferred it until, having completed the work of our redemption and finished the time of his humiliation, he received from the Father "the time which is above every name . . . before which every knee should bow" [Phil. 2:9–10 p.]. For this reason, since the time was not yet ripe, he denied to the woman of Canaan that he had been sent to any but "the lost sheep of the house of Israel" [Matt. 15:24]; and he did not permit the apostles on their first mission to go beyond the boundaries of Israel. He said: "Go nowhere among the Gentiles, and enter no town of the Samaritans, but go rather to the lost sheep of the house of Israel." [Matt. 10:5].[62]

Furthermore, Calvin demonstrated that the original apostles did not properly understand "the calling of the Gentiles" in the beginning of their ministry because it seemed "so new and strange to them." However, eventually the apostles accepted the mission to the Gentiles "tremblingly

---

61. Ibid., 2.11.11.
62. Ibid., 2.11.12.

and not without misgiving." Calvin continued to argue that the Lord called the Gentiles "not only were made equal to the Jews," but also "taking the place of dead Jews." Therefore, Paul proclaims the calling of the Gentiles in Christ under the New Covenant as a profound "mystery hidden for ages and generation" as he manifests it in Colossians 1:26 and Ephesians 3:9. As such, Calvin demonstrated his understanding of a progressive development of redemptive history in light of "the calling of the Gentiles," making a contrast between the Old and New Covenants:

> But however many testimonies of Scripture proclaimed the calling of the Gentiles, when the apostles were about to undertake it the call so new and strange to them that they shrank back from it as a monstrous thing. At last they set about it tremblingly and not without misgiving. And no wonder! For it seemed completely unreasonable that the Lord, who for so many ages had singled out Israel from all other nations, should suddenly change his plan and abandon that choice. Prophecies had indeed foretold this. But men could not heed these prophecies without being startled by the newness of the thing that met their eyes. And these evidences of the future calling of the heathen which God had given them of old were not sufficient to convince them. Besides the fact that he had called very few, he in a manner engrafted them into Abraham's family, thus adding them to his people. But by this public calling the Gentiles not only were made equal to the Jews, but it also was manifest that they were, so to speak, taking the place of dead Jews. Besides this, all those strangers whom God had previously received into the body of the Church had never been made equal to the Jews. Paul with good reason, therefore, proclaims this a great "mystery hidden for ages and generations" [Col. 1:26; cf. Eph. 3:9], and says that it is wonderful even to the angels [cf. 1 Peter 1:12].[63]

Meanwhile, it is very important to note that in Calvin's mind, "the covenant of the law" (*foedus legale*) was not the means of justification not only under the Old Covenant but also in the Abrahamic Covenant because Abraham was justified by faith alone, not by works. Not works but faith was a sole means to Abraham for his justification. In that sense, Abraham's circumcision, as an element of the *foedus legale*, was not the means of justification, but rather, his circumcision was the sign of the

---

63. Ibid.

covenant. Calvin's point is that the law cannot be the way to justification in the postlapsarian state:

> I also grant, that Paul, for this reason, contends that works are not meritorious, except under the covenant of the law, of which covenant, circumcision is put as the earnest and the symbol ... Both arguments are therefore of force; first, that the righteousness of Abram cannot be ascribed to the covenant of the law, because it preceded his circumcision; and, secondly, that the righteousness even of the most perfect characters perpetually consists in faith; since Abram, with all the excellency of his virtues, after his daily and even remarkable service of God, was, nevertheless, justified by faith.[64]

As such, we find that Calvin was a great redemptive historical theologian, not falling into either legalism, neonomianism, covenantal legalism or antinomianism, brilliantly applying typology. Particularly, Calvin used and carefully applied typology as a hermeneutical tool to denote and to expound the rich concept of eschatology already deeply embedded in the history of Israel, especially under the Old Covenant under the notion of "the covenant of the law" (*foedus legale*).

It is important to note that Calvin's contrast between the Old and New Covenant, applying the concept of the covenant of the law (*foedus legale*) for blessings or curses to the chosen nation of Israel as a *type* of everlasting blessings in heaven and everlasting curse in hell, is not fundamentally different from the Reformed orthodox understanding of a republication of the covenant of works under the Old Covenant. However, the concept of the republication of the covenant of works under the Old Covenant has been significantly misunderstood by the Federal Visionists because of their monocovenantal reading of redemptive history under the Old Covenant without the implication of typological significance of either the covenant of the law or the covenant of works with redemptive historical adjustment.

For example, as a promoter of the Federal Vision, Sandlin disagrees with Francis Turretin's concept of "a republication of a covenant of works" under the Old Covenant. However, our problem with Sandlin is not his critique to Turretin. Rather, it is whether he understands correctly why Turretin and other Reformed orthodox theologians categorize the Mosaic Covenant or Old Covenant as "a republication of a covenant of works"

---

64. Calvin, *Genesis*, 15:6.

within redemptive historical adjustment. Furthermore, Sandlin provides a critique of both Turretin's and Scofield's understandings of the Old Covenant, without making a theological clarification and difference between the two, which are very important:

> And what about the Mosaic economy? Was it something of a republication of a covenant of works? Shall we say with C. I. Scofield that even the Mosaic Law as a mere system of moralistic law-keeping (apart from Jesus!) was a "condition of eternal life" in the Old Testament period, as though salvation was in something or someone other than Jesus Christ? Of course not.
>
> Well, we must ask again, did the Mosaic Law present two ways of salvation, one, flawless law-keeping, and another trusting in Christ alone for salvation? Again, of course not. Paul tells us in Romans 10:6–9 that Deuteronomy 30 teaches that the Law is not some requirement of extraordinary, meritorious virtue, but that it is near us, right next our hearts. It is something that by the grace of God, we *can* obey.[65]

However, we know that Romans 10:5–9 is a classical passage to make a distinction between law and gospel whereby Calvin used as a hermeneutical and theological tool to denote the principle of the sovereign grace in sinners' salvation and justification after Adam's Fall. This is another reason why the hermeneutics and theology of the Federal Vision are not compatible to the biblical religion, as well as, to Calvin.

I would argue that Turretin's understanding of the republication of the covenant of works (*foedus* operum) with redemptive adjustment is fundamentally harmonious with Calvin's concept of "the covenant of the law" (*foedus legale*) and rightly so. To be sure, Turretin did not apply the concept of the republication of the covenant of works under the Old Covenant to the level of personal salvation but only to the earthly blessings or curses whereas Calvin applied the concept of the covenant of the law to the temporal earthly blessings or curses, which is the key to a proper understanding of the Old Covenant eschatology.

In addition, Turretin's notion of the covenant of works under the Old Covenant is to emphasize the pedagogical function of the moral law, revealed on the Mount Sinai ultimately pointing to Jesus Christ. It is also

---

65. Sandlin, "Covenant in Redemptive History," 74. For the brief analysis on Francis Turretin's covenant theology and the doctrine of justification by faith and other related issues, see Jeon, *Covenant Theology*, 56–69.

closely tied to the concept of the antithesis between law and gospel. Here, we need to interact with Turretin because Sandlin as the other Federal Visionists provides critique to the notion of the republication of the covenant of works under the Old Covenant, represented by Turretin and the Reformed orthodox theologians. The following is Turretin's analysis:

> Strictly, however, it denotes the covenant of works or the moral law given by Moses—the unbearable burden (*abastakto*) of legal ceremonies being added, absolutely and apart from the promise of grace. The former was signified properly and of itself (if the scope and intention of the lawgiver be considered) because in that first economy he joined together these three things by giving the old covenant or legal dispensation, not to abolish the promises, but to lead unto Christ. The latter is accessory and accidental, springing from an ignoring of the true end and the desiring of a false. The true end was Christ for righteousness to every believer (Rom. 10:4), but the self-righteous Jews did not obtain this end because it was proposed under a veil (2 Cor. 3:14), i.e., under a wrappage of types and of figures because the promise of grace on account of Christ was clothed with legal rites. Hence they invented a false end, maintaining that the law was given in order that by its observance they might be justified before God and be saved (Rom. 10:3–5). Against this error the apostle everywhere disputes from that hypothesis which takes the law strictly and opposes it to the promise.[66]

Sandlin reads and interprets the soteriology under the Mosaic Covenant in light of monocovenantalism by which he denies the distinction between law and gospel, which is crucial for the *sola gratia* and the *sola fide*. As faith and obedience were the means of the inheritance of the everlasting life in the prelapsarian era, according to Sandlin, faith and obedience, which he defines as a soteriological paradigm of "trust and obey," are also the means of everlasting life under the Mosaic Covenant. Thus, Sandlin writes the monocovenantal concept of salvation under the Mosaic Covenant as follows:

66. Francis Turretin, *Institutes of Elenctic Theology*. Vol. 2. trans. George Musgrave Giger and ed. James T. Dennison, Jr. (Phillipsburg: Presbyterian and Reformed Publishing, 1994), 234. I briefly explored Turretin's brilliant depiction of the Old Covenant in light of the republication of the covenant of works with redemptive adjustment, which is perfectly harmonious with Calvin's concept of the covenant of the law. And it is significant to note the Old Covenant eschatology, developed after the pattern of Calvin's hermeneutics and theology by Turretin and other Reformed orthodox theologians. Cf. Jeon, *Covenant Theology*, 63–66.

Of course, we cannot obey it apart from the work of Jesus Christ and the power of the Holy Spirit, but that was no less true in the Old Testament than it was in the New Testament. In Exodus 19 we read of the formalization of the Mosaic covenant. How can we summarize it? Simply, trust and obey (vv. 5–8)—the same essential scheme as in the Garden of Eden, though, of course, now adapted to man's sinful condition.[67]

It is true that the Federal Visionists have redemptive historical consciousness as they identify their hermeneutics and theology with Calvin and the Westminster Standards. However, it is important to separate them from Calvin and the Westminster Standards. The redemptive historical continuity between the Old and New Covenants, expounded by the Federal Visionists is, at best, tainted by monocovenantalism, which is a short cut to covenantal legalism. For example, Sandlin argues that the gospel preached under the New Testament was the same "Gospel preached to the Jews in the wilderness," emphasizing redemptive historical continuity between the Mosaic and New Covenants:

> We know from Hebrews that the same Gospel preached in the New Testament era was preached to the Jews in the wilderness, but since their response was not governed by faith, they were condemned (Heb. 4:2). The basic substance and requirements of the Gospel in the Mosaic economy were not different from those preached to the recipients of Hebrews.[68]

Once again, the Chrisitocentric hermeneutics and theology in the Federal Vision have been deeply tainted by monocovenantalism. Sandlin interprets sacrificial system under the Mosaic Covenant in light of the Christocentric theology and redemptive historical continuity in the milieu of the New Covenant. He properly argues that "holy Law-keeping included trusting in the Redeemer to come, confessing one's sins, and gaining (temporary relief by the blood of bulls and goats" typified "Christ's efficacious blood-shedding on the Cross." However, he radically falls into covenantal legalism when he argues that there was a dynamic relationship between "Trust and Obey" in personal salvation in that era, which is a thorough revision of the profound Christ-centered theology, developed by Calvin and adapted by the Reformed orthodoxy:

---

67. Sandlin, "Covenant in Redemptive History," 74.
68. Ibid.

The sacrificial system was an essential component of the Mosaic economy. This meant (among other things) that holy Law-keeping included trusting in the Redeemer to come, confessing one's sins, and gaining (temporary) relief by the blood of bulls and goats, which prefigured Christ's efficacious blood-shedding on the Cross. In other words, there was not some revelation of salvation and eternal life *apart from* the Law and its requirements. There were not two ways of salvation in the Law—one that said, "Trust in the Redeemer Who is to come," and another one that said, "Obey the Law." To trust in the Redeemer Who is to come *was* to obey the Law, and to obey the Law *was* to trust the Redeemer Who was to come. "Trust and Obey."[69]

Reflecting wisdom literature, Sandlin rereads the concept of the law from the perspective of covenantal legalism, which is a hallmark of the Federal Vision. In his interpretation of Psalm 119, Sandlin argues law "as a gracious, merciful, reviving, life-giving revelation." Here, Sandlin falls into radical legalism because he views law as a *gracious revelation* in his interpretation of the Davidic Psalm as a stepping stone to deny the distinction between law and gospel, which is an absolute path to the *sola gratia* and the *sola fide* even under the Old Covenant:

> And what intent Christian has not read the psalmist's (presumably David's) exaltation (and exultation) of the Law in Psalm 119? If you have, you must have identified with his love for that Law as a gracious, merciful, reviving, life-giving revelation ... We discover from a careful reading of this psalm that David oriented his entire life—including his eternal life—to Jehovah by means of God's revelation in the Law. We do not read here two messages—a cumbersome law versus a gracious Gospel. We detect not a single hint that David considered the Law *only* a compendium of commands and threatenings terrifying all who even slightly swerve from it, or that the Law contains nothing of God's grace. Rather, the Law is filled with gracious, vivifying force to all who submit to it—or, more accurately, who submit to the loving, covenant God who gave it.[70]

In his interpretation of the prophetic messages, Sandlin injects his monocovenantalism to interpret Isaiah 55 as a way of understanding prophetic soteriology. He argues that Isaiah 55 is a representative example of "the clearest samples of the Gospel in the Old Testament." In addition,

69. Ibid., 74–75.
70. Ibid., 75.

he emphasizes that soteriology in Isaiah 55 is "one of grace, not merit" as presented in verses 5 and 7. However, Sandlin mixes faith and obedience while he appears to affirm the grace-oriented soteriology in Isaiah 55. In this manner, he notices that the gracious salvation requires "faith, repentance and obedience." So, Sandlin's understanding of the redemptive historical continuity in Jesus Christ during the period of the Old Testament prophets, at best, is deeply painted with monocovenantalism through and through, mixing law and gospel, although he argues that his soteriology is a grace-oriented soteriology:

> Isaiah 55 presents one the clearest samples of the Gospel in the Old Testament. The prophet urges Israel to eat the good food of salvation (v. 2): "Hear, and your soul shall live" (v. 3). God will make an everlasting covenant with Israel, "the sure mercies of David" (v. 3). The Lord makes clear that this salvation is one of grace, not merit (v. 5, 7). Yet this gracious salvation requires faith, repentance and obedience. "Seek the Lord," "Call upon Him," "Let the wicked forsake his way" "And He [God] will have mercy on him" (vv. 6–7). Grace and obligation, Gospel and Law, salvation and requirement are united in God's single message: "Trust and Obey."[71]

Likewise, it is important to remember that the hermeneutics and soteriology of the Federal Vision are governed by monocovenantalism by which they interpret the redemptive historical continuity in light of "Trust and Obey," which is another expression of the denial of the antithesis between law and gospel in soteriology.

SUMMARY

We have traced Calvin's covenant theology. In doing so, we have found that Calvin laid out all the hermeneutical and theological ingredients for the development of the distinction between the covenant of works and the covenant of grace though he did not use the term the covenant of works (*foedus operum*) in respect to the prelapsarian Adamic status. In short, Calvin was a great redemptive historical theologian.

In his redemptive historical analysis, eschatological motif was deeply embedded, especially in his analysis of the Old Covenant under the rubric of "the covenant of the law" (*foedus legale*) in contrast with the New Covenant. In that sense, Calvin's hermeneutics may be identified as escha-

71. Ibid.

tological hermeneutics. In addition, we found that Calvin's identification of the Old Covenant as "the covenant of law" (*foedus legale*) decisively contributed to the idea of the republication of the covenant of works under the Old Covenant with redemptive adjustment among the Reformed orthodox theologians.

Calvin did not mix the law and gospel or grace in his analysis of the historical and logical orders in his depiction of the redemptive history, covering creation, fall, redemption, and consummation along with his analysis on the principles of *sola gratia* and *sola fide*. Neoorthodox theologians, after the pattern of Barth's existential monocovenantalism, reject historical and logical orders, law and gospel, while they identify themselves in one way or another with Calvin's theology, creating a deep wedge between Calvin and the Calvinists. Meanwhile, Federal Visionists, after Norman Shepherd, reject the historical and logical orders, law and gospel, though they do not identify themselves with neoorthodox theology after the pattern of Karl Barth. But they rather identify themselves with the theologies of Calvin and the Westminster Standards. To be sure, for Calvin, the historical and logical orders of law and gospel are not dualism as critics falsely argue. Rather, they are essential components of biblical religion. Calvin's theological vision was clear: if there is no distinction between law and gospel, then there is no union with Christ. For Calvin, the good news of the Gospel stands and falls together with the Pauline evangelical distinction between law and gospel.

3

Covenant and Election

THE FEDERAL VISIONISTS FOLLOW a theological paradigm, namely "covenantal paradigm," which has been developed and promoted by Norman Shepherd. Shepherd perceives divine election primarily not from the perspective of sovereign grace but of covenantal obedience. He substantially denies the sovereign grace character in the divine election although he claims that his concept of covenant and election has substantial agreement with Calvin and the Westminster Standards.[1] The exponents of the Federal Vision follow the lead of Shepherd in their exposition of covenant and election. Examining the relationship between covenant and election, Barach locates a great tension between covenant and election, arguing that it is actually a view point of Calvin and the Westminster Standards:

> According to Scripture, not everyone who is in the covenant has been predestined to eternal glory with Christ. God establishes His covenant with believers and their households, including some who will later apostatize and be cut off from covenantal fellowship with Him. Put another way, all those who are baptized are genuinely baptized *into Christ* (Galatians 3:27), and brought into Christ's body, the church (1 Corinthians 12:13), and are members of God's covenant, at least until they are cut off, whether by Christ's church (excommunication) or directly by Christ (death as judgment).
>
> Like the previous view, this view has been held by many Reformed people. You find it taught by Calvin, the Three Forms of Unity, and many Reformed and Presbyterian theologians. It is not

---

1. For critical analysis on the Federal Visionists' view on covenant and election, including Shepherd, see Jeon, *Covenant Theology and Justification by Faith*, 97–105; Carl D. Robbins, "A Response to 'Covenant and Election,'" in *The Auburn Avenue Theology, Pros and Cons: Debating the Federal Vision*, ed. E. Calvin Beisner (Fort Lauderdale: Knox Theological Seminary, 2004), 157–61; Waters, *The Federal Vision and Covenant Theology*, 96–124.

the case that there has been only *one* accepted Reformed view on the relationship between covenant and election.

This third view is biblical: God does not make His covenant exclusively with those who have been predestined to eternal salvation. Rather, He establishes His covenant with all who have been baptized, with professing believers and their children. The whole church, head for head, is in covenant with God.[2]

Unlike Norman Shepherd and the Federal Visionists, I will demonstrate that Calvin did not use the concept of covenant to blur the distinction between election and reprobation. In that sense, I will explore how Calvin safeguarded divine election from the perspective of sovereign grace, articulating the biblical doctrine of double predestination and posing a radical distinction between election and reprobation in light of soteriological benefits and blessings in Christ. Calvin's *Brief Articles Concerning Predestination* concretely demonstrates that Calvin's doctrine of double predestination was controlled by "the distinction between elect and reprobate," which is lost in the theological perspective of the Federal Vision due to the influence of monocovenantalism:

> Upon the same decree depends the distinction between elect and reprobate: as he adopted some for himself for salvation, he destined others for eternal ruin.
>
> While the reprobate are the vessels of the just wrath of God, and the elect vessels of his compassion, the ground of the distinction is to be sought in the pure will of God alone, which is the supreme rule of justice.[3]

In addition, we will argue that the concept of covenant and election, understood by the exponents of the Federal Vision, is not compatible to Calvin although they identify their ideas with those of Calvin, the Westminster Standards, other Reformed confessional standards and the Bible.

2. John Barach, "Covenant and Election," in *The Auburn Avenue Theology, Pros and Cons: Debating the Federal Vision*, ed. E. Calvin Beisner (Fort Lauderdale: Knox Theological Seminary, 2004), 150–51.

3. John Calvin, *Calvin: Theological Treatises*, ed. & trans. J. K. S. Reid, in *The Library of Christian Classics* (London: SCM Press, 1954; reprint, Louisville: Westminster John Knox Press, 2006), 179.

DOUBLE PREDESTINATION

During the Protestant Reformation, there was a great deal of debate on whether double predestination, namely election and reprobation, is a biblical doctrine or not.[4] Erasmus, Eck, and Albert Pighiu were the representative theologians who objected the doctrine of double predestination. Against them, Calvin plainly wrote that God's "eternal election," illumining his sovereign free grace in salvation necessarily entails its counter part, which is reprobation. Calvin pointed out that it is important to know that salvation "from the well spring of God's free mercy" (*ex fonte gratuitae misericordiae Dei*) has a concrete divine background, which is "his eternal election" (*aeterna eius election*):

> A baffling question this seems to many. For they think nothing more inconsistent than that out of the common multitude of men some should be predestined to salvation, others to destruction . . . We shall never be clearly persuaded, as we ought to be, that our salvation from the wellspring of God's free mercy until we come to know his

4. For the excellent discussion on Calvin's adaptation and exposition of the biblical doctrine of double predestination in the context of the Protestant Reformation with historical sensitivity and its practical implication, see R. Scott Clark, "Election and Predestination: The Sovereign Expressions of God," in *Theological Guide to Calvin's Institutes*, eds. David W. Hall and Peter A. Lillback (Phillipsburg: Presbyterian and Reformed Publishing, 2008), 90–122.

Clark comprehensively discusses that the basic pattern of the doctrine of double predestination was a commonly shared theological idea among the major Protestant Reformers after the theological pattern of Augustine of Hippo (354–430): "One of the most striking and rhetorically powerful statements of double predestination was Luther's 1525 *De servo arbitrio* (*On the Bondage of the Will*) written and published in response to Erasmus's critique of Luther's doctrine of predestination. Among the English Protestants, William Tyndale's (c. 1494–1536) doctrine of predestination focused, in his preface to Romans, on the comfort it brings to the believer. On the continent, Huldrych Zwingli (1484–1531) taught clearly the doctrine of double predestination in his 1530 treatise *On Providence*. Calvin's sometime colleague Martin Bucer (1491–1551) defended the doctrine of double predestination in his massive commentary on Romans. It has been claimed that Heinrich Bullinger (1504–1575), Zwingli's successor in Zurich, rejected double predestination. Cornelis Venema has shown, however, that Bullinger's concerns about double predestination were not theological but homiletical and practical.

It is evident that the doctrines of predestination and double predestination were not unique to Calvin at all but the common property since Augustine." Ibid., 95–96. For the comprehensive exploration of Calvin's doctrine of double predestination in relation to Christology and its adaptation by the early Reformed orthodoxy in the sixteenth-century European context, see Richard A. Muller, *Christ and the Decree: Christology and Predestination in Reformed Theology from Calvin to Perkins* (The Labyrinth Press, 1986; reprint, Grand Rapids: Baker, 2008).

eternal election, which illumines God's grace by this contrast: that he does not indiscriminately adopt all into the hope of salvation but gives to some what he denies to others.[5]

In the discussion of Calvin's understanding of Pauline double predestination, it is important to grasp that Calvin viewed the divine election in light of the antithesis between works and grace, which is closely related to the antithesis between law and gospel in the doctrine of justification by faith alone (*sola fide*) and salvation by grace alone (*sola gratia*) in his soteriology. Likewise, the genius of Calvin's analysis on the doctrine of double predestination lies in that he made a harmonious connection between the divine election by sovereign grace and *sola gratia* and *sola fide* in soteriology, which was lacking even in Augustine's soteriology. The classical passage that Calvin appealed is Romans 11:5–6. Calvin wrote that there is "a remnant," who has been saved "according to the election of grace" among the descendents of Abraham. Again, characteristically, in Calvin's election theology, there is a close connection between "the election of grace" and salvation "solely from God's mere generosity":

> How much the ignorance of this principle detracts from God's glory, how much it takes away from true humility, is well known. Yet Paul denies that this which needs so much to be known can be known unless God, utterly disregarding works, chooses those whom he has decreed within himself. 'At the present time,' he says, 'a remnant has been saved according to the election of grace. But if it is by grace, it is no more of works; otherwise grace would no more be grace. But if it is of works, it is no more of grace; otherwise work would not be work.' [Rom. 11:5–6] If-to make it clear that our salvation comes about solely from God's mere generosity-we must be called back to the course of election, those who wish to get rid of all this are obscuring as maliciously as they can what ought to have been gloriously and vociferously proclaimed, and they tear humility up by the very roots.[6]

From the perspective of historical theology, Calvin, in his discussion of double predestination, self-consciously followed the theological principle of Augustine. Augustine in his exposition of the divine predestination in his book, *On the Gift of Perseverance*, emphasized the importance

5. Calvin, *Institutes*, 3.21.1.

6. Ibid.

of making a balance between the hidden and revealed will of God in the proper understanding of the doctrine of double predestination:

> Augustine admits that for these reasons he was frequently charged with preaching predestination too freely, but, as it was easy for him, he overwhelmingly refuted the charge. We, moreover, because many and various absurdities are obtruded at this point, have preferred to dispose of each in its own place. I desire only to have them generally admit that we should not investigate what the Lord has left hidden in secret, that we should not neglect what he has brought into the open, so that we may not be convicted of excessive curiosity on the one hand, or of excessive ingratitude on the other. For Augustine also skillfully expressed this idea: we can safely follow Scripture, which proceeds at the pace of a mother stooping to her child, so to speak, so as not to leave us behind in our weakness.[7]

In his biblical articulation of the doctrine of double predestination, Calvin faced some who denied the doctrine of reprobation where they argued that it is the doctrine against biblical witness. J. Faber and Pighius wrote their view against the doctrine of reprobation, appealing their objection to Ezekiel 33:11; 1 Timothy 2:3–4 and others that might be used as definitive poof texts against the doctrine of reprobation. However, Calvin argued that those passages may not be used as biblical examples of rejection to the doctrine of reprobation. Interpreting 1 Timothy 2:3–4, Calvin briefly explored redemptive history, represented in the history of Israel in the Old Testament. Afterward, Calvin argued that the election of Israel out of many pagan nations is a good example of the biblical doctrine of reprobation. In light of this redemptive historical reflection, Calvin brilliantly avoided universalism, and he explained "all men" as "any order of men," considering the literal context of 1 Timothy 2:1–2:

> Secondly, they quote a passage from Paul in which he states that God "wills all men to be saved" [I Tim. 2:3–4]. I reply: first, it is clear from the context how he wills it. For Paul couples the two points: that He wills them to be saved, and to come to a recognition of the truth. If they mean that this has been fixed by God's eternal plan so that they may receive the doctrine of salvation, what does that saying of Moses' mean: "What nation is so glorious that God should draw nigh unto it as he does unto you?" [Deut. 4:7 p., cf. Comm.]. How did it happen that God deprived many peoples of the light of his gospel while others enjoyed it? How did it happen that the pure

7. Ibid., 3.21.4.

recognition of the doctrine of godliness never came to some, while others barely tasted some obscure rudiments of it? From this it will be easy to determine the drift of Paul's reasoning. He had enjoyed upon Timothy to make solemn prayers in the church for kings and rulers [I Tim. 2:1–2]. But since it seemed somewhat absurd to pour out prayers to God for an almost hopeless class of men (not only strangers all to the body of Christ, but intent upon crushing his Kingdom with all their strength), he adds, "This is acceptable to God, who wills all men to be saved" [1 Tim. 2:3–4 p.]. By this, Paul surely means only that God has not closed the way unto salvation to any order of men; rather, he has so poured out his mercy that he would have none without it.[8]

Calvin argued that the doctrine of the divine predestination is neither abstract nor a speculative doctrine. God arranged it covenantally. So,

8. Ibid., 3.24.16. Albert Pighius (1490–1542) was a Roman Catholic apologist, who engaged in a theological discussion against Calvin in respect to the doctrine of double predestination. He wrote a theological treatise "on free will which sought to make predestination dependent on foreknowledge of merits and jeopardized acceptance of original sin." Calvin considered Pighius' view seriously, and he wrote a treatise entitled *Concerning the Eternal Predestination* (*De aeterna Praedestinatione Dei*, 1552), which is a major refutation against Pighius after his death in 1542. See J. D. Douglas, "Pighius, Albert," in *Evangelical Dictionary of Theology*, ed. Walter E. Elwell (Grand Rapids: Baker, 1984), 858. For Calvin's critical engagement against Pighius' view and his followers on "the freewill of man" over against the biblical doctrine of double predestination, see John Calvin, *Concerning the Predestination of God*, trans. J. K. S. Reid (Cambridge, James Clarke & Co., 1961; reprint, Louisville: Westminster John Knox Press, 1997). In addition, for Calvin's comprehensive and critical analysis over against Pighius' concept of "free choice," see idem, *The Bondage and Liberation of the Will: A Defense of the Orthodox Doctrine of Human Choice against Pighius*, ed. A.N.S. Lane, trans G.I. Davies. in *Texts and Studies in Reformation and Post-Reformation Thought*. vol. II (Grand Rapids: Baker Book House, 2002), 1–244. Calvin responded to Pighius' criticism to his doctrine of double predestination after eleven years since Pighius' death. He referred to Pighius as "a dead dog." I do not endorse Calvin's inflammatory language to his theological counterpart although I consider the harsh Reformation theological and practical contexts: "Nine years have now elapsed since Albertus Pighius the Campanian, a man of clearly frenzied audacity, tried in the same book both to establish the freewill of man and to overthrow the secret counsel of God whereby He chooses some to salvation and destines others for eternal destruction. But because he attacked me by name, so as to stab at pious and sound doctrine through my side, it has become necessary for me to curb the sacrilegious fury of the man. However, I was at that time distracted by other business and was unable to embrace the discussion of both matters in a short space of time. But the first part being discharged, I undertook to write later, when occasion served, about predestination. Shortly after my book on freewill appeared, Pighius died. So, not to insult a dead dog, I turned attention to other studies." Calvin, *Concerning the Eternal Predestination of God*, 53–54.

God "compacted with himself" (*apud se constitutum habuit*) everyone into the category of either election unto "eternal life" (*vita aeterna*) or reprobation unto "eternal damnation" (*damnatio aeterna*). It is safe to say, then, in Calvin's view of predestination, there is no middle ground between election and reprobation. Calvin summarized the biblical doctrine of double predestination as follows:

> We call predestination God's eternal decree, by which he compacted with himself what he willed to become of each man. For all are not created in equal condition; rather, eternal life is foreordained for some, eternal damnation for others. Therefore, as any man has been created to one or the other of these ends, we speak of him as predestined to life or to death.[9]

Meanwhile, the Federal Visionists self-consciously develop their new theology, based upon the monocovenantal concept where they deny the distinction between law and gospel along with the distinction between the covenant of works and the covenant of grace as I have already explored in their doctrine of covenant and justification by faith. In that sense, I am not surprised that they also modify the doctrine of double predestination under their hermeneutical and theological principle which is monocovenantalism. In word, however, they appear to approve the doctrine of double predestination as a biblical doctrine, but with a new and monocovenantal interpretation while they identify their view with Calvin, the Westminster Standards and the Bible. For example, Barach apparently endorses the classical formulation of the doctrine of double predestination which Calvin adopted and expounded after the pattern of the Augustinian double predestination, namely election and reprobation:

> The Bible teaches that all things happen according to God's will, so that if anyone enters into final glory with Christ Jesus, that is the outworking of God's eternal plan. God has predestined some people who deserve eternal damnation to eternal glory with Christ instead, while not so predestining others. This is the Bible's teaching from Genesis 1:1 on through the whole of Scripture. God didn't predestine anyone to glory because of something in that person, but simply out of His sheer love and grace in Christ. God initiates, not because He sees anything in us, but out of sheer grace.
>
> That predestination choice is unchangeable. The number of people who will enter into final glory is the number of people

9. Calvin, *Institutes*, 3.21.5.

God always *intended* to enter into final glory with Christ. That predestining choice is also unthwartable. Apostasy, we are told in Romans 9, doesn't thwart God's people. Yes, some people fall away. Yes, Israel has fallen away. Yes, Israel has been cut off, but that has not thwarted God's plan. God preserves a remnant, and even that apostasy happens in accord with God's will, we are told, to show His wrath, to make His power and His justice known.[10]

However, in the discussion of apostasy and perseverance in relation to covenant and election, Barach creates a new group, which does not belong to either the elect or the reprobate. Barach argues that there are some people in the covenant community who "do not persevere to the end." God chose them and showed His "grace and love for a time," but "their subsequent rejection of His grace and love is the historic outworking of His predestinating decree." In that fashion, Barach creates a new group between election and reprobation, which is an idea alien to Calvin and the Bible:

> For those who do not persevere to the end, God's choice to have them belong to His covenant was His choice to show them grace and love for a time. Both their entrance into His covenant and their subsequent rejection of His grace and love is the historic outworking of His predestinating decree.
>
> For those who do persevere to the end, God's choice to have them belong to His covenant *just is* His choice to have them belong to Him forever. Their entrance into His covenant, their perseverance in faith, and their rich entry into the everlasting kingdom of Jesus Christ (2 Peter 1:11) are the historic outworking of His predestinating decree.[11]

Barach and the Federal Visionists move toward *triple predestination* as they create a new group within the covenant community who do not persevere to the end. It is a logical byproduct due to their rejection of a clear distinction between election and reprobation as Robbins provides a critique against Barach's formulation on covenant and election:

"Any view that states that reprobate men will receive any of the salvific benefits of Christ's work (i.e. *effectual* calling, regeneration, faith, adoption, justification, etc.), seems to shatter the clear divide between God's

10. John Barach, "Covenant and Election," in *The Federal Vision*, eds. Steve Wilkins & Duane Garner (Monroe: Athanasius Press, 2004), 17–18.

11. John Barach, "Covenant and Election," in *The Auburn Avenue Theology*, 154–55.

eternal people and all others. Barach's view would tend towards erecting a third class of men (like Lewis Sperry Chafer's and Campus Crusade for Christ's "carnal Christian") who are neither fish nor fowl."[12]

A DISTINCTION BETWEEN THE NATIONAL ELECTION OF ISRAEL AND INDIVIDUAL ELECTION

Examining the redemptive history of Israel, Calvin made a careful distinction between the national election of Israel as the descendents of Abraham and individual election and reprobation among the Israelites. He noted that Abraham's descendents composed "the church" (*ecclesia*). However, within the church among the descendents of Abraham, some were elected to be saved while others were cut off although "the spiritual covenant" (*spirituale foedus*) was "equally sealed by the sign of circumcision":

> We must now add a second, more limited degree of election, or one in which God's more special grace was evident, that is, when from the same race of Abraham God rejected some but showed that he kept others among his sons by cherishing them in the church. Ishmael had at first obtained equal rank with his brother, Isaac, for in him the spiritual covenant had been equally sealed by the sign of circumcision. Ishmael is cut off; then Esau; afterward, a countless multitude, and well-nigh all Israel. In Isaac the seed was called; the same calling continued in Jacob. God showed a similar example in rejecting Saul. This is also wonderfully proclaimed in the psalm: 'He rejected the tribe of Joseph, and chose not the tribe of Ephraim but chose the tribe of Judah' [Ps. 78:67–68; cf. LXX and Ps. 77:67–68, Vg. And Comm.].[13]

Calvin explained that only for some among the descendents of Abraham, individual election became "effectual and truly enduring, ascend to the Head, in whom the Heavenly Father has gathered his elect together, and has joined them to himself by an indissoluble bond." Here again, Calvin used covenantal language, using the phrase, "an indissoluble bond" where God unites the elect to his Son, who is the Head of the church through the work of the Holy Spirit. It is true that God bestowed his "generous favor" to "the adoption of the race of Abraham" while he

---

12. Carl D. Robbins, "A Response to 'Covenant and Election,'" in *The Auburn Avenue Theology, Pros and Cons: Debating the Federal Vision*, ed. E. Calvin Beisner (Fort Lauderdale: Knox Theological Seminary, 2004), 160.

13. Calvin, *Institutes*, 3.21.6.

has denied its access to others. Calvin continued to argue that only some within the race of Abraham received "a covenant of eternal life" (*vitae aeternae pacto*) as "a special mode of election" (*specialem electionis modum*). It is exemplified representatively in the case of Jacob and Esau. The contrast between Jacob and Esau, Calvin wrote, may be applied to "the whole offspring of the patriarch":

> So, indeed God's generous favor, which he has denied to others, has been displayed in the adoption of the race of Abraham; yet in the members of Christ a far more excellent power of grace appears, for engrafted to their Head, they are never cut off from salvation. Therefore Paul skillfully argues from the passage of Malachi that I have just cited that where God has made a covenant of eternal life and calls any people to himself, a special mode of election is employed for a part of them, so that he does not with indiscriminate grace effectually elect all [Rom. 9:13].[14]

In the context of the discussion of the national election of Israel as the descendents of Abraham and individual election and reprobation within the elected nation of Israel, Calvin carefully located the status of the national election of Israel as "general election" (*generalis election*) while he put individual election unto salvation as actual election in which he specified as "a special mode of election" (*specialem electionis modum*). Here, Calvin made a clear distinction between "general election" and "special election," in viewing the Old Testament Israel as a chosen nation. According to Calvin, both Esau and Jacob received the outward blessings of "general election" as the descendents of Abraham who were members of the church. However, Esau was not the member of "special election" although he was the member of the covenant community or the church. Examining the biblical example of election and reprobation within the category of "general election" (*generalis electio*), Calvin emphasized that God does not bestow saving grace for those who are not members of "special election":

> It is easy to explain why the general election of a people is not always firm and effectual: to those with whom God makes a covenant, he does not at once give the spirit of regeneration that would enable them to persevere in the covenant to the very end. Rather, the outward change, without the working of inner grace, which might have availed to keep them, is intermediate between the re-

14. Ibid., 3.21.7

jection of mankind and the election of a meager number of the godly. The whole people of Israel has been called 'the inheritance of God' [Deut. 32:9; 1 Kings 8:51; Ps. 28:9; 33:12; etc.], yet many of them were foreigners.[15]

We need to pay special attention to how Calvin used the word, "a covenant" in his analysis about "the general election of a people" (*generalis electio populi*) in relation to the implication of saving grace. Calvin emphasized that God made "a covenant" with "the whole people of Israel," but within the covenant community of the Israelites, some did not receive "the spirit of regeneration" (*Spiritu regenerationis*) because they were reprobate although they were the members of "general election," who could enjoy the outward blessings of the covenant community such as worship, circumcision and other religious outward benefits and blessings.

Calvin, in his interpretation of Galatians 4:28, made a distinction between "the children of Abraham according to the flesh" and "the spiritual children." Calvin continued to write that the genuine spiritual blessings have been applied only to "the spiritual children" of Abraham who were elected by "God's unchangeable plan":

> For the fact that God was continually gathering his church from Abraham's children rather than from profane nations had its reason in his covenant, which, when violated by that multitude, he confined to a few that it might not utterly cease. In short, that adoption of Abraham's seed in common was a visible image of the greater benefit that God bestowed on some out of the many. This is why Paul so carefully distinguishes the children of Abraham according to the flesh from the spiritual children who have been called after the example of Isaac [Gal. 4:28]. Not that it was a vain and unprofitable thing simply to be a child of Abraham; such could not be said without dishonoring the covenant! No, God's unchangeable plan, by which he predestined for himself those whom he willed, was in fact intrinsically effectual unto salvation for these spiritual offspring alone.[16]

In his discussion of predestination through the examination of the redemptive history of Israel among the descendents of Abraham, Calvin used the word "church" (*ecclesia*) with a very careful redemptive historical and theological intention. According to Calvin, God continually composed

15. Ibid.
16. Ibid.

"his church from Abraham's children." Here, Calvin suggested that within the "church," elect and reprobate coexist as seen in the history of Israel. Calvin's discussion of "the church" within the context of the doctrine of predestination, exploring the history of Israel among the descendents of Abraham, is important for his comprehensive and biblical understanding of the doctrine of the Church.

The distinction between the individual elect and reprobate within the chosen nation of Israel in the Old Testament of Israel is decisively lacking in the theology of the Federal Vision because the hermeneutics of the Federal Vision does not balance continuity and discontinuity in their understanding of the relationship between the Old and New Covenants. The Federal Visionists' *exclusive emphasis* on the continuity of the Old and New Covenants becomes a hermeneutical barrier to read a legitimate discontinuity, which obviously exists. For Calvin, the Old Testament of Israel in the promise land was a *type* of eternal heaven, which will be fulfilled after the Second Coming of Jesus Christ. In that sense, the proper understanding of *typology* is so pertinent in Calvin's grand and comprehensive description of redemptive history as we already explored extensively.

However, the Federal Visionists do not maintain the distinction between the national election of Israel and individual election, which is vital in Calvin's understanding of the typological nature of the Old Testament Israel and the doctrine of double predestination revealed in redemptive history. John Barach writes:

> Each Israelite was grafted into God's people as an act of God's electing love. That election, that choice belong to the people of God, that choice of Israel as a nation, involves a special calling and a special responsibility. God chose His people unconditionally, not because of anything that was true of them. He chose them to belong to Him, but their life in covenant with God was *conditional*. It involved faith and obedience and perseverance.
>
> All through history we see that individual Israelites apostatize. Israel as a whole apostatizes, though God preserves a remnant. It is out of the whole of Israel that God selects some whom He preserves according to His eternal plan and predestination. That is how God works out His eternal plan in the course of history. Though God declares Israel "my people" early in her history, we discover in Hosea that God later calls Israel "not my people" (Hos. 1:9). He made them His special people, and then He reprobated them in history: "Not my people." Later in Hosea He promises to

call Israel "my people" again. He promises to preserve a remnant and to bring in the Gentiles as well. He promises to choose, to elect, Israel one more time.[17]

Unlike the Federal Visionists, the genius of Calvin's theology lies in the fact that he beautifully harmonized the doctrine of double predestination, soteriology, church, and eschatology. In fact, Calvin had a deep consciousness of double predestination in his discussion of soteriology, church and eschatology. In that sense, Calvin's distinction between general and special election within the chosen nation of Israel was to demonstrate biblical validity of election and reprobation within the covenant community of the chosen Israel through the Old Testament history of Israel. In this manner, Calvin made a distinction between the invisible and visible churches to differentiate the elect and reprobate within the church:

> How we are to judge the church visible, which falls within our knowledge, is, I believe, already evident from the above discussion. For we have said that Holy Scripture speaks of the church in two ways. Sometimes by the term "church" it means that which is actually in God's presence, into which no persons are received but those who are children of God by grace of adoption and true members of Christ by sanctification of the Holy Spirit. Then, indeed, the church includes not only the saints presently living on earth, but all the elect from the beginning of the world. Often, however, the name "church" designates the whole multitude of men spread over the earth who profess to worship one God and Christ. By baptism we are initiated into faith in him; by partaking in the Lord's Supper we attest our unity in true doctrine and love; in the Word of the Lord the ministry instituted by Christ is preserved. In this church are mingled many hypocrites who have nothing of Christ but the name and outward appearance. There are very many ambitious, greedy, envious persons, evil speakers, and some of quite unclean life. Such are tolerated for a time either because a vigorous discipline does not always flourish as it ought.
>
> Just as we must believe, therefore, that the former church, invisible to us, is visible to the eyes of God alone, so we are commanded to revere and keep communion with the latter, which is called "church" in respect to men.[18]

---

17. Barach, "Covenant and Election," in *the Federal* Vision, 26.

18. Calvin, *Institutes*, 4.1.7.

We need to pay attention to Calvin's remark that the invisible church is only "visible to the eyes of God alone" (*solius Dei oculis conspicuam ecclesiam*) because it embraces all the elect from the beginning of redemptive history, inaugurated with the proclamation of 'the primitive gospel' (*proto Evangelium*) to the consummation, which will be completed in the everlasting heaven after the Second Coming of Jesus Christ. According to Calvin, all the elect members of God in Christ are not visible to our eyes. In that sense, Calvin's identification of the invisible and visible church is based upon the distinction between election and reprobation. And it is also biblically warranted.

Meanwhile, the Federal Visionists offer criticism about the concept of the distinction between the invisible and visible church which was developed by Augustine, used and sophisticated by Calvin and adopted by the Westminster Standards. In his article on *The Church: Visible or Invisible*, Douglas Wilson demonstrates a very insightful argument about the nature and character of the church, describing it as historical and eschatological. Wilson's description of the church as historical and eschatological has a strong emphasis on the historical nature of the church. Wilson reasons that he had an idea from Murray to rethink the traditional concept of the distinction between the invisible and visible church. Afterwards, he becomes negative about this distinction because he believes that it is not biblical:

> If, like John Murray, we expressly guard against that kind of ontological division, I have no problem with it. It was John Murray incidentally who drove me most of the way down this particular road. Certainly the Church has invisible aspects. But to *define* the Church this way is, according to Murray, "invalid." "There are liabilities that can be avoided if other terms are employed." As he put it, the Church "in the New Testament never appears as an invisible entity and therefore may never be *defined* in terms of invisibility." As he continues, invisibility is a "term that is liable to be loaded with the misconceptions inherent in the concept 'invisible church', and tends to support the abuses incident thereto." And I agree with him that this is no matter of theological gnat-strangling. This matter is of "deep practical significance."[19]

---

19. Douglas Wilson, "The Church: Visible or Invisible," in *The Federal Vision*, eds. Steve Wilkins & Duane Garner (Monroe: Athanasius Press, 2004), 266. Wilson also discusses "the visible and invisible church" extensively, critically engaging with the Westminster Confession of Faith. See Wilson, "'Reformed' Is Not Enough," 69–78.

Critiquing the distinction between the invisible and visible church, Wilson appears to follow the critique offered by John Murray. Nevertheless, Wilson's critique is fundamentally different from Murray's. Murray never lost the consciousness of double predestination, sharply distinguishing between election and reprobation in his biblico-systematic theology. However, the Federal Visionists, including Wilson, loses the consciousness of a legitimate divide of election and reprobation in their covenantal approach to predestination and its implication to the doctrine of church. Furthermore, Wilson misinterprets the classical distinction between the invisible and visible church, relating it to "the Platonic categories of the Greeks instead of the historical and eschatological categories of the Jews." In that sense, Wilson undermines and bypasses the significance of the distinction between the invisible and visible church, which is a biblical way to denote that the earthly church in distinction to the heavenly church includes and embraces both the elect and reprobate:

> Our problem is that we have tended to think in the Platonic categories of the Greeks instead of the historical and eschatological categories of the Jews. (This is *not* a charge of Hellenism against the Westminster Confession of Faith.) That which is heavenly (and hence invisible) is true, we assume, and that which is earthly can at best be only a dim shadow of that which is true. Thus, because we think of the heavenly and earthly as two separate and distinct ontological realms, existing at the same time, and because we *tend* to think of a Church in each realm, we find ourselves stuck with two separate and distinct churches. But Christ is the Head of only *one* Church.[20]

Certainly, there is merit in Wilson's description and analysis of the church as historical and eschatological; it is very insightful. We can develop the doctrine of the church from the perspective of historical and eschatological identity in which we may emphasize and enrich the historical character of the church. Nevertheless, Wilson's description of historical church embraces a significant theological problem because he sees that some in the historical church may fall away from the saving grace of God, appealing to Jesus' Parable about the Vineyard in John 15:1–8. Our complaint to Wilson and the Federal Visionists lies in the fact that their description of the church as a historical may be used as a theological justification to reject a sharp divide of elect and reprobate in the church,

20. Wilson, "The Church: Visible or Invisible," 267.

which is warranted in the Biblical witness as Calvin correctly read it. Wilson writes as follows:

> This distinction helps us to understand the relationship of un-converted professing Christians to the Church as well. The Bible teaches clearly that in the historical Church there are fruitless branches (but real branches nontheless) which will not be there in the eschatological Church. Jesus sternly warns that, "If a man abide not in me, he is cast forth as a branch, and is withered; and men gather them, and cast them into the fire, and they are burned" (John 15:6). And Paul says the same. "For if God spared not the natural branches, take heed lest he also spare not thee" (Rom. 11:21).
>
> This does not mean that the elect can lose their salvation. But it *does* mean that branches can lose their position on the tree. The elect always bear fruit, and their fruit remains. And yet some false pro-fessors, with a genuine historical connection to the tree, never bear lasting fruit, and consequently fall under the judgment of God.[21]

Again, we need to pay special attention to Wilson's discussion about his concept of the historical Church as a replacement of the classical con-cept of the visible church. He argues that "in the historical Church there are fruitless branches (but real branches nontheless) which will not be there in the eschatological Church" in his exposition of John 15:6 and Romans 11:21. In doing so, he rightly denies that "the elect can lose their salvation." However, he adds that "branches can lose their position on the tree." Here, we find theological inconsistency and a contradiction in Wilson's mind. Wilson falsely argues that in the historical Church some people who receive the blessings of union with Christ may be broken off from Christ through apostasy and may not belong to the blessings of the eschatological Church in the everlasting heaven. It is a primary reason why I argue that the Federal Visionists' doctrine of Church in relation to double predestination is incompatible to the view points of Calvin, the Westminster Standards and the Bible.

REFUTATION AGAINST THE FOREKNOWLEDGE
OF MERIT IN ELECTION

As a counter to Calvin during the Protestant Reformation in respect to the doctrine of election, Pighius and others emphasized the divine foreknowl-edge of merit or good works as the condition of election. Calvin, against

---

21. Ibid., 268–9.

Pighius and others who promoted the concept of conditional election, examined Scriptural testimonies for the confirmation of "the free election of believers." In doing so, Calvin primarily appealed to the classical Pauline passages about the divine free election, described in Ephesians 1:

> Now it behooves us to pay attention to what Scripture proclaims of every person. When Paul teaches that we were chosen in Christ 'before the creation of the world' [Eph. 1:4a], he takes away all consideration of real worth on our part, for it is just as if he said: since among all the offspring of Adam, the Heavenly Father found nothing worthy of his election, he turned his eyes upon his Anointed, to choose from that body as members those whom he was to take into the fellowship of life. Let this reasoning, then prevail among believers: we were adopted in Christ into the eternal inheritance because in ourselves we were not capable of such great excellence.[22]

Interpreting Ephesians 1:4–5, Calvin wrote that Paul's analysis on the divine election "before the creation of the world" signifies that election absolutely eliminates "foreknowledge of merit." Calvin further elaborated that believers' holiness or sanctification is not the condition of election, but it is "the result of election" (*electionis effectum*):

> By saying that they were 'elect before the creation of the world' [Eph. 1:4], he takes away all regard for worth. For what basis for distinction is there among those who did not yet exist, and who were subsequently to be equals in Adam? Now if they are elect in Christ, it follows that not only is each man elected without respect to his own person but also certain ones are separated from others, since we see that not all are members of Christ. Besides, the fact that they were elected 'to be holy' [Eph. 1:4b] plainly refutes the error that derives election from foreknowledge, since Paul declares all virtue appearing in man is the result of election. Now if a higher cause be sought, Paul answers that God has predestined it so, and that this is 'according to the good pleasure of his will' [Eph. 1:5b].[23]

It is fascinating to observe that in Calvin's theology believers' personal holiness or sanctification is "the result of election," which emphasizes the nature or character of "the free election of believers" as Calvin located believers' sanctification or good works as the *fruit* or the *result* of

22. Calvin, *Institutes*, 3.22.1.
23. Ibid., 3.22.2. Cf. Ibid., 3.22.3.

justification in his soteriology. Thus, Calvin refuted the idea of "election from foreknowledge" (*electionem ex praescientia*).

Pighius and his supporters over against Calvin insisted that the divine election is based upon his foreknowledge of merit or good works. They argued that "the reprobation of Esau" and "the election of Jacob" are the representative examples of election, based upon the foreknowledge of merit. Calvin, carefully examining Romans 9:11–13, countered their argument that indeed the examples of Esau and Jacob are the classical biblical paradigm of predestination, namely election and reprobation. Indeed "the election of Jacob" is a biblical paradigm for "the free election of believers." Calvin persuasively wrote:

> From the example of Jacob and Esau, Paul then develops the matter further. For although both were sons of Abraham, enclosed together in their mother's womb, the honor of the first born was transferred to Jacob. Here was a change like a portent, which, as Paul contends, testified to the election of Jacob and the reprobation of Esau. When one asks the origin and cause, the teachers of foreknowledge would locate it in the virtues and vices of the men. Here is the sum of their facile argument: in the person of Jacob, God showed that he chooses those worthy of his grace; in the person of Esau, that he repudiates those whom he foresees as unworthy. So, indeed, they boldly argue. But what does Paul say? "Though they were not yet born and had done nothing either good or bad, in order that God's purpose of election might continue, not because of works but because of his call, it was said, 'The elder will serve the younger.' As it is written, 'Jacob I loved but Esau I hated.'" [Rom. 9:11–13; cf. Gen. 25:23] If foreknowledge had any bearing upon this distinction between the brothers, the mention of time would surely have been inopportune.[24]

Likewise, Calvin effectively countered the concept of meritorious conditional election, based upon foreknowledge of merit, using the example of Esau and Jacob. Refuting the unbiblical view of meritorious conditional election, Calvin laid out the concrete biblical principle of unconditional free election. Furthermore, Calvin argued that the divine free election and salvation by grace alone (*sola gratia*) are closely tied together. In that manner, Calvin concretely argued that believers' salvation is based upon nothing else but "the decision of divine election alone" (*solius divi-*

---

24. Ibid., 3.22.4.

nae electionis arbitrio), examining the Pauline analysis on Esau and Jacob in relation to election and reprobation:

> For we have it from the words of the apostle that the salvation of believers has been founded upon the decision of divine election alone, and that this favor is not earned by works but comes from free calling. We have, as it were, an example of this thing set before us. Esau and Jacob are brothers, born of the same parents, as yet enclosed in the same womb, not yet come forth into the light. In them all things are equal, yet God's judgment of each is different. For he receives one and rejects the other.[25]

It is remarkable to observe that Calvin emphasized the characteristics of election by grace alone along with salvation by grace alone (*sola gratia*) over against human merit or obedience. Again, Calvin found and adopted its representative biblical paradigm from "Jacob's spiritual election" in the context of Esau's reprobation in Romans 9:15–16:

> Jacob, therefore, is chosen and distinguished from the rejected Esau by God's predestination, while not differing from him in merits. If you ask the reason, the apostle gives this: 'For he says to Moses, 'I will have mercy on whom I have mercy, and I will have compassion on whom I have compassion'" [Rom. 9:15]. And what does this mean I ask? It is simply the Lord's clear declaration that he finds in men themselves no reason to bless them but takes it from his mercy alone [Rom. 9:16]; therefore the salvation of his own is his own work. Inasmuch as God establishes your salvation in himself alone, why do you descend to yourself? Since he appoints for you his mercy alone, why do you have recourse to your own merits? Seeing that he confines your thought within his mercy alone, why do you turn your attention in part to your own works?[26]

In relation to the divine election, there was on going debate between Calvin and others whether "the universality of God's invitation and the particularity of election" are biblically warranted. For those who objected "the particularity of election" in relation to "the universality of God's invitation," Calvin employed the distinction between the universality of God's call and "special grace":

> Some object that God would be contrary to himself if he should universally invite all men to him but admit only a few as elect.

25. Ibid., 3.22.5.
26. Ibid., 3.22.6.

Thus, in their view, the universality of the promises removes the distinction of special grace; and some moderate men speak thus, not so much to stifle the truth as to bar thorny questions, and to bridle the curiosity of many. A laudable intention, this, but the design is not to be approved, for evasion is never excusable. But those who insolently revile election offer a quibble too disgusting, or an error too shameful.

I have elsewhere explained how Scripture reconciles the two notions that all are called to repentance and faith by outward preaching, yet that the spirit of repentance and faith is not given to all. Soon I shall have to repeat some of this.[27]

In Calvin's doctrine of election and soteriology, the distinction between special grace and general grace plays out a very important background to penetrate a concrete balance between the universal offer of the Gospel and its effectual call to the elect. Thus, Calvin carefully elaborated that "God's special grace" is only applicable for those who are elect. However, "the general grace of God" (*generalem Dei gratiam*) is applicable to all for both elects and reprobates. In that sense, Calvin's divide of election and reprobation is closely related to the distinction between God's "general grace" and "God's special grace" (*specialis Dei gratia*). According to Calvin, the cultivation and promotion of culture, science, art, and politics in the world history are possible as the result of "God's general grace" to all without any discrimination. So, Calvin's concept of "general grace" in light of the distinction of general grace and special grace not only provided a concrete hermeneutical provision for a legitimate divide of election and reprobation but also a comprehensive biblical worldview:

We see among all mankind that reason is proper to our nature; it distinguishes us from brute beasts, just as they by possessing feeling differ from inanimate things. Now, because some are born fools or stupid, that defect does not obscure the general grace of God. Rather, we are warned by that spectacle that we ought to ascribe what is left is us to God's kindness. For if he had not spared us, our fall would have entailed the destruction of our whole nature. Some men excel in keenness; others are superior in judgment; still others have a readier wit to learn this or that art. In this variety God commends his grace to us, lest anyone should claim as his own what flowed from the sheer bounty of God. For why is one person more excellent than another? Is it not to display in common nature God's

27. Ibid., 3.22.10.

special grace, which, in passing many by, declares itself bound to none? Besides this, God inspires special activities, in accordance with each man's calling.[28]

Meanwhile, Calvin focused on the redemptive history of Israel to show and to demonstrate the representative biblical paradigm about "the particularity of election":

> Through Isaiah he still more openly shows how he directs the promises of salvation specifically to the elect: for he proclaims that they alone, not the whole human race without distinction, are to become his disciples [Isa. 8:16]. Hence it is clear that the doctrine of salvation, which is said to be reserved solely and individually for the sons of the church, is falsely debased when presented as effectually profitable to all.
>   Let this suffice for the present: although the voice of the gospel addresses all in general, yet the gift of faith is rare. Isaiah sets forth the cause: that 'the arm of the Lord has' not 'been revealed' to all [Isa. 53:1].[29]

Following Paul's teaching on the doctrine of election, Calvin stated that election is "the mother of faith" (*fidei mater*). Calvin's point is that faith in Christ is not for every one "because election is special" (*quia specialis est electio*), which in nature logically excludes reprobates:

> Besides, if election, as Paul testifies, is the mother of faith, I turn back upon their head the argument that faith is not general because election is special. For from this series of causes and effects we may readily draw this inference: when Paul states that 'we have been supplied with every spiritual blessing ... even as he chose us from the foundation of the world' [Eph. 1:3–4 p.], these riches are therefore not why Paul in another place commends faith to the elect [Titus 1:1]: that no one may think that he acquires faith by his own effort but that this glory rests with God, freely to illumine whom he previously had chosen.[30]

Once again, Calvin highlighted that God's rejection towards reprobates does not take place "on the basis of works" but solely according to

---

28. Ibid., 2.2.17. For Calvin's comprehensive discussion on "God's general grace" and its implication in the fallen world in the areas of art, philosophy, science, and others, see Ibid., 2.2.12–16.

29. Ibid., 3.22.10.

30. Ibid.

his sovereign will. Calvin again went back to the example of Esau and Jacob for the representative biblical paradigm for double predestination, namely election and reprobation. Here, Calvin found a key principle of the double predestination arguing that "the foundation of divine predestination is not in works" (*divinae praedestinationis fundamentum in operibus non esse*). It is so peculiar to understand that in Calvin's understanding of double predestination there is no place of foreknowledge of merit or good works. Simply, we as mere creatures cannot argue against God as an unjust God because predestination is based upon his sovereign will for His own glory, not considering any foreknowledge of merit or good works:

> For as Jacob, deserving nothing by good works, is taken into grace, so Esau, as yet undefiled by any crime, is hated [Rom. 9:13]. If we turn our eyes to works, we wrong the apostle, as if he did not see it, since he specifically emphasizes the point that when as yet they had done nothing good or evil, one was chosen, the other rejected. This is to prove that the foundation of divine predestination is not in works. Then when he raised the objection, whether God is unjust, he does not make use of what would have been the surest and clearest defense of his righteousness: that God recompensed Esau according to his own evil intention. Instead, he contents himself with a different solution, that the reprobate are raised up to the end that through them God's glory may be revealed. Finally, he adds the conclusion that 'God has mercy upon whomever he wills, and he hardens whomever he wills' [Rom. 9:18].[31]

Thus, Calvin persuasively argued that "the foundation of divine predestination" (*divinae praedestinationis fundamentum*) is not based upon works but his own sovereign grace. In addition, God's reprobation in the case of Esau may reveal his own glory in the end.

Meanwhile, some accepted only election, rejecting reprobation. Against the background of the rejection of reprobation, Calvin reasoned that reprobation is the concomitant of election, and it is an act of God's sovereign will. Calvin followed biblical logic that election can only stand as the counter of reprobation. Therefore, Calvin insisted that if there is no reprobation, then there is no election as well:

> Indeed many, as if they wished to avert a reproach from God, accept election in such terms as to deny that anyone is condemned. But they do this very ignorantly and childishly, since election itself

31. Ibid., 3.22.11.

could not stand except as set over against reprobation. God is said to set apart those whom he adopts into salvation; it will be highly absurd to say that others acquire by chance or obtain by their own effort what election alone confers on a few. Therefore, those whom God passes over, he condemns; and this he does for no other reason than that he wills to exclude them from the inheritance which he predestines for his own children.[32]

As such, some rejected the doctrine of reprobation, only affirming the doctrine of election. According to Calvin, they wrongly perceived that the biblical revelation of "the universal promises of salvation" (*universals salutis promissiones*) is logically inconsistent to the concept of "the predestination of the reprobate" (*reproborum praedestinatione*). But Calvin countered that double predestination and the announcement of salvation "to all men indiscriminately" are perfectly harmonious to one another:

> But, you will say, if this is so, there will be little faith in the gospel promises, which, in testifying to the will of God, assert that he wills what is contrary to his inviolable decree. Not at all. For however universal the promises of salvation may be, they are still in no respect inconsistent with the predestination of the reprobate, provided we pay attention to their effect. When we receive the promises in faith, we know that then and only then do they become effective in us. On the contrary, when faith is snuffed out, the promise is abolished at the same time. If this is their nature, let us see whether they disagree with one another. God is said to have ordained from eternity those whom he wills to embrace in love, and those upon whom he wills to vent his wrath. Yet he announces salvation to all men indiscriminately. I maintain that these statements agree perfectly with each other. For by so promising he merely means that his mercy is extended to all, provided they seek after it and implore it. But only those whom he has illumined do this. And he illumines those whom he has predestined to salvation. These latter possess the sure and unbroken truths of the promises, so that one cannot speak of any disagreement between God's eternal election and the testimony of his grace that he offers to believers.[33]

When Calvin viewed the doctrine of double predestination, he endeavored to understand it in light of the concrete balance between the two horizons of the hidden and revealed will of God. This is one of the

32. Ibid., 3.23.1.
33. Ibid., 3.24.17.

reasons why Calvin emphasized believers' holiness in relation to the mysterious biblical doctrine of double predestination. Representatively, the Renaissance humanistic philosopher and theologian Erasmus (1466–1536), and J. Faber objected to the doctrine of election, insisting that it hinders and destroys every effort for believers' holy life:

> To overthrow predestination our opponents also raise the point that, if it stands, all carefulness and zeal for well-doing go to ruin. For who can hear, they say, that either life or death has been appointed for him by God's eternal and unchangeable decree without thinking immediately that it makes no difference how he conducts himself, since God's predestination can neither be hindered nor advanced by his effort?[34]

Answering critics, Calvin went back to the biblical passage, especially Ephesians 1:4. Following Paul's theological logic in relation to the doctrine of election, Calvin insisted that "holiness of life" (*vitae sanctimonia*) is the goal of the divine free election. In addition, Calvin argued that believers must pursue continual goodness and holiness "as the appointed goal of election" (*et electioni propositum esse finem*). In such a concretely balanced manner, Calvin answered to the critics who argued that the doctrine of double predestination may promote immorality and lawlessness. So, Calvin advised his readers to treat the doctrine of double predestination with "so much more reverence and piety" (*quanto maiori et reverential et religione*) because it is a "great mystery" (*de tanto mysterio*), which unfolds "God's unattainable secrets" (*inaccessa Dei secreta*):

> But Scripture, while it requires us to consider this great mystery with so much more reverence and piety, both instructs the godly to a far different attitude and effectively refutes the criminal madness of these men. For Scripture does not speak of predestination with intent to rouse us to boldness that we may try with impious rashness to search out God's unattainable secrets. Rather, its intent is that, humbled and cast down, we may learn to tremble at his judgment and esteem his mercy. It is at this mark that believers aim . . . Yet Paul teaches that we have been chosen to this end: that we may lead a holy and blameless life [Eph. 1:4]. If election has its goal holiness of life, it ought rather to arouse and goad us eagerly to set our mind upon it than to serve as a pretext for doing nothing. What a great difference there is between these two things: to

---

34. Ibid., 3.23.12.

cease well-doing because election is sufficient for salvation, and to devote ourselves to the pursuit of good as the appointed goal of election! Away, then, with such sacrileges, for they wickedly invert the whole order of election.[35]

Now, let us turn to the discussion of the relationship between election and effectual call, which is a turning point from the divine election to soteriology in Calvin's theology.

RELATIONSHIP BETWEEN ELECTION AND EFFECTUAL CALL

Calvin considered effectual calling as "a testimony of election" (*electionis testimonium*) and believers' justification by faith as "another sign" of the manifestation of election. In that respect, according to Calvin, "the Lord seals his elect by call and justification" (*vocatione et iustificatione electos suos Dominus signat*). However, God withholds all the genuine spiritual blessings to the reprobate, including "knowledge of his name" (*notitia sui nominis*) or "the sanctification of his Spirit" (*Spiritus sui sanctificatione*):

> Now among the elect we regard the call as a testimony of election. Then we hold justification another sign of its manifestation, until they come into the glory in which the fulfillment of that election lies. But as the Lord seals his elect by call and justification, so, by shutting off the reprobate from knowledge of his name or from the sanctification of his Spirit, he, as it were, reveals by these remarks what sort of judgment awaits them.[36]

Pondering upon the above quotation, we may ask a question of why Calvin identified effectual calling and justification as the seals of election. In soteriological blessings, Calvin identified effectual calling and justification as the monergistic works of God, eliminating any human cooperation or works as divine election eliminates the foreknowledge of good works or merits in its own realm. Then, it is not hard to project that in Calvin's mind "the free election of believers" and justification by faith alone (*sola fide*) are closely tied together. In other words, "the free election of believers" and *sola fide* in Calvin stand or fall together.[37]

35. Ibid.

36. Ibid., 3.21.7.

37. Calvin's doctrine of double predestination is closely related to his doctrine of justification by faith alone (*sola fide*). Here, my interpretation is harmoniously supported

Barach, as a promoter of the Federal Vision, appears to affirm Calvin's distinction between general and special election. However, he essentially denies it. Barach wrongly argues that some, who are covenantally united with Christ, may fall away from grace because God chose that they may not persevere. Again, he appeals his analysis based upon John 15:1–8 and Hebrews 6:4–6. Reflecting Calvin's distinction between general and special election, Barach argues that people who fall away may be identified as "'generally elect' but not 'specially elect.'" However, we have to understand that Calvin never used the concept of general election to justify that some people may fall away actually and finally from the saving grace of God. This is another good example of the Federal Visionists have the form of Calvin's theology but they deny it, misreading and misrepresenting Calvin's theology as a whole:

> But in God's wisdom, He has decreed that some of those whom He has chosen to bring into a covenant relationship with Him will enjoy that relationship only for a time. God brings those people into His covenant and unites them to Christ for a time (John 15; Hebrews 6). They really experience His love, but they do not respond with repentance and faith and love.
>
> God chooses not to work in these people so that they persevere. When they fall into sin, in His unsearchable wisdom, He allows them to harden themselves and He hardens them Himself. They have a privileged status, but they fall from privilege. They harden their hearts. They grieve the Spirit (Ephesians 4:30) and quench Him (1 Thessalonians 5:19). And there comes a point when the Spirit will no longer strive with them and they apostatize.
>
> Using our traditional language, we would say that these were non-elect members of the covenant. Using Calvin's terminology, these people were "generally elect" but not "specially elect." They

by Clark and Wiley: "'Scripture shows clearly' that election to life is not conditioned by human dignity (*nullo humane dignitatis respectu*), but rather by God's 'eternal and immutable counsel.' His election to salvation is grounded in 'his gracious mercy' (*in gratuita eius misericordia*), and his reprobation is a 'holy, irreproachable but incomprehensible judgment.' For those who are elect, prior to glorification there are two testimonies of election. The first is efficacious, inward *vocation*. The second is *iustificatio*. 'By vocation and justification the Lord seals the elect' and excludes the reprobate 'from the knowledge of his name and from his Spirit of sanctification.' These comments, as Calvin summarizes his doctrine of election and reprobation, validate Wiley's conclusion that, through his doctrine of justification, Calvin 'defended the theological validity of the Reformation's doctrine of gratuitous justification apart from meritorious works.'" Clark, "Election and Predestination," 111–12.

were among God's chosen people, joined covenantally to Christ, the elect cornerstone, but they have stumbled and fallen, as Peter says, just as they were appointed to do (1 Peter 2:8), and they have been cut off from Christ.[38]

As such, the Federal Visionists apply Calvin's concept of "general election" as if Calvin taught that there are some who fall away from God's saving grace through apostasy, and in the end, God may cut them off from covenantal union with Christ.

Calvin, interpreting Romans 8:29–30, which is the classic Pauline passage about 'the order of salvation' (the *ordo salutis*) emphasized that the beginning of the true realization of the divine election to the elect is the effectual calling through the powerful works of the Holy Spirit by the means of the preaching of the Word. Furthermore, Calvin noted that effectual calling is the manifestation of election by God:

> But to make the matter clearer, we must deal with both the calling of the elect and the blinding and hardening of the wicked.
>
> Of the former I have already said something, when refuting the error of those who think that the universality of the promises makes all mankind equal. Yet it is not without choice that God by his call manifests the election, which he otherwise holds hidden within himself; accordingly, it may properly be termed his 'attestation.' 'For those whom he foreknew, he also appointed beforehand to be conformed to the image of his son.' [Rom. 8:29] 'Those whom he appointed beforehand, he also called; those whom he called, he also justified' [Rom. 8:30] that he might sometime glorify them. Although in choosing his own the Lord already has adopted them as his children, we see that they do not come into possession of so great a good except when they are called; conversely, that when they are called, they already enjoy some share of their election. For this reason, Paul calls the Spirit, whom they receive, both 'Spirit of adoption' [Rom. 8:15] and the 'seal' and 'guarantee of the inheritance to come' [Eph. 1:13–14; cf. 2 Cor. 1:22; 5:5]. For he surely establishes and seals in their hearts by his testimony the assurance of the adoption to come.
>
> Even though the preaching of the gospel streams forth from the wellspring of election, because such preaching is shared also with the wicked, it cannot of itself be a full proof of election. But God effectively teaches his elect that he may lead them to faith.[39]

38. Barach, "Covenant and Election," in *The Auburn Avenue Theology*, 154.

39. Calvin, *Institutes*, 3.24.1.

In Calvin's soteriology, God the Father unites himself with believers "by calling," which is a soteriological means to unite the elect to himself. He receives the elect "into his family and unites them to him so that they may together be one." Calvin beautifully connected election and calling as a decisive turning point from election to salvation for the elect. Calvin reasoned that if election is by "God's free mercy," then effectual calling as the manifestation and implication of election is also by "God's free mercy" (*gratuitam Dei misericordiam*) alone. Again, Calvin pointedly emphasized that election is based upon God's "mercy alone" (*sola misericordia*) which is coterminous with *sola gratia* interpreting Romans 9:16:

> Therefore, God designates as his children those whom he has chosen, and appoints himself their Father. Further, by calling, he receives them into his family and unites them to him so that they may together be one. But when the call is coupled with election, in this way Scripture sufficiently suggests that in it nothing but God's free mercy is to be sought. For if we ask whom he calls, and the reason why, he answers: whom he had chosen. Moreover, when one comes to election, there mercy alone appears on every side. Here Paul's statement truly has significance: 'It depends not upon him who wills, or upon him who runs but upon God, who shows mercy' [Rom. 9:16]. And it is not as those commonly understand it who divide it between God's grace and man's willing and running.[40]

Calvin portrayed that when God calls his elect, he uses not only "the preaching of the Word" (*verbi praedicatione*) but also "the illumination of the Spirit" (*Spiritus illuminatione*) concomitantly. Calvin reasoned that "the preaching of the Word" itself is the manifestation of God's abundant goodness to all, including reprobates. However, God, even withdrawing "the effectual working of his Spirit" (*Spiritus sui efficaciam*) from the reprobates, demonstrates his own glory. Interpreting 1 John 3:24 and 4:13, Calvin stated that "inner call" (*interior vocatio*) as effectual calling to the elect is indeed "a pledge of salvation" (*pignus salutis*). Calvin wrote:

> Besides, even the very nature and dispensation of the call clearly demonstrates this fact, for it consists not only in the preaching of the Word but also in the illumination of the Spirit . . . Here, then, God's boundless goodness is already manifesting itself but not to the salvation of all; for a heavier judgment remains upon the

40. Ibid.

wicked because they reject the testimony of God's love. And God also, to show forth his glory, withdraws the effectual working of his Spirit from them. This inner call, then, is a pledge of salvation that cannot deceive us. To it applies John's statement: "We recognize that we are his children from the Spirit, which he has given us" [I John 3:24; cf. ch. 4:13].[41]

Calvin was very clear that election does not rely on faith. Rather, Calvin viewed that faith is the outworking of election which is one of the aspects of immeasurable richness of soteriological blessings in Christ:

But here we must beware of two errors: for some make man God's co-worker, to ratify election by his consent. Thus, according to them, man's will is superior to God's plan. As if Scripture taught that we are merely given the ability to believe, and not, rather, faith itself! Others, although they do not so weaken the grace of the Holy Spirit yet led by some reason or other, make election depend upon faith, as if it were doubtful and also ineffectual until confirmed by faith. Indeed, that it is confirmed, with respect to us, is utterly plain; we have also already seen that the secret plan of God, which lay hidden, is brought to light, provided you understand by this language merely that what was unknown is now verified-sealed, as it were, with a seal. But it is false to say that election takes effect only after we have embraced the gospel, and takes its validity from this; for if we try to penetrate to God's eternal ordination, that deep abyss will swallow us up.[42]

Calvin's soteriology is deeply anchored with the idea of in Christ alone, which may be summarized with 'union with Christ' (*unio cum Christo*). It is also the case in the doctrine of election. Calvin argued that Christ alone is "the fountain of life, the anchor of salvation, and the heir of the Kingdom of Heaven." Furthermore, Calvin, following the logic of Paul in Ephesians 1:4, argued that God chose his children "not in themselves but in his Christ." In that sense, we should not have "assurance of our election in ourselves," but in Christ alone:

First, if we seek God's fatherly mercy and kindly heart, we should turn our eyes to Christ, on whom alone God's Spirit rests [cf. Matt. 3:17]. If we seek salvation, life, and the immortality of the Heavenly Kingdom, then there is no other to whom we may flee, seeing that he alone is the fountain of life, the anchor of salvation, and the heir

41. Ibid., 3.24.2.
42. Ibid., 3.24.3.

of the Kingdom of Heaven. Now what is the purpose of election but that we, adopted as sons by our Heavenly Father, may obtain salvation and immortality by his favor? ... Accordingly those whom God has adopted as his sons are said to have been chosen not in themselves but in his Christ [Eph. 1:4]; for unless he could love them in him, he could not honor them with the inheritance of his Kingdom if they had not previously become partakers of him. But if we have been chosen in him, we shall not find assurance of our election in ourselves; and not even in God the Father, if we conceive him as severed from his Son. Christ, then, is the mirror wherein we must, and without self-deception may contemplate our own election.[43]

Calvin guides us to have the assurance of election in nothing else but in Christ alone as we have seen. Then, he extended his discussion further about the assurance of election. He put effectual calling as another means to have the assurance of election on our part. Calvin argued that for those who are called by God in Christ will be persevered unto glorious eternal life to the end because Christ takes care of and protects them through the work of the Holy Spirit. Dealing with this complex theological matter, Calvin went into the Scripture where he beautifully connected together election, effectual calling, and perseverance of saints, interpreting John 6:37, 39 and 17:6, 12:

The fact that, as we said, the firmness of our election is joined to our calling is another means of establishing our assurance. For those whom Christ has illumined with the knowledge of his name and has introduced into the bosom of his church, he is said to receive into his care and keeping. All whom he receives, the Father is said to have entrusted and committed to him to keep unto eternal life. What would we have? Christ proclaims aloud that he has taken under his protection all whom the Father wishes to be saved [cf. John 6:37, 39; 17:6, 12]. Therefore, if we desire to know whether God cares for our salvation, let us inquire whether he has entrusted us to Christ, whom he has established as the sole Savior of all his people.[44]

Calvin argued that God provides all the necessary spiritual means for those who are the elect in Christ, who may be persevered unto the end. So, in Calvin's theology, perseverance, as one aspect of believer's salvation,

43. Ibid., 3.24.5
44. Ibid., 3.24.6.

is God's gracious gift as salvation itself. In that manner, Calvin used the word "the gift of perseverance" (*dono perseverantiae*), which highlights the sovereign grace work of God in the process of perseverance of believers. In doing so, Calvin paid attention to the biblical testimony to expound the concrete validity of the doctrine of perseverance. He explored extensively Jesus' testimony about the doctrine of perseverance, harmoniously written in the Johannine Gospel and the Gospel of Matthew. And it is perfectly harmonious with Paul's teaching in his epistles such as Romans and Philippians:

> But anxiety about our future state steals in; for as Paul teaches that they are called who were previously chosen [Rom. 8:30], so Christ shows that "many are called but few are chosen" [Matt. 22:14]. Indeed, Paul himself also dissuades us from overassurance: "Let him," he says, "who stands well, take heed lest he fall" [1 Cor. 10:12]. Again: You are grafted into the people of God? "Be not proud but fear" [Rom. 11:20]. For God can cut you off again that he may engraft others [cf. Rom. 11:21–23]. Finally, we are taught by this very experience that call and faith are of little account unless perseverance be added; and this does not happen to all. But Christ has freed us from this anxiety, for these promises surely apply to the future: "All that the Father gives me will come to me; and him who will come to me I will not cast out" [John 6:37]. Likewise: "This is the will of him who sent me, the Father, that I should lose nothing of all that he has given me but should raise it up again at the last day." [John 6:39, cf. Vg.]... Now when he declares, "Every tree that my Father has not planted will be uprooted" [Matt. 15:13], he conversely implies that those rooted in God can never be pulled up from salvation. With this John's statement agrees: "If they had been of us, they would not have gone out from us" [1 John 2:19 p.]. And here is why Paul magnificently lords it over life and death, things present and to come [Rom. 8:38]; and this boasting must be grounded upon the gift of perseverance. There is no doubt that he applies this idea to all the elect. Elsewhere, Paul says the same thing: "He who has begun a good work in you will bring it to completion at the day of Jesus Christ" [Phil. 1:6].[45]

Calvin logically analyzed the relationship between election and soteriological blessings where the elect receives through the sovereign work of the Holy Spirit. In doing so, Calvin argued that only the elect may have "true faith" (*vera fide*) in Christ, which may be applicable to all the elect. However,

45. Ibid.

there are some apparent believers, who appear to be falling away from Christ again. For example, Calvin pointed out "the son of perdition" (*filium perditionis*), representatively in John 17:12. Calvin went on to argue that apparent believers indeed "never cleaved to Christ with the heart felt trust in which certainty of election" has been manifested. If we analyze Calvin's argument from the perspective of the union with Christ, then God unites only the elect with Christ through effectual calling, and the elect with the blessings of the union with Christ cannot fall away from it. Indeed, Calvin appealed to Jesus' self claim in John 3:16 and 6:39 that he will not perish any one, who has "true faith" (*vera fide*) in him that the Father has given to him. Here, Calvin convincingly argued that those who are not elected by God may manifest temporarily "the signs of a call" which are similar to the signs of the elect. But, the elect only will ultimately persevere to the end because Christ is "their guardian and shepherd":

> Yet it daily happens that those who seemed to be Christ's, fall away from him again, and hasten to destruction. Indeed in that same passage, where he declares that none of those whom the Father had given to him perished, he nevertheless except the son of perdition [John 17:12]. True indeed, but it is equally plain that such persons never cleaved to Christ with the heart felt trust in which certainty of election has, I say, been established for us. "They went out from us," says John, "but they were not of us. For if they had been of us, they would no doubt have continued with us." [1 John 2:19] And I do not deny that they have signs of a call that are similar to those of the elect, but I by no means concede to them that sure establishment of election which I bid believers seek from the word of the gospel. So then, let not such instances induce us at all to abandon a quiet reliance upon the Lord's promise, where he declares that all by whom he is received in true faith have been given to him by the Father, no one of whom, since he is their guardian and shepherd, will perish [cf. John 3:16; 6:39].[46]

Calvin developed and adopted the distinction between general and special calling in his discussion of God's calling, ordinarily in the context of the preaching of the word. Calvin explained that general calling (*universalis vocatio*) is universal call without exception, including reprobates "through the outward preaching of the word." On the other hand, special calling (*specialis vocatio*) is God's special call, which may be applied to the elect

46. Ibid., 3.24.7

alone "by the inward illumination of his Spirit." Calvin explained the biblical concept of the distinction between general and special calling, appealing to Jesus' parable about the wedding banquet in Matthew 22:1–14:

> The statement of Christ "Many are called but few are chosen" [Matt. 22:14] is, in this manner, very badly understood. Nothing will be ambiguous if we hold fast to what ought to be clear from the foregoing: that there are two kinds of call. There is the general call, by which God invites all equally to himself through the outward preaching of the word-even those to whom he holds it out as a savor of death [cf. 2 Cor. 2:16], and as the occasion for severer condemnation. The other kind of call is special, which he deigns for the most part to give to the believers alone, while by the inward illumination of his Spirit he causes the preached Word to dwell in their hearts. Yet sometimes he also causes those whom he illumines only for a time to partake of it; then he justly forsakes them on account of their ungratefulness and strikes them with even greater blindness.[47]

Interestingly, Calvin argued that the phrase in Jesus' parable about the wedding banquet in Matthew 22:11–13 illustrates that there are some in the church among who profess faith although they do not have authentic or saving faith in Jesus Christ where the elect may have it as the gift of God. According to Calvin, they are the people in the church, who are not the elect although they may "enter the church on profession of faith" (*fidei professione in ecclesiam ingrediuntur*). However, Calvin argued that they with their "profession of faith," are "not clothed with Christ's sanctification" (*sed Christi sanctificatione nequaquam induti*). And only the elect may receive the spiritual blessing of special call "with the Spirit of regeneration," who is "the guarantee and seal of the inheritance to come." So, in the end, believers may participate in the eschatological heavenly banquet at the last day:

> Hence, since they refuse, he is compelled to call in off the crossroads all met there [Matt. 22:2–9]. Up to this point everyone sees that the parable is to be understood of the outward call. He afterward adds that God acts like a good host, who circulates from table to table, affably greeting his guests. But if he finds one not dressed in a wedding garment, he will not allow him, unfitly dressed, to dishonor the festivity of the banquet with his unclean attire [Matt. 22:11–13]. This phrase ought, I admit, to be understood as ap-

47. Ibid., 3.24.8.

plying to those who enter the church on profession of faith but not clothed with Christ's sanctification. God will not forever bear such dishonors, even cancers, of his church but as their baseness deserves, will cast them out. Few, therefore, were chosen from the great number of those called [cf. Matt. 20:16]; however, we do not say that this is the call by which believers ought to reckon their election. For this call is common also to the wicked, but the other bears with the Spirit of regeneration [cf. Titus 3:5], the guarantee and seal of the inheritance to come [Eph. 1:13–14], with which our hearts are sealed [2 Cor. 1:22] unto the day of the Lord.[48]

As such, it is important to understand that we need to read Calvin's distinction between general and special call as one of the windows for the proper biblical understanding of double predestination. In Calvin, the biblical doctrine of double predestination is organically related to the distinction between general and special call.

Some people held that there is "seed of election" (*semen electionis*) during the Protestant Reformation. They viewed that the elect, even before regeneration and conversion, may demonstrate "the seed of piety" (*pietatis seminaria*). Calvin countered the unbiblical idea about "the seed of election" and "the seed of piety." In doing so, Calvin explained that all human beings as "Adam's offspring" are totally corrupt so that they are spiritually dead although some of them may manifest outward moral goodness or holiness before regeneration. Calvin argued that God in his sovereign time gathers his elect through his effectual calling. Once again, Calvin emphasized not natural birth but effectual calling as the temporal moment of bestowing God's sovereign saving grace to the elect. Examining the Pauline passages such as Ephesians 2:1–3; 2:12, and 5:8–9, Calvin persuasively concluded that there is no endowment of "the spirit of piety" (*pietatis spiritu*) before effectual calling even for the elect:

> The elect are gathered into Christ's flock by a call not immediately at birth, and not all at the same time, but according as it pleases God to dispense his grace to them. But before they are gathered unto that Supreme Shepherd, they wander scattered in the wilderness common to all; and they do not differ at all from others except that they are protected by God's special mercy from rushing headlong into the final ruin of death. If you look upon them, you will see Adam's offspring, who savor of the common corruption of the mass. The fact that they are not carried to utter and even

48. Ibid.

desperate impiety is not due to any innate goodness of theirs but because the eye of God watches over their safety and his hand is outstretched to them!

For those who imagine that some sort of seed of election was sown in them from birth itself, and that by its power they have always been inclined to piety and the fear of God, are not supported by Scriptural authority and are refuted by experience itself.[49]

Meanwhile, in word, the Federal Visionists insist that they adopt the biblical doctrine of double predestination, namely election and reprobation. However, their covenantal approach or paradigm to the doctrine of election becomes a hermeneutical and theological barrier to maintain the biblical doctrine of double predestination, which was brilliantly adopted and developed by Calvin after the pattern of Augustine. The decisive breach between Calvin and the Federal Vision takes place partly on the denial of the distinction between law and gospel and partly on the denial of the distinction between general and effectual calling through the proclamation of the Word. Calvin used the distinction between general and effectual calling as a hermeneutical guide to differentiate the elect and the reprobate from the perspective of God's eyes. For Calvin, the distinction between general and effectual calling is a divinely ordained biblical means to differentiate between the elect and the reprobates, even within the church or the covenant community. Then, from the perspective of Calvin's theology, without maintaining the distinction between general and effectual calling, the doctrine of double predestination is an impossible doctrine to maintain.

No implication of the distinction between general and effectual calling is the major reason why the Federal Visionists' description of the doctrine of election manifests a strong tension and confusion between election and reprobation. In Calvin's theology, it is very obvious that God bestows his saving grace through effectual calling, and uniting with Christ for those who are the elect in the specific moment of history. Calvin made a beautiful harmony and balance, relating election to salvation through the means of effectual calling. In other words, Calvin always located the *proper place* for the doctrine of election and soteriology to draw out biblical doctrines.

But in the theology of the Federal Vision, the biblical doctrine of election is eclipsed because the proper place of effectual calling, a cru-

49. Ibid., 3.24.10.

cial means for the testimony of the elect from the perspective of God, is definitely lost. They locate and replace with "covenant union with Christ" in the proper place of effectual calling. In such a manner, Steve Wilkins argues that salvation is "found only in covenant union with Christ." In addition, he insists that the biblical term "the elect" usually indicates "those in covenant union with Christ who is *the* elect one." In doing so, a biblical distinction between election and reprobation is eclipsed. Wilkins writes:

> Salvation is relational. It is found only in covenant union with Christ. As we abide in Him, all that is true of Him is true of us. As we abide in Him, all that is true of Him is true of us. It has been the common practice in Reformed circles to use the term "elect" to refer only to those who are predestined to eternal salvation. Since God has ordained all things "whatsoever comes to pass" (Eph. 1:11), He has certainly predestined the number of all who will be saved at the last day. This number is fixed and settled, not one of these will be lost. The Lord will accomplish all His holy will. But the term "elect" (or "chosen") as it is used in the Scriptures most often refers to those in covenant union with Christ who is *the* Elect One.[50]

As we explored, Romans 8:28–34 is a classical passage that Calvin used to demonstrate that God may bestow saving grace by the means of effectual calling to the elect, making a transition from election to salvation. However, mentioning the passage, Wilkins directs his argument that the elect may have "the possibility of apostasy" where they may be broken off from "covenant union with Christ":

> Think of the promise Paul relates to the members of the church at Rome (Rom. 8:28–34). Throughout this passage, Paul refers to the "elect," those whom God "foreknew" and "predestined," and then asks these questions: "What shall *we* say to these things? If God is for *us*, who can be against *us*? Christ died, rose again and makes intercession for *us*, who can separate *us* from the love of God?" Clearly, Paul is not stating promises that are true only for some unknown group called the "elect." Nor is he speaking only to a portion of the congregation whom he judges to be "regenerate." Rather, he is applying these promises to all the members of the Church who have been baptized and united to Christ in His death, burial, and resurrection (Rom. 6). Yet, in spite of these clear af-

---

50. Wilkins, "Covenant, Baptism and Salvation," 56.

firmations of their elect status, Paul does not hesitate to warn them against the possibility of apostasy (Rom. 11:9–22).[51]

As we have carefully examined, Calvin correctly viewed that Romans 8:28–34 is a classic Pauline passage relating the doctrine of election to soteriology. He expounded that God sovereignly bestows his saving grace for the elect only through effectual calling and uniting them with Christ. In that sense, believers may enjoy the blessings of justification, sanctification and glorification, ultimately persevering to the end. But, Wilkins does not operate according to this kind of concrete hermeneutical and theological vision. Rather, he wrongly argues that the promises of Romans 8:28–34 are the promises to "all the members of the Church who have been baptized and united to Christ in His death, burial, and resurrection (Rom. 6)." Then, it is important to notice that the Federal Vision falsely identifies the elect with "all the members of the Church," who received water baptism because they do not maintain the distinction between general calling and effectual calling, which is a necessary means to maintain the biblical doctrine of double predestination.

ELECTION AND APOSTASY: A TEST CASE
FROM JOHN 15:1–8 AND HEBREWS 6:4–8

The Federal Visionists insist that believers with covenant union with Christ may actually lose their saving grace, appealing to several biblical passages, representatively John 15:1–8 and Hebrews 6:4–8.[52] For example, Wilkins argues that believers through their apostasy may lose "the blessings of covenant, including the forgiveness of sins, adoption, possession of the kingdom, sanctification." Wilkins writes:

> This is not a hypothetical impossibility but a very real possibility
> for those who are in covenant with Christ and members of His
> Church. We must not view these and similar warnings as mere
> devices which are placed in the Scriptures in order to frighten the
> elect into heaven. The clear implication of these passages is that
> those who ultimately prove to be reprobate may be in covenant

51. Ibid., 57.

52. For critical exploration on the Federal Visionists' understanding of covenant and apostasy, see Orthodox Presbyterian Church, *Justification*, 151–53; Waters, *The Federal Vision and Covenant Theology*, 125–67; R. Fowler White, "Covenant and Apostasy," in *The Auburn Avenue Theology, Pros and Cons: Debating the Federal Vision*, ed. E Calvin Beisner (Fort Lauderdale: Knox Theological Seminary, 2004), 206–23.

with God. They may enjoy for a season the blessings of the covenant, including the forgiveness of sins, adoption, possession of the kingdom, sanctification, etc., and yet apostatize and fall short of the grace of God.[53]

Meanwhile, dealing with the problem of apostasy, Calvin had a consciousness of the distinction between election and reprobation along with general and effectual calling when he interpreted the biblical passages whether it is possible for those who received the saving grace to lose it through apostasy. However, in the theological minds of the Federal Vision, a distinction between election and reprobation along with the distinction between general and effectual calling is eclipsed as we already explored extensively. In light of that, the classical biblical doctrines of election, effectual calling and the perseverance of the saints that as faithfully expounded in Calvin and the Westminster Standards are destroyed in the theology of the Federal Vision.

John 15:1–8

Calvin, in his interpretation of Jesus' Parable about the Vineyard, did have a deep consciousness of the distinction between "universal grace" and "special grace," along with distinction between the elect and the reprobates. In the milieu of these important distinctions, Calvin began to exposit Jesus' famous parable. Calvin argued that "universal grace" does not have any power to bestow spiritual power and strength. In that sense, all spiritual life, strength, and goodness proceed from Christ alone. Under the universal grace, however, "the nature of man" cannot produce any spiritual goodness and fruits because no one has "the nature of a *vine*" until one is implanted in Jesus Christ by the Father. Calvin emphasized that "the nature of a *vine*" with the implantation in Christ is given by God the Father "to the elect alone by special grace." In other words, the blessings of the spiritual union with Christ may be applied only to the elect. In such a careful manner, Calvin wrote:

> There is scarcely any one who is ashamed to acknowledge that every thing good which he possesses comes from God; but, after making this acknowledgment, they imagine that a universal grace has been given to them, as if it had been implanted in them by nature. But Christ dwells principally on this, that the vital sap—that

---

53. Wilkins, "Covenant, Baptism and Salvation," 62.

is, all life strength—proceeds from himself alone. Hence it follows, that the nature of man is unfruitful and destitute of everything good; because no man has the nature of a *vine*, till he be implanted in him. But this is given to the elect alone by special grace. So then, the Father is the first Author of all blessings, who plants us with his hand; but the commencement of life is in Christ, since we begin to take root in him. When he calls himself *the* TRUE *vine*, the meaning is, *I am* TRULY *the vine*, and therefore men toil to no purpose in seeking strength anywhere else, for from none will useful fruit proceed but from *the branches* which shall be produced by me.[54]

Interpreting John 15:2, Calvin carefully argued that there are some apparent believers in the church who have only "outward profession" without any inward spiritual blessings from God. But those apparent believers from the perspective of men do not have "root in the vine," who is Jesus Christ. Calvin went on to argue that those apparent believers as the branches in the vine which will ultimately be "unfruitful will be cut off from *the vine*." What Calvin emphatically argued is that every branch, "ingrafted into Christ" will bear good fruits under the guidance of the Holy Spirit in the process of progressive sanctification:

2. *Every branch in me that beareth not fruit.* As some men corrupt the grace of God, others suppress it maliciously, and others choke it by carelessness, Christ intends by these words to awaken anxious inquiry, by declaring that all *the branches* which shall be unfruitful will be cut off from *the vine*. But here comes a question, Can any one who is ingrafted into Christ be without fruit? I answer, many are supposed to be *in the vine*. Thus, in the writings of the prophets, the Lord calls the people of Israel *his vine*, because, by outward profession, they had the name of the Church.

And every branch that beareth fruit he pruneth. By these words, he shows that believers need incessant culture, that they may be prevented from degenerating; and that they produce nothing good, unless God continually apply his hand; for it will not be enough to have been once made partakers of adoption, if God do not continue the work of his grace in us ... When he says that vines are *pruned, that they may yield more abundant fruit*, he shows what ought to be the progress of believers in the course of true religion.[55]

54. Calvin, *Gospel According to John*, 15:1.
55. Ibid., 15:2.

Calvin had a consciousness about the *necessity* of believers' bearing good fruits in relation to vital or spiritual union with Christ in his interpretation on John 15:4. According to Calvin, the Holy Spirit may dwell in all the genuine believers, helping them to persevere eventually to the end because the Holy Spirit as the Spirit of Jesus will always be "efficacious" in believers. Likewise, in the process, all the genuine believers, having "a living root" in Jesus will be "fruit-bearing *branches*" without exception:

> In order to prove that he did not begin the work of our salvation for the purpose of leaving it imperfect in the middle of the course, he promises that his Spirit will always be efficacious in us, if we do not prevent him. *Abide in me,* says he; *for I am ready to abide in you.* And again, *He who abideth in me beareth much fruit.* By these words he declares that all who have a living root in him are fruit-bearing *branches*.[56]

Calvin, in his interpretation of John 15:6, insisted that the perseverance of believers is indeed "the gift of God." However, not the members of the elect but hypocrites in the church, who are apparent believers "in outward appearance," "to wither like a dead branch," will eventually be "cut off from Christ":

> 6. *If any one abide not in me.* He again lays before them the punishment of ingratitude, and, by doing so, excites and urges them to perseverance. It is indeed the gift of God, but the exhortation to fear is not uncalled for, lest our flesh, through too great indulgence, should root us out.
>
> *He is cast out, and withered, like a branch.* Those who are cut off from Christ are said to *wither* like a dead branch; because, as the commencement of strength is from him, so also is its uninterrupted continuance. Not that it ever happens that any one of the elect is *dried up,* but because there are many hypocrites who, in outward appearance, flourish and are green for a time, but who afterwards, when they ought to yield fruit, show the very opposite of that which the Lord expects and demands from his people.[57]

Meanwhile, the Federal Visionists consider John 15:1–8 as one of the definitive proof texts for the affirmation that apostasy may break "a vital union" between Christ and believers. Wilson writes as follows:

56. Ibid., 15:4.
57. Ibid., 15:6.

This seems to be the point of John 15:1–8. Jesus here declares that He is the vine and His hearers are branches united to Him. He then exhorts them to continue abiding in Him so that they might bear fruit. If they refuse to abide in Him, they will be fruitless and incur the wrath of the Divine husband man and, finally, will be cast into the fire. Here, then, we have those who are joined to Christ in a vital union (i.e., a union that could and should be fruitful) and yet who end up cursed and condemned.[58]

However, in Calvin's theology, only the elect receive the blessings of effectual calling and mystical or real union with Christ, which may be identified also as a vital and spiritual union with Christ. So, the reprobate in the church or covenant community may receive only the external religious blessings in the realm of common grace. In the exposition and analysis of John 15:1–8, Wilson denies external and inward distinction in light of receiving the saving grace, following the exegetical and theological pattern of the foremost hero of the Federal Vision, Norman Shepherd:

Often this passage is interpreted along these lines: There are two kinds of branches. Some branches are not really in Christ "in a saving way," but only in an *external* sense—whatever fruit they bear is not genuine and they will eventually be destroyed. Other branches are truly joined to Christ *inwardly* and savingly, and they bear more and more fruit as they are pruned and cultivated by the Father. As Norman Shepherd has noted,

If this distinction is in the text, it is difficult to see what the point of warning is. The outward ("external") branches cannot profit from it, because they cannot in any case bear genuine fruit. They are not related to Christ inwardly and draw no life from him. The inward branches do not need the warning, because they are vitalized by Christ and therefore cannot help but bear good fruit. Cultivation by the Father, with its attendant blessing, is guaranteed.[59]

Calvin certainly interpreted John 15:1–8 with the consciousness of the distinction between election and reprobation, the distinction between general and effectual calling, and the perseverance of the saints.

58. Wilson, "Covenant, Baptism and Salvation," 62.

59. Ibid., 62–63. For Shepherd's discussion on John 15:1–8 from a typical monocovenantal perspective, denying the distinction between outward and inner spiritual blessings, which is a major component of the doctrine of double predestination, *sola gratia* and *sola fide*, see Shepherd, *The Call of Grace*, 88–91. I have provided a brief critique against Shepherd's interpretation. See Jeon, *Covenant Theology and Justification by Faith*, 102–5.

But, Wilson's adaptation of monocovenantal hermeneutics and theology, exemplified by Norman Shepherd, draws him to deny necessary hermeneutical ingredients to safeguard the distinction between external and internal union, which is also closely related to the distinction between the invisible and visible church:

> The Calvinist embraces this implausible interpretation because he (understandably) does not want to deny election, effectual calling, or the perseverance of the saints. The exegetical problems one must embrace with this position, however, are nearly insurmountable. If the branches are not truly joined to the vine, how can they be held accountable for their lack of fruit? The distinction of "external" and "internal" union seems to be invented and is not in the text. All the branches are truly and vitally joined to the vine. All can and should be fruitful. The pressure to preserve the Scriptural teaching of God's sovereignty in salvation ought not to be allowed to push us to deny these obvious points. But in order to resist this pressure the text must be interpreted as it is intended to be interpreted—i.e., covenantally.[60]

Wilson compares and identifies "the picture of the vine and branches" in John 15:1–8 with God's "covenant people Israel in the Old Testament." In conclusion, he argues that covenant people will be "cut off from covenant with God" and will "lose the blessings of His grace and mercy." Moreover, their curse from God will be greater because they abused "the grace of God," which was "really and truly given to them in Christ." In such a manner, interpreting John 15:1–8 in comparing the Old Testament Israelites, Wilson fails to make a distinction between outward and internal blessings of the Spirit.

Another of Wilson's failures is his inability to grasp the discontinuity between the Old and New Covenants. Certainly, the Old Covenant at the level of *typology* was a breakable covenant. So, when Israelites, as the chosen nation, disobeyed to "the covenant of the law" (*foedus legale*), God punished them based upon the covenant, and they were ultimately expelled from the promised land due to their disobedience and apostasy. In such a manner, Calvin brilliantly affirmed *the presence of the Old Covenant eschatology* through the proper implication of typology as we already explored it. However, Calvin was certain that even under the Old Covenant, the Israelite's individual salvation was safeguarded by the sov-

---

60. Wilson, "Covenant, Baptism and Salvation," 63.

ereign grace of God in light of individual election and not national election. As such, Wilson's concept of *radical continuity* between the Old and New Covenants, without the recognition of the *legitimate discontinuity* leads him to conclude that believers may lose the blessings of true and vital union with Christ through apostasy and disobedience. Wilson writes:

> The picture of the vine and branches was a common way in which God referred to His covenant people Israel in the Old Testament (Ps. 80:8–16; Isa. 5:1–7; Jer. 2:21). The Jews were used to thinking of themselves as the vineyard of Jehovah. "The vine" was a figure of God's chosen people. Here in John 15 Jesus says that "He is the real vine." He identifies Himself with His people. He is their covenant head. He is their life. He is not only their Creator but their Redeemer. They are His body, united to Him by God's gracious inclusion of them in covenant.
>
> Jesus is merely reiterating what the prophets had proclaimed. If they do not abide faithful to God, they are going to bring judgment upon themselves. They will be cut off from covenant with God. They will lose the blessings of His grace and mercy and will be destroyed like the ungodly (only their condemnation will be greater since they despised the grace of God and have done despite to the Spirit of grace—which was really and truly given to them in Christ).[61]

Likewise, in the interpretation of John 15:1–8, Wilson is not aware of the distinction between the elect and the reprobate along with the distinction between general calling and effectual calling as well as universal or common and special grace, which are the divinely ordained means to differentiate the elect and the reprobate in the bestowment of His sovereign saving grace. In that sense, Wilson, along with other Federal Visionists, fails to maintain the distinction between saving grace and common grace, which is vital not only for biblical soteriology, including the doctrine of election but also a comprehensive worldview that Calvin properly envisioned.

Hebrews 6:4–8

In interpreting Hebrews 6:4–8, Calvin had a deep consciousness of the radical distinction between election and reprobation where he rightly conceived that only the elect may receive the genuine saving grace from God through effectual calling. This profound concept of a radical distinc-

---

61. Ibid.

tion between the elect and the reprobate from the perspective of God was a guiding principle to interpret such a difficult passage. Reflecting Romans 8:14, Calvin reasoned that God bestows the saving grace through effectual calling *only* for the elect. And the elect are free from "the danger of finally falling away" from saving grace. And God bestows and blesses "the elect alone with the Spirit of regeneration," distinguishing "from the reprobate." In this careful manner, Calvin wrote:

> But here arises a new question, How can it be that he who has once made such a progress should afterwards fall away? For God, it may be said, call none effectually but the elect, and Paul testifies that they are really his sons who are led by his Spirit, (Rom. Viii. 14;) and he teaches us, that it is a sure pledge of adoption when Christ makes us partakers of his Spirit. The elect are also beyond the danger of finally falling away; for the Father who gave them to be preserved by Christ his Son is greater than all, and Christ promises to watch over them all so that none may perish. To all this I answer, That God indeed favours none but the elect alone with the Spirit of regeneration, and that by this they are distinguished from the reprobate; for they are renewed after his image and receive the earnest of the Spirit in hope of the future inheritance, and by the same Spirit the Gospel is sealed in their hearts.[62]

Laying out a profound presupposition that only the elect may receive genuine saving grace through effectual calling, Calvin discussed that the reprobate may experience "also some taste of his grace," "some sparks of his light," "some perception of his goodness," and "his word on their hearts." Afterward, Calvin reasoned that those spiritual experiences that the reprobate may have, are not genuine saving faith but *the temporary faith* as described in Mark 4:17:

> But I cannot admit that all this is any reason why he should not grant the reprobate also some taste of his grace, why he should not irradiate their minds with some sparks of his light, why he should not give them some perception of his goodness, and in some sort engrave his word on their hearts. Otherwise where would be the temporary faith mentioned by Mark iv. 17? There is therefore some knowledge even in the reprobate, which afterwards vanishes away, either because it did not strike roots sufficiently deep, or because it withers, being choked up.[63]

62. Calvin, *Epistle to the Hebrews*, 6:4.
63. Ibid.

In the interpretation of the pericope of Hebrews 6:3–6, Calvin recognized that the proper understanding of "fall away" of verse 6 is the key terminology to correctly and comprehensively understand this difficult passage. Calvin argued that there is "a twofold falling away, one particular, and the other general." The author of Hebrews meant here "fall away" not general fall, committed as a genuine Christian, but "a total defection or falling away from the Gospel," which is entire renouncement of God's grace. It is important to note that Calvin viewed that any sin committed by a genuine Christian is falling away in a general sense:

> The knot of the question is in the word, *fall away*. Whosoever then understands its meaning, can easily extricate himself from every difficulty. But it must be noticed, that there is a twofold falling away, one particular, and the other general. He who has in anything, or in anyways offended, has fallen away from his state as a Christian; therefore all sins are so many fallings. But the Apostle speaks not here of theft, or perjury, or murder, or drunkenness, or adultery; but he refers to a total defection or falling away from the Gospel, when a sinner offends not God in some one thing, but entirely renounces his grace.[64]

Interpreting Hebrews 6:7–8, Calvin had a consciousness of the distinction between the elect and the reprobate. Calvin insisted that the elect who receive "the seed of the Gospel into their hearts and bring forth genuine shoots, will always make progress until they produce ripe fruit." However, the reprobates, destroying "the seed of the Gospel either by their indifference or by corrupt affections" do not manifest "sign of good progress in their life," facing the ultimate judgment in the presence of God. In light of producing good fruits in the process of progressive sanctification, Calvin wrote:

> The earth, he says, which by sucking in the rain immediately produces a blade suitable to the seed sown, at length by God's blessing produces a ripe crop; so they who receive the seed of the Gospel into their hearts and bring forth genuine shoots, will always make progress until they produce ripe fruit. On the contrary, the earth, which after culture and irrigation brings, forth nothing but thorns, affords no hope of a harvest; nay, the more that grows which is its natural produce, the more hopeless is the case. Hence the only remedy the husbandman has is to burn up the noxious and useless

---

64. Ibid., 6:6.

weeds. So they who destroy the seed of the Gospel either by their indifference or by corrupt affections, so as to manifest no sign of good progress in their life, clearly shew themselves to be reprobates, from whom no harvest can be expected.[65]

Meanwhile, in the hermeneutical and theological minds of the Federal Vision, a distinction between the elect and the reprobates, which was a key hermeneutical and theological concept to Calvin, is lost. Following the hermeneutical and theological tradition of Calvin, the great Puritan preacher and theologian, John Owen made a careful distinction between "feeding" and "tasting" within the covenant community or the visible church, which is analogous to the divide of the elect and the reprobates from God's perspective. In his interpretation of Hebrews 6:4–6, however, Rich Lusk provides a false critique to John Owen's proper distinction between "feeding" and "tasting":

> Let us imagine, for the sake of the argument, that there is some qualitative difference between what the truly regenerate experience and what future apostates experience, *and* that this distinction is in view in Hebrews 6:4–6. The question every believer has to ask himself, then, is, "How do I know I won't apostatize? How do I know I won't fall away?" To take one example, Puritan John Owen, in his work *Nature and Causes of Apostasy from the Gospel*, says we must distinguish between merely "tasting" (6:5) the heavenly gift (which future apostates may do) and really "feeding" upon it (which the genuinely regenerate do). But subtle psychological distinctions of this sort are bound to make one hopelessly introspective, always digging deeper into the inner recesses of one's heart to find some irrefutably genuine mark of grace. We are always left asking, "How do I know I am feeding on the heavenly gift, and not merely tasting of it? How do I know I've experienced *real* regeneration, and not its evil apostate twin? How do I know I have the real thing and not merely a counterfeit?" One's assurance is swallowed up in the black hole of self-examination.[66]

Lusk injects his monocovenantal theological mind into the inspired mind of the author of Hebrews, denying that there is a *qualitative* "difference between the truly regenerate person" and others in the covenant community when the author of Hebrews describes it in Hebrews 6:4–6. This is a clear hermeneutical and theological evidence that the Federal

65. Ibid., 6:7–8.
66. Lusk, "New Life and Apostasy," 272.

Visionists do not have a *deep consciousness* of a distinction between the elect and the reprobates, which was a foundational principle in Calvin's theology of the doctrine of double predestination and apostasy:

> But there is a more serious problem with this way of reading Hebrews 6. *Nothing in the text calls those warned to engage in a process of self-examination.* Rather, *Hebrews as a whole functions as an extended exhortation to perseverance.* In fact, the writer never calls into question whether or not he and his readers have experienced the grace of God. That is taken for granted. What is called into question, again and again, is whether or not they will *continue* in that grace. In terms of the theology of the book of Hebrews, the difference between the truly regenerate person and the person who will fail to persevere is not clear on the front end; rather, it only becomes clear as the one continues on in the faith and the other apostatizes. Hebrews does not call us to construct two differing psychologies of conversion (or regeneration), one for those who will persevere and one for those who will not. Instead, it calls us to look away from ourselves to Jesus, the Author and Finisher of our faith. We are assured not by figuring out if we've received "real" regeneration, but by keeping our eyes fixed on Christ, the One who persevered to the end (cf. Heb. 12:1ff.).[67]

Dealing with the problem of "falling away" passages in the New Testament, including Hebrews 6:4–8, Leithart interprets it in light of monocovenantalism. At the same time, he does not grasp the consciousness of the distinction between elect and reprobate, which is foundational in reading the passages of "falling away" and apostasy properly. In doing so, he argues that reprobates genuinely experience "favor, fellowship, and knowledge," although these spiritual blessings are temporary. Furthermore, he insists that believers, through apostasy, may lose "a relationship with the Spirit, union with Christ, and knowledge of the Savior":

> Yet, all of these passages describe a real, although temporary, experience of favor, fellowship, and knowledge of God. These reprobates really were joined to Christ, really shared in the Spirit, and yet they did not persevere and lost what they had been given. Ultimately, these blessings and gifts are no help. Like the exorcized man who is infested with the seven demons, their last state, Peter says, is worse than the first (2 Pet. 2:20). But the New Testament says pretty plainly

67. Ibid., 272–73.

that they have lost something real, which includes a relationship with the Spirit, union with Christ, and knowledge of the Savior.[68]

Contrastingly, in Calvin's theology, there is no apostasy, committed by believers, who may eventually and finally fall away from salvation. God will enable true believers to persevere to the end through the gift of perseverance, which is the biblical way of understanding. Likewise, Calvin's understanding of the sovereign grace in the outworking of individual salvation is concretely biblical. Certainly, it is based upon a theological vision, which is the distinction between the elect and the reprobates. Contrastingly, the Federal Visionists argue that even true believers may lose salvation through apostasy.

In that manner, Lusk falsely argues that believers may fall away from saving grace through apostasy. TULIP is wonderfully harmonious with Calvin's theology as we know, but it cannot be maintained without a firm affirmation of a clear distinction between election and reprobation. However, Lusk, denying the distinction between the elect and the reprobates in light of receiving the blessings of saving grace, falsely argues that his view on predestination and apostasy is comprehensively harmonious with TULIP:

> Clearly, then, Hebrews 6:4–8 teaches the possibility of a real apostasy. Some people do indeed fall away, and it is a *real* fall *from* grace. Apostates actually lose blessings they once possessed. Apostasy is so terribly heinous precisely because it is sin against grace.
>
> So how can this be reconciled with the TULIP? We satisfy the doctrinal requirements of Calvinism by insisting that all those God elected to eternal salvation will receive the gift of perseverance and will not fall away. Their perseverance is assured not by their own power or by some inner, irreversible metaphysical change that has taken place. Rather, their final glorification is guaranteed because God continues to work in them until he has brought their salvation to completion (e.g., John 10:28–29; Phil. 1:6).
>
> Meanwhile, non-elect covenant members sooner or later will turn away from Christ and will perish because God withholds from them the gift of perseverance. The TULIP remains important because it reminds us that *all* of our salvation, including our perseverance, is a gift of God's grace. Those who fall away have no one to blame but themselves; those who persevere have no one to

68. Leithart, *The Baptized Body*, 91.

thank but God. He is the Sovereign Lord of salvation as well as apostasy.[69]

TULIP, as the summary of Calvin's theology, can be maintained only with the affirmation of a distinction between the elect and the reprobates. However, in the theology of the Federal Vision, the distinction between the elect and the reprobates is sharply eclipsed. Logically, then, there is no room for the affirmation of TULIP in the theology of the Federal Vision. Nevertheless, Lusk emphasizes that their covenantal theology is still harmonious with TULIP.

Lusk appears to affirm that there is a qualitative difference "between the grace that the 'truly regenerate' (e.g., elected to persevere) receive and the grace that future apostates receive." But, we need to remember that Calvin rightly affirmed that only the elect receive saving grace through effectual calling. In addition, Calvin correctly argued that God does not bestow saving grace through effectual calling to the reprobates within the covenant community although some of them may have "temporary faith" which is not saving faith at all. In that sense, Calvin properly differentiates saving grace from common grace. So, the reprobates only receive the common operations of the Holy Spirit in the realm of religion, which may help outward religious and moral life without the blessings of the Spirit of regeneration. But Lusk falsely argues that even "reprobate covenant members" may receive saving grace but without the gift of perseverance:

> Second, this is not to say that there is no actual difference between the grace that the "truly regenerate" (e.g., elected to persevere) receive and the grace that future apostates receive. No doubt, there *is* a difference, since God has decreed and made provision for the perseverance of the one and not for the other (Eph. 1:11). Systematic theologians certainly have a stake in making such distinctions a part of their theology, so the TULIP must stand unchallenged. Whatever grace reprobate covenant members receive is qualified by their lack of perseverance.[70]

After the pattern of Calvin's theology, the Westminster divines had a deep consciousness of the distinction between effectual call and universal call along with the distinction between the elect and the reprobates as Calvin had. So, in the minds of the Westminster divines the reprobates

69. Lusk, "New Life and Apostasy," 274.
70. Ibid., 275.

within the covenant community do not receive the blessings of saving grace, which may be bestowed only to the elect. Rather, they may receive only the outward religious blessing, which is in the realm of common grace. Likewise, the Westminster divines safeguarded the distinction between saving grace and common grace as well as the elect and the reprobates. They carefully stated the blessings of the reprobates within the covenant community as "some common operations of the Spirit," which are the blessings of not saving grace but common grace:

> IV. Others, not elected, although they may be called by the ministry of the Word, and may have some common operations of the Spirit, yet they never truly come unto Christ, and therefore cannot be saved: much less can men, not professing the Christian religion, be saved in any other way whatsoever, be they never so diligent to frame their lives according to the light of nature, and the laws of that religion they do profess. And to assert and maintain that they may, is very pernicious, and to be detested (WCF, 10.4).

The Westminster divines had a clear understanding that the reprobates within the covenant community do not receive the blessings of saving grace. They only receive the blessings of "some common operations of the Spirit." Likewise, the Westminster divines made a distinction between special and common operations of the Holy Spirit not only to safeguard the elect and the reprobate but also to provide a very comprehensive biblical worldview.[71]

However, Lusk misinterprets Westminster Confession of Faith 10.1 and 10.4, failing to notice the distinction between universal call and effectual call:

71. The Westminster divines understood that those who experience "fall away," described in Hebrews 6:4–8, are not the elect but the reprobate, who do not receive genuine saving grace. In that sense, the hermeneutical and theological tradition of the Westminster divines is harmonious with Calvin as we have already explored: "[16] MAT 7:22 Many will say to me in that day, Lord, Lord, have we not prophesied in thy name? and in thy name have cast out devils? and in thy name done many wonderful works? 13:20 But he that received the seed into stony places, the same is he that heareth the word, and anon with joy receiveth it; 21 Yet hath he not root in himself, but dureth for a while: for when tribulation or persecution ariseth because of the word, by and by he is offended. HEB 6:4 For it is impossible for those who were once enlightened, and have tasted of the heavenly gift, and were made partakers of the Holy Ghost, 5 And have tasted the good word of God, and the powers of the world to come." The Westminster Confession of Faith, 10.4. Footnote no. 16 for the biblical proof text.

Thus, I fully affirm WCF 10.1 and 10.4: only those actually pre-destinated unto life are effectually called and the reprobate never "truly" come to Christ. There are numerous passages which dif-ferentiate the grace of the elect and the reprobate within the cov-enant (e.g., John 8:35, Rom. 8:29–30, etc.). But this differentiation between elect and reprobate covenant members only becomes evident over time. Insofar as history is real to us (and to God!), we must take undifferentiated covenant grace seriously.[72]

Likewise, Lusk fails to make a distinction between universal call and effectual call as well as a distinction between saving grace and com-mon grace, which are vitally important hermeneutical theological tools to make a divide of the elect and reprobate in terms of bestowing God's saving grace. He mistakenly argues that Calvin taught that "the eternally reprobate can, for a season, share in the special, effectual call of the Holy Spirit." Blurring the distinction between saving grace and common grace, Lusk appeals his monocovenantal theology to Calvin and falsely identifies his theology with Calvin's, which is a result of a grave misrepresentation of Calvin's thoughts on election, apostasy, and covenant:

The teaching offered here is not un-Reformed in any sense. Calvin is known for his doctrine of double predestination, but he was also the covenant theologian par excellence. Calvin had a robust doctrine of apostasy. In various places, he speaks of apostates as those who had been formerly "reconciled to God" and "adopted" by Him, joined in "sacred marriage" to Him, recipients of "illumi-nation" and "grace," having "faith," and so on. He says the eternally reprobate can, for a season, share in the special, effectual call of the Holy Spirit. Those who fall away have forsaken their salvation and forgotten that they were cleansed. He clearly says the warnings are for those elected by the Father and redeemed by the Son-in other words, they're for us![73]

Moreover, Lusk also appeals to the theology of John Murray as if Murray did not make a distinction between saving grace and common grace. In doing so, Lusk puts Norman Shepherd in the line of the theology of Murray, which misrepresents Murray's biblico-systematic theology:

In more recent Reformed theology, John Murray has had quite a bit to say about the relationship of the work of Christ to com-

72. Lusk, "New Life and Apostasy," 292. End note no. 10.
73. Ibid., 286.

mon grace and the non-elect within the covenant. For Murray, many benefits from Christ's work accrue to people who ultimately do not reach final salvation. And yet, the "L" in TULIP (limited atonement) remains in tact because the atonement does in history precisely what God designed for it to do. Following on the heels of Murray, Norman Shepherd sought to reformulate some Reformed doctrines, not to alter their substance, but to take into account more fully the Bible's covenantal perspective. In particular, Shepherd points out that biblical writers frequently look at election through the lens of the covenant.[74]

However, we need to point out that Murray as a reformed biblico-systematic theologian carefully maintained the distinction between saving grace and common grace, affirming limited atonement as well as the divide of the elect and the reprobate in terms of bestowing saving grace. Murray safeguarded a clear distinction between saving grace and common grace in terms of bestowing God's grace to both the elect and reprobate, although he argued that all the blessings that we receive in the present world is the result of "the mediatorial dominion of Christ." Murray carefully noted that "many benefits accrue to the non-elect from the redemptive work of Christ." And they are not the bestowment of saving grace but common grace in the realm of religion, moral, and social life whereby God bestows them both to the elect and the reprobate without any distinction or discrimination in light of Christ's mediatorial sacrifice and ministry:

> Many benefits accrue to the non-elect from the redemptive work of Christ. There is more than one consideration to establish this proposition. Many blessings are dispensed to men indiscriminately because God is fulfilling his redemptive purpose in the world. Much in the way of order, equity, benevolence, and mercy is the fruit of the gospel, and the gospel is God's redemptive revelation centered in the gift of his Son. Believers are enjoined to 'do good to all men' (Gal. 6:10) and compliance has a beneficent result. But their identity as believers proceeds from redemption. Again,

74. Ibid. Lusk mistakenly argues as though Murray did not maintain a sharp distinction between special grace and common grace in his discussion of Murray's view of atonement, referring to Murray's article on "The Atonement and the Free Offer of the Gospel": "The theology of apostasy laid out in this paper can be thought of as simply an unpacking of Murray's provocative statement on page 63: 'Many benefits accrue to the non-elect from the redemptive work of Christ.' We are not abandoning effectual atonement; we are making nuances within its parameters." Ibid., 298.

it is by virtue of what Christ had done that there is a gospel of salvation proclaimed to all without distinction. Are we to say that the unrestricted overture of grace is not grace to those to whom it comes? Furthermore, we must remember that all the good dispensed to this world is dispensed within the mediatorial dominion of Christ. He is given all authority in heaven and in earth and he is head over all things. But he is given this dominion as the reward of his obedience unto death (cf. Phil. 2:8, 9), and his obedience unto death is but one way of characterizing what we mean by the atonement.[75]

Likewise, we must be aware that Murray had a deep consciousness of the distinction between saving grace and common grace in his discussion of "The Atonement and the Free Offer of the Gospel." Murray's point lies in the fact that Christ's perfect obedience to the law through his life and atoning death is the fountainhead of all the soteriological blessings for the elect as well as the blessings of common grace in the world which are shared by both the elect and reprobates until the second Coming of the exalted King Jesus Christ, who is ruling the visible and invisible world as the sovereign Lord:

Thus all the good showered on this world, dispensed by Christ in the exercise of his exalted lordship, is related to the death of Christ and accrues to man in one way or another from the death of Christ. If so, it was designed to accrue from the death of Christ. Since many of these blessings fall short of salvation and are enjoyed by many who never become the possessors of salvation, we must say that the design of Christ's death is more inclusive that the blessings that belong specifically to the atonement. This is to say that even the non-elect are embraced in the design of the atonement in respect of those blessings falling short of salvation which they enjoy in this life. This is equivalent to saying that the atonement sustains this reference to the non-elect and it would not be improper to say that, in respect of what is entailed for the non-elect, Christ died for them.[76]

Having the consciousness of the radical distinction between the elect and the reprobates in terms of receiving saving grace, Murray paid special at-

75. John Murray, "The Atonement and the Free Offer of the Gospel," in *Collected Writings of John Murray*, vol. 1 (Edinburgh and Carlisle: Banner of Truth Trust, 1976), 63–64.

76. Ibid., 64.

tention to the biblical passages about those who fall away after experiencing "the sanctifying effect," "the transforming effects" and others:

> We have in the Scripture itself an indication of this kind of reference and of the sanctifying effect it involves in some cases. In Hebrews 10:29 we read: 'Of how much sorer punishment, think ye, shall he be accounted worthy, who hath trodden under foot the Son of God, and hath counted the blood of the covenant wherewith he was sanctified an unholy thing, and hath done despite unto the Spirit of grace? The person in view we must regard as one who has abandoned his Christian profession and for whom 'there remaineth no more sacrifice for sins, but a certain fearful expectation of judgment' (Heb. 10:26, 27). It is the person described in Hebrews 6:4,5 in terms of the transforming effects experienced but who falls away and cannot be renewed unto repentance. In 2 Peter 2:20–22 the same person is described as having 'escaped the defilements of the world', as having 'known the way of righteousness', but as having turned back and returned as the dog to his vomit or the sow to wallowing in the mire. This is-terrible to contemplate!-the apostate.[77]

As such, Murray was very careful in his analysis on apostasy, described in Hebrews 6:4–5. According to Murray, the apostate in Hebrews 6:4–5 does not experience transformation itself which is the authentic spiritual experience bestowed by the Holy Spirit for the elect alone, but "the transforming effects" which are temporary spiritual experience for the reprobates within the covenant community.

Murray continued to argue that the reprobates may experience "sanctifying effects" or "transforming effects" within the covenant community as a result of Christ's atoning sacrifice. In that sense, it is legitimate to say that "Christ died for non-elect persons" also, broadly speaking. However, Murray was clear that "transforming effects," experienced by the reprobates, "fall short of salvation." In that sense, Murray carefully safeguarded the radical distinction between the elect and the reprobates in terms of the quality of spiritual experience within the covenant community in his analysis and affirmation on the biblical doctrine of limited atonement:

> We have found that there are included in the design of atonement benefits which accrue to the non-elect. The fruits of the atonement enjoyed by some non-elect persons are defined in very lofty terms.

77. Ibid.

Non-elect are said to have been sanctified in the blood of Christ, to have tasted the good word of God and the powers of the age to come, to have escaped the pollutions of the world through the knowledge of the Lord and Saviour, and to have known the way of righteousness (cf. Heb. 6:4,5; 10:29; 2 Pet. 2:20, 21). In this sense, therefore, we may say that Christ died for non-elect persons. It must, however, be marked with equal emphasis that these fruits or benefits all fall short of salvation, even though in some cases the terms used to characterize them are such as could properly be used to describe a true state of salvation. Theses non-elect persons, however reforming may have been the influences excerted upon them and however uplifting their experiences, come short of the benefits accruing from the atonement, which the truly and finally saved enjoy.[78]

Murray had a clear consciousness of the radical distinction between the elect and the reprobates in terms of spiritual experience, bestowed by God. In doing so, Murray not only safeguarded the biblical doctrine of the limited atonement but also the *qualitative difference* of the spiritual experience between the elect and the reprobates within the covenant community. In conclusion, therefore, Murray argued that the reprobates "do not participate in the benefits *of* atonement and the elect do":

It is, therefore, apparent that the atonement has an entirely different reference to the elect from that which it sustains to the non-elect on the highest level of their experience. It is this radical differentiation that must be fully appreciated and guarded; it belongs to the crux of the question respecting the extent of the atonement. The difference can be stated bluntly to be that the non-elect do not participate in the benefits *of* the atonement and the elect do. The non-elect enjoy many benefits that accrue *from* the atonement but they do not partake of the *atonement*.[79]

Thus, we must reject Lusk's notion that Murray recognized that those who experienced the spiritual blessings of salvation may finally fall away through apostasy. It is simply a misrepresentation of Murray's biblico-systematic theology, whereby he carefully maintained the radical distinction between the elect and the reprobates in terms of both personal spiritual experience and bestowment of saving grace from God.

78. Ibid., 68.
79. Ibid., 68–69.

SUMMARY

Calvin portrayed the biblical doctrine of double predestination, namely election and reprobation, against the background of rejection to it in his own historical context. In doing so, he self-consciously followed the theological pattern of Augustine, who maintained the doctrine of double predestination against the backdrop of the Pelagian rejection to it. Furthermore, Calvin responded to his opponents about the doctrine of double predestination from the perspectives of the Pauline theology, the redemptive history of the Old Testament Israel, the comprehensive testimonies of the four Gospels, and others. The most decisive hermeneutical principle of the double predestination that Calvin applied is the distinction between law and gospel, which is also applied to the doctrine of *sola gratia* and *sola fide* in his soteriology. In addition, Calvin made a careful distinction between general call and effectual or special call to offer a biblical harmony between the universal offer of the gospel and particular application of it to the elect only.

Meanwhile, the Federal Visionists approach the doctrine of double predestination not from the perspective of the divine sovereign grace which Calvin properly did. Rather, they approach it from their narrowly defined covenantal perspective, following the pattern of Shepherd and others because they deny the validity of the distinction between law and gospel in hermeneutics and theology. In doing so, they lose the hermeneutical and theological ground of the biblical doctrine of double predestination. So, their apparent affirmation of double predestination after the theological pattern of Calvin cannot be maintained. In conclusion, their doctrine of the double predestination is incompatible to Calvin, and the Westminster Standards although they identify their view with Calvin, and the Westminster Standards.

4

Covenant and Baptism

CALVIN INTERPRETED SACRAMENTAL THEOLOGY in light of the covenant, and redemptive historical continuity and discontinuity. In his understanding of the theology of baptism and the Lord's Supper, Calvin carefully viewed it from the perspective of the sign and seal of the covenant of grace, which is a decisive hermeneutical standpoint to exposit the biblical understanding and practice of sacramental theology.[1] As such, Calvin viewed sacraments as the signs and seals of the covenants, and Calvin's biblical definition of sacraments dictates his sacramental theology against the Medieval meritorious sacerdotalism:

> And our adversaries cannot boast that this comparison has been recently devised by us, since Paul himself used it, calling circumcision a 'seal' [Rom. 4:11]. There Paul expressly argues that Abraham's circumcision was not for his justification but for the seal of that covenant by faith in which he had already been justified . . . Since the Lord calls his promises 'covenants' [Gen. 6:18; 9:9; 17:2] and his sacraments 'tokens' of the covenants, a simile can be taken from the covenants of men . . . Yet when words precede, the laws of covenants are by such signs ratified, although they were first conceived, established, and decreed in words. The sacraments, therefore, are exercises which make us more certain of the trustworthiness of God's Word. And because we are of flesh, they are shown us under things of flesh, to instruct us according to our dull capacity, and to lead us by the hand as tutors lead children. Augustine calls a sacrament 'a visible word' for the reason that it represents God's

---

1. For the concise yet comprehensive analysis of Calvin's views on worship and the sacramental theology in light of the Reformation context, see W. Robert Godfrey, "Calvin, Worship, and the Sacraments," in *Theological Guide to Calvin's Institutes: Essays and Analysis*, eds. David W. Hall & Peter A. Lillback (Phillipsburg: Presbyterian and Reformed Publishing, 2008), 368–89.

promises as painted in a picture and sets them before our sight, portrayed graphically and in the manner of images.[2]

Meanwhile, we will find out that the sacramental theology of the Federal Vision loses the theological sensitivity of baptism and the Lord's Supper as the sign and seal of the covenant of grace because they reinterpret it from the monocovenantal perspective. Leithart as one of the representative voices of the Federal Vision denies the profound validity of sacraments as the signs and seals of the covenant of grace, which has been a controlling motif for biblical sacramental theology since Augustine:

> Sacramental theology has employed this idea of signs for a long time. Augustine defined a sign as 'a thing which of itself makes something come to mind, besides the impression that it presents to the senses' (*On Christian Teaching*, 2.1), and Augustine's definition was the basis for sacramental theology throughout the Middle Ages and into the Reformation. The seventeenth-century Reformed theologian Francis Turretin explained that sacramental signs work in such a way that 'the thing promised is so represented to our minds that it is caused also to be truly communicated.'
>
> Though not wrong as far as he goes, Augustine does not go nearly far enough, and the application of his definition of sign to sacraments has been the source of much confusion ... Augustine's definition robs sacraments of much of any objective, real-world efficacy. On these assumptions, sacraments do nothing but provoke pious thoughts.[3]

The dictum, "sacraments are not signs" of the covenant of grace is the heart of sacramental theology of the Federal Vision. And, from that theological point of view, the Federal Visionists actively promote baptismal regeneration in their discussion of baptismal efficacy, which is covenantal sacerdotalism, at best although they argue that it is compatible to Calvin and the Westminster Standards.[4]

---

2. Calvin, *Institutes*, 4.14.5–6.

3. Leithart, *The Baptized Body*, 12–13.

4. For critical interaction against sacramental theology of the Federal Vision, see George W. Knight III, "1 Corinthians 11:17–34: The Lord's Supper: Abuses, Words of Institution and Warnings with An Addendum on 1 Corinthians 10:16–17," in *The Auburn Avenue Theology, Pros & Con: Debating the Federal Vision*, ed. E. Calvin Beisner (Fort Lauderdale: Knox Theological Seminary, 2004), 282–96; The Orthodox Presbyterian Church, *Justification*, 153–63; Richard D. Phillips, "A Response to 'Sacramental Efficacy in the Westminster Standards,'" in *The Auburn Avenue Theology, Pros & Con: Debating the*

THE IMPORTANCE OF FAITH IN BELIEVER'S BAPTISM

Calvin emphasized that baptism is the mark of an open confession of *faith* before men. In doing so, we testify that we worship "the same God, in one religion with all Christians," affirming our faith openly and publicly. In addition, through water baptism in the name of Jesus Christ, we have committed to devote ourselves to him, making "sworn allegiance to his name." We pledge our faith to Christ publicly, confessing no other name, "but Christ alone." In this manner, Calvin wrote:

> But baptism serves as our confession before men. Indeed, it is the mark by which we publicly profess that we wish to be reckoned God's people; by which we testify that we agree in worshiping the same God, in one religion with all Christians; by which finally we openly affirm our faith. Thus not only do our hearts breathe the praise of God, but our tongues also and all members of our body resound his praise in every way they can . . . Paul had this in mind when he asked the Corinthians whether they had not been baptized in Christ's name [1 Cor. 1:13]. He thus implied that, in being baptized in his name, they had devoted themselves to him, sworn allegiance to his name, and pledged their faith to him before men. As a result, they could no longer confess any other but Christ alone, unless they chose to renounce the confession they had made in baptism.[5]

Calvin stated that we not only publicly affirm our faith through baptism but we also nourish our faith. So, we have to be sure that Christ speaks to us through baptism, which is the sign of thing itself. In baptism, Christ purifies and washes away our sins, and he even blots out the memory of our sins. In that sense, Calvin argued that we must see "spiritual things" in physical elements in the sacraments as if they are before our own eyes. In baptism, the Lord attests "his will toward us" by the sacramental token whereby he is pleased to bestow all the spiritual blessings upon us:

> For inasmuch as it is given for the arousing, nourishing, and con-firming of our faith, it is to be received as from the hand of the Author himself. We ought to deem it certain and proved that it is

---

Federal Vision, ed. E. Calvin Beisner (Fort Lauderdale: Knox Theological Seminary, 2004), 245–53; Joseph A. Pipa Jr., "A Response to 'Covenant, Baptism, and Salvation,'" in *The Auburn Avenue Theology, Pros & Con: Debating the Federal Vision,* ed. E. Calvin Beisner (Fort Lauderdale: Knox Theological Seminary, 2004), 270–81; Waters, *The Federal Vision and Covenant Theology,* 168–257.

5. Calvin, *Institutes,* 4.15.13

he who speaks to us through the sign; that it is he who purifies and washes away sins, and wipes out the remembrance of them; that it is he who makes us sharers in his death, who deprives Satan of his rule, who weakens the power of our lust; indeed, that it is he who comes into a unity with us so that, having put on Christ, we may be acknowledged God's children. These things, I say, he performs for our soul within as truly and surely as we see our body outwardly cleansed, submerged, and surrounded with water. For this analogy or similitude is the surest rule of the sacraments: that we should see spiritual things in physical, as if set before our very eyes.[6]

Calvin boldly argued that baptism is not the means of forgiveness of sins. Rather, it is a means of "a surer exercise of faith" (*certiorem fidei exercitationem*), increasing "assurance from a pledge" as it was exemplified by the baptismal episode of Cornelius the centurion in Acts 10:48:

Let us take as proof of this, Cornelius the centurion, who, having already received forgiveness of sins and the visible graces of the Holy Spirit, was nevertheless baptized [Acts 10:48]. He did not seek an ampler forgiveness of sins through baptism, but a surer exercise of faith—increase of assurance from a pledge. Perhaps someone will object: why, then, did Ananias tell Paul to wash away his sins through baptism [Acts 22:16; cf. ch. 9:17–18] if sins are not washed away by the power of baptism itself? I reply: we are said to receive, obtain, and acquire what, according as our faith is aware, is shown forth to us by the Lord, whether when he first testifies to it, or when he confirms more fully and more surely what has been attested. Ananias meant only this: "To be assured, Paul, that your sins are forgiven, be baptized. For the Lord promises forgiveness of sins in baptism; receive it, and be secure."[7]

In his interpretation of Acts 22:16, Calvin analyzed that "the blood of Christ" is "the only means whereby our sins are washed away." In addition, the Holy Ghost makes believers clean continually "by the sprinkling thereof through faith." In that sense, Calvin highlighted that "God alone" washes away "from our sins by the blood of his Son." So, the washing away of our sins may be "effectual in us" "by the hidden power of his Spirit." As such, in Calvin's baptismal theology, "the blood of Christ" is only "material cause," and the Holy Ghost is the chief "formal cause" while "the heavenly Father" stands as "author." In that sense, I can safely argue that Calvin

6. Ibid., 4.15.14.
7. Ibid., 4.15.15.

focused on the triune God while thinking about the baptismal washing away of our sins. Calvin viewed "the preaching of the word and baptism itself" as "an inferior instrument" of washing away of our sins. In such a manner, Calvin did not tie "the grace of God to the sacraments" because "the administration of baptism" profits nothing in terms of saving grace unless God bestows his saving grace through his sovereign will:

> Surely, forasmuch as the blood of Christ is the only means whereby our sins are washed away, and as it was once shed to this end, so the Holy Ghost, by the sprinkling thereof through faith, doth make us clean continually. This honor cannot be translated unto the sign of water, without doing open injury to Christ and the Holy Ghost; and experience doth teach how earnestly men be bent upon this superstition . . . Wherefore, we must hold this, first, that it is God alone who washeth from our sins by the blood of his Son; and to the end this washing may be effectual in us, he worketh by the hidden power of his Spirit. Therefore, when the question is concerning remission of sins, we must seek no other author thereof but the Heavenly Father, we must imagine no other material cause but the blood of Christ; and when we be come to the formal cause, the Holy Ghost is the chief. But there is an inferior instrument, and that is the preaching of the word and baptism itself. But though God alone doth work by the inward power of his Spirit, yet that doth not hinder but that he may use, at his pleasure, such instruments and means as he knoweth to be convenient; not that he includeth in the element anything which he taketh either from his Spirit or from the blood of Christ, but because he will have the sign itself to be an help for our infirmity . . . Notwithstanding, we must again beware that we tie not the grace of God to the sacraments; for the external administration of baptism profiteth nothing, save only where it pleaseth God it shall.[8]

---

8. Calvin, *Acts of the Apostles*, 22:16. Calvin provided a succinct critique against the Medieval Schoolmen's understanding that water baptism removes original sin. In responding to the Medieval Schoolmen's interpretation, Calvin argued that water baptism provides God's unfailing *promise* to the believer for "the forgiveness of all sins for the whole of life." On the other hand, in the process of lifelong fighting against sin, water baptism becomes a constant reminder of "a present promise and encouragement to Christians" that God is working constantly to sanctify the believers as Godfrey correctly reads Calvin's balanced interpretation: "Second, Calvin rejected the doctrine that baptism removed original sin—a doctrine taught by the medieval church. Such teaching, Calvin believed, made both too much and too little of baptism. This medieval teaching promised too much in saying that the water of baptism removed the original sin of everyone baptized. But it also promised too little by reducing baptism to dealing with only with

Calvin emphasized the importance of faith in the reception and participation of baptism and the Lord's Supper because we receive "reality and truth to the sign" when we receive it in faith:

> Yet it is not my intention to weaken the force of baptism by not joining reality and truth to the sign, in so far as God works through outward means. But from this sacrament, as from all others, we obtain only as much as we receive in faith. If we lack faith, this will be evidence of our ungratefulness, which renders us chargeable before God, because we have not believed the promise given there.
>
> But as far as it is a symbol of our confession, we ought by it to testify that our confidence is in God's mercy, and our purity in forgiveness of sins, which has been procured for us through Jesus Christ; and that we enter God's church in order to live harmoniously with all believers in complete agreement of faith and love. This last point was what Paul meant when he said, "We have all been baptized in one Spirit that we may be one body" [1 Cor. 12:13].[9]

Meanwhile, in the discussion of baptismal efficacy in relation to faith, the Federal Visionists self-consciously separate themselves from the baptismal efficacy of the Medieval Church in which the theology of *ex opera operato* was actively advocated and promoted. In that respect, we can categorize the Roman Catholic's view as *meritorious sacerdotalism* while we can identify the Federal Visionists' view as *covenantal sacerdotalism*. For example, with water baptism, Lusk argues that "baptism does not automatically guarantee salvation." Rather, he combines "the waters of baptism with a living faith," affirming baptismal regeneration:

> Baptismal efficacy raises a red flag for many in the Reformed community. In part, this is due to the specter of *ex opera operato* from the Medieval Church and is very understandable. We must carefully guard against any view that would lead people to believe that simply because they have been baptized, all is well no matter how they live their lives. In this sense, baptism does not automatically guarantee salvation. We must combine the waters of baptism with a living faith.[10]

---

original sin and having little significance for the rest of life. Instead Calvin taught that baptism promised the believer the forgiveness of all sins for the whole of life (4.15.10). In the lifelong and sometimes discouraging fight against sin, baptism always remained a present promise and encouragement to Christians that God was at work in them to sanctify (4.15.11)." Godfrey, "Calvin, Worship, and the Sacraments," 378.

9. Calvin, *Institutes*, 4.15.15.

10. Lusk, "Paedobaptism and Baptismal Efficacy," 103. For the brief analysis of the

In his discussion of baptismal efficacy, Lusk appeals to the Westminster Standards for the affirmation of baptismal regeneration, arguing for "a certain limited version of *ex opera operato*." However, we have to be reminded that the Westminster divines affirmed that water baptism is a sacramental means to invite God's covenant people to "the visible church" with rich covenantal and spiritual blessings and promises. The Westminster divines had a clear theological consciousness whereby they believed that water baptism is not a divinely ordained means for regeneration and salvation in light of *ex opera operato*. God saves his chosen people in his appointed moment, and it may be a moment of water baptism through the sovereign work of the Holy Spirit:

> What then is the relationship of baptism to faith? If faith is demanded, how does this requirement qualify our notions of baptismal efficacy? It is easy to draw caricatures here, so we must be careful. For example, I know of no theologian in history, Roman Catholic or otherwise, who has taught baptism *automatically guarantees* final salvation, come what may. By contrast, at the same time, the Reformed confessions do bind us to believe in a certain limited version of *ex opera operato*: Everyone baptized, no matter their subjective heart condition, is joined to the "visible church" at the time of their baptism—automatically and without exception, right then and there, you might say (cf. WCF 28.1). So baptismal efficacy, and its relation to faith, is something that deserves careful and nuanced consideration. We must avoid making hasty and sloganized judgments.[11]

Having covenantal sacerdotalism in their thoughts, the Federal Visionists begin to reinterpret baptismal theology, represented by Calvin and the Reformed tradition. Quoting Calvin's *Strasbourg Catechism* and *Catechism of the Church of Geneva*, Lusk falsely argues that Calvin taught "the sacraments as effectual means of salvation and assurance." To be

---

major theological problem of "by the work performed" (*ex opera operato*) by medieval scholasticism and Roman Catholicism, see Muller, "Dictionary of Latin and Greek Theological Terms," 108: "With reference to the sacraments, the assumption of medieval scholasticism and Roman Catholicism that the correct and churchly performance of the rite conveys grace to the recipient, unless the recipient places a spiritual impediment (*obex*) in the way of grace. Sacraments themselves, therefore, have a *virtus operativa*, or operative power. This view of sacraments is denied by both Lutherans and Reformed, who maintain that faith must be present in the recipient if the sacraments are to function as means of grace; the mere performance of the rite will not convey grace."

11. Lusk, "Paedobaptism and Baptismal Efficacy," 103.

sure, Calvin properly located water baptism and the Lord's Supper not as "effectual means of salvation and assurance" but as *the means of grace*. Calvin did not force to dogmatize that water baptism *is* "effectual means of salvation." Lusk argues as follows:

> Beginning with the prince of Reformed theologians, John Calvin, the Reformed church had strongly emphasized the sacraments as effectual means of salvation and assurance. In Calvin's Strasbourg catechism, he asks the student, "How do you know yourself to be a son of God in fact as well as in name?" The answer is, "Because I am baptized in the name of God the Father, and of the Son, and of the Holy Ghost." In his Geneva catechism, he asks, "Is baptism nothing more than a mere symbol [i.e., picture] of cleansing?" The answer: "I think it to be such a symbol that the reality is attached to it For God does not disappoint us when he promises us his gifts. Hence, both pardon of sins and newness of life are certainly offered and received by us in baptism."[12]

In the discussion of baptismal efficacy in the Reformed tradition, Lusk injects the Federal Visionists' dogmatic concept of baptismal regeneration into Calvin's baptismal theology. However, we need to remember that Calvin never dogmatized baptismal regeneration as the Federal Visionists do. Thus, Lusk mistakenly writes as follows:

> For Calvin, regeneration began at the font. The Christian life took its source and shape from the baptismal rite. Of course, baptism was not a complete salvation in itself; the one baptized had to grow in faith and repentance, living out the grace received in baptism. But as the foundation and touchstone of the Christian life, baptism was of unparalleled importance.
>
> Early on in his discussion of baptism in the *Institutes*, Calvin claims,
>
> > We must realize that at whatever time we are baptized, we are once for all washed and purged for our whole life. Therefore, as often as we fall away, we ought to recall the memory of our baptism and fortify our mind with it, that we may always be sure and confident of the forgiveness of sins.[13]

Injecting the dogmatic concept of baptismal regeneration, Lusk argues that Calvin viewed water baptism as a focal point of regeneration. He fails to understand Calvin's remarks on the forgiveness of sins for those

12. Ibid., 89.
13. Ibid.

who are in Christ. He impresses how Calvin taught that regeneration and forgiveness of sins come from water baptism, quoting his *Institutes* 4.15.3. But we have to be aware that Lusk misinterprets Calvin's writing on baptismal efficacy. Indeed, Calvin emphasized how water baptism is *a visible sign* for the washing away of sins from the entire life "through the sprinkling of Christ's blood." In Calvin's baptismal theology, we must understand that water baptism is a visible sign or token of how our sins are "once for all washed and purged for our whole life."[14]

Likewise, it is very clear that Lusk fails to read Calvin's theology correctly on baptismal efficacy. Calvin was very careful to note that water baptism itself does not have the power for "cleansing and salvation." Moreover, he clearly stated that water baptism does not contain "in itself the power to cleanse, regenerate, and renew; nor that here is the cause of salvation." But, Calvin emphasized that we receive "the knowledge and certainty of such gifts." Water baptism provides us with God's *sure promise* that our sins are cleansed "through the sprinkling of Christ's blood, which is represented by means of water from the resemblance to cleansing and washing":

> In this sense we are to understand what Paul has written: that the church "has been sanctified" by Christ, the bridegroom, and "cleansed with the washing of water in the Word of life" [Eph. 5:26 p]. And another passage: "He saved us . . . in virtue of his own mercy, through the washing of regeneration and of renewal in the Holy Spirit" [Titus 3:5]. And by Peter: "Baptism . . . saves us" [1 Peter 3:21].
>
> For Paul did not mean to signify that our cleansing and salvation are accomplished by water, or that water contains in itself the power to cleanse, regenerate, and renew; nor that here is the cause of salvation, but only that in this sacrament are received the knowledge and certainty of such gifts. This the words themselves explain clearly enough. For Paul joins together the Word of life and the baptism of water, as if he had said: "Through the gospel a message of our cleansing and sanctification is brought to us; through such baptism the message is sealed." And Peter immediately adds that this baptism is not a removal of filth from the flesh but a good conscience before God [1 Peter 3:21], which is from faith. Indeed, baptism promises us no other purification than through the sprinkling of Christ's blood, which is represented by means of water from the resemblance to cleansing and washing.[15]

14. Calvin, *Institutes*, 4.15.3.

15. Ibid., 4.15.2.

Lusk misinterprets Calvin's theology especially on baptismal efficacy, assuming baptismal regeneration, which is against Calvin's self-conscious theological will whereby he was against the dogmatic assumption of baptismal regeneration. Again, Lusk refers to Calvin's *Institutes* 4.17.1 as if Calvin taught baptismal regeneration, affirming that "new life begins in baptism and is continued at the Table."[16] But, Calvin did not affirm baptismal regeneration in that literal context. Rather, he viewed that the Eucharistic bread and wine are the representation of "the invisible food that we receive from the flesh and blood of Christ":

> First, the signs are bread and wine, which represent for us the invisible food that we receive from the flesh and blood of Christ. For as in baptism, God, regenerating us, engrafts us into the society of his church and makes us his own by adoption, so we have said, that he discharges the function of a provident householder in continually supplying to us food to sustain and persevere us in that life into which he has begotten us by his Word.
>
> Now Christ is the only food of our soul, and therefore our Heavenly Father invites us to Christ, that, refreshed by partaking of him, we may repeatedly gather strength until we shall have reached heavenly immortality.[17]

16. Lusk, "Paedobaptism and Baptismal Efficacy," 89–90.

17. Calvin, *Institutes*, 4.17.1. James Cassidy makes some helpful comments in his discussion of baptismal efficacy while he correctly refutes the contention that Calvin affirmed the doctrine of baptismal regeneration in reference to *Institutes*, 4.17.1: "Again, context is everything. Those who would make Calvin to be a supporter of their position have indeed here taken him out of context. These words find themselves in the chapter on the Lord's Supper, not baptism. Moreover, the section in which these words are found addresses the issue we just left above, namely, the relation between the *signa* and *res*. Calvin explains in the sentence before our quotation that bread and wine are signs that represent invisible food. The bread and the wine are the signs. The invisible food of Christ and his blessings are the things signified. Then Calvin proceeds to draw an analogy with baptism in saying that we have already quoted . . . Therefore, it makes better sense to interpret Calvin as saying in this quotation that in baptism we have represented God's regeneration of us and his engrafting us into the society of his church. In fact, the phrase in the citation should be taken into serious consideration. Calvin teaches that the new life the Christian has is one begotten 'by his Word.' In other words, God begets new life in us. He regenerates us through the means of the Word, and then we receive the visible sign of that invisible grace. It is not the baptism that begets us; it is the Word. Baptism visibly points to that regeneration given by the Spirit by means of the Word of God. Or, to put it another way, Calvin here is clearly employing the two ways of speaking, the *duplex loquendi modus*, because he has in view a body of believers. Therefore he can, as Scripture itself does, employ language proper to the *res* for the *signa*." James J. Cassidy, "Calvin on Baptism: Baptismal Regeneration or the *Duplex Loquendi Modus*?" in *Resurrection and*

More interestingly, Douglas Wilson argues that "water baptism now saves us" in his interpretation of 1 Peter 3:18–22 while he identifies his view with Calvin and the Westminster Standards, which is a typical approach by the Federal Visionists:

> When the Scriptures speak of water baptism, what kind of language is commonly used? A good place to begin is with the text quoted earlier. Water baptism now saves us. Peter tells us that baptism saves, and his subsequent qualifier does not mean that baptism does not save. He is not taking away with one hand what he has given with the other. It means that baptism saves in this fashion, but not in that fashion.
>
> Baptism does not save by means of the water (not putting away physical dirt), but baptism does save by the resurrection of Jesus Christ accompanied by the answer of a good conscience. This reference to a removal of physical dirt is likely not addressing those who thought that their morning shower washed away their sins, but rather addressed certain aspects of the Jewish ceremonial.[18]

Wilson argues that water baptism bestows "the remission of sins" on the one hand, and regeneration, on the other hand. Wilson affirms that Peter's response to his audience after "the first sermon of the New Covenant era" in Acts 2:38 and Ananias's response to Saul after Saul's Damascus Road Conversion experience in Acts 22:16 warrant his argument that water baptism actually washes away sins:

> When Peter was preaching the first sermon of the New Covenant era, his message cut his listeners to the heart. They cried out, "What should we do?" How many of us would give Peter's answer? "Then Peter said unto them, Repent, and be baptized every one of you in the name of Jesus Christ for the remission of sins, and ye shall receive the gift of the Holy Ghost" (Acts 2:38). This is where the phrase in the Nicene Creed came from—baptism for the remission of sins.
>
> When Saul was first converted, Ananias knew just what was called for and apparently did not adequately guard against superstition in his language. "And now why tarriest thou? Arise, and be baptized, and wash away thy sins, calling on the name of the Lord" (Acts 22:16). In blunt language, Ananias told Saul to come to the baptismal font in order to wash away his sins.[19]

Eschatology: Theology in Service of the Church: Essays in Honor of Richard B. Gaffin Jr., eds. Land G. Tipton and Jeffrey C. Waddington (Phillipsburg: Presbyterian and Reformed Publishing, 2008), 550.

18. Wilson, *"Reformed" Is Not Enough*, 100.

19. Ibid., 101.

Wilson refers to the baptism and washing away passages in relation to regeneration, founded in passages such as Mark 16:16, Ephesians 5:26, and Titus 3:5. He interprets them *literally* to support his dogmatic assumption of baptismal regeneration. In doing so, he argues that the context of water baptism is actually "the *font* of regeneration." It is remarkable to discover how Wilson's dogma on baptismal regeneration is directly against Calvin's baptismal theology, although he identifies himself with Calvin:

> The Bible also speaks of the washing of regeneration. The word for *washing* in Titus 3:5 is literally *laver*: "Not by works of righteousness which we have done, but according to his mercy he saved us, by the washing of regeneration, and renewing of the Holy Ghost." We find the reality referred to in Ephesians 5:26. This is one of the few places where the Bible refers to regeneration, and it is the only place where it does so in reference to the conversion of individuals. In doing this, Paul speaks of the *font* of regeneration.
>
> When Jesus tells His apostles to preach the gospel throughout the world, He teaches them what the response to that gospel needs to be. "He that believeth and is baptized shall be saved; but he that believeth not shall be damned" (Mk. 16:16).[20]

Wilson identifies the Federal Visionists' view on baptismal regeneration as not Roman Catholic but "the magisterial Reformation." Wilson, along with other Federal Visionists, is massively confused about Calvin's view on baptismal efficacy, as well as the Westminster Standards. He reinterprets Calvin and the Westminster Standards in respect to baptismal efficacy in light of baptismal regeneration. This interpretation is unknown to Calvin and the Reformed orthodox formulation, which was beautifully encapsulated in the Westminster Standards. Wilson is critical of "modern evangelicals" who object to their radical understanding of baptismal regeneration, unfairly labeling them as "heirs of the radical Anabaptist reformation":

> All this seems to be pretty plain. What are we to do with this? Are we Roman Catholics yet? For the historically astute, the answer is *of course not*. But it has to be confessed that the biblical response to these things (and the historic Reformed formulation of them) looks Roman Catholic to many modern evangelicals. But this is because they are heirs of the radical Anabaptist reformation, and not of the magisterial Reformation. We have gotten to such a low point in our awareness of our heritage that a man can be thought

20. Ibid.

to be quoting Roman Catholic formulae when he is actually quoting that old papists, John Knox.[21]

Referring to the Westminster Confession of Faith 28.1, Wilson argues as though the Westminster divines affirmed baptismal regeneration, which is an alien concept to them. Of course, they considered baptism as "a sign and seal of the covenant of grace." We have to be reminded that the Westminster divines' designation of baptism as "a sign and seal of the covenant of grace" necessarily excludes the concept of baptismal regeneration, as well as sacerdotalism, which was adopted and actively promoted by the Roman Catholics:

> Raise your hand if you knew that the Westminster Confession taught baptismal regeneration–but more on this in a moment. We have discussed sacraments generally; we now come to discuss the two sacraments specifically, in turn. Baptism is one of the sacraments of the new covenant. It was ordained by Jesus Christ as a sacrament in the words of the Great Commission. He told His disciples that the mark of His disciples was to be baptism. Disciple the nations, He said, *baptizing* them. The signification of baptism is twofold, that is, it points in two directions. The first is the solemn recognition that the one baptized has been admitted into the historical Church of Christ. At the same time, the baptism also points *away* from the person, to the objective meanings of baptism. Baptism means that the one baptized has a sign and seal of the covenant of grace, the one baptized has been grafted into Christ, he has the sign and seal of regeneration, forgiveness of sins, and the obligation to walk in newness of life. This sacrament is perpetual in history.[22]

Wilson again reinterprets the Westminster Confession of Faith from the theological perspective of the Federal Vision's dogmatic presupposition of baptismal regeneration. Quoting WCF 28.5, Wilson argues that we must consider "baptism and regeneration together." In doing so, he makes baptismal regeneration not "an absolute," but "the norm," putting "the connection between water baptism and grace and salvation" together:

> Although it be a great sin to condemn or neglect this ordinance, yet grace and salvation are not so inseparably annexed unto it, as that no person can be regenerated,

21. Ibid., 101–2.
22. Ibid., 103–4.

> or saved, without it: or, that all that are baptized are
> undoubtedly regenerated. (28.5)

Neglect of baptism is a great sin but not an unforgivable one. We are to consider baptism and regeneration together, but we are not to treat this as an absolute. In other words, some who are not baptized will be saved, and not all who are baptized are saved. But as discussed earlier, while we do not take the connection between water baptism and grace and salvation as an absolute, we do take it as the norm.[23]

As such, Wilson and other Federal Visionists are critical towards those who go against baptismal regeneration and covenantal sacerdotalism, injecting their presupposition of baptismal regeneration into the baptismal theologies of Calvin and the Westminster Standards.

Interestingly, Wilson critiques Warfield, who was one of the representative orthodox Reformed theologians in the Old Princeton, along with Charles Hodge. Wilson points to the Westminster Confession of Faith 28.6 as a confessional reference to provide a critique against Warfield:

> The efficacy of Baptism is not tied to that moment of
> time wherein it is administered; yet, not withstanding,
> by the right use of this ordinance, the grace promised is
> not only offered, but really exhibited, and conferred, by
> the Holy Ghost, to such (whether of age or infants) as
> that grace belongeth unto, according to the counsel of
> God's own will, in His appointed time. (28:6)

Contrary to Warfield, baptism is efficacious. But the efficacy of the sacrament is not tied to the moment when it is administered. By means of baptism, this efficacious grace is *conferred* on the elect at the appropriate time, the time of conversion, and it is *the applied grace of their baptism*.[24]

Wilson unfairly criticizes that Warfield's denial of baptismal regeneration is due to the influence of rationalism, arguing that Warfield's view is "a reductionistic one." Furthermore, he notes that Warfield's view has "the clear tendency of the rationalist system" which is "to disparage the means of grace." Wilson quotes from Warfield's famous book, *The Plan of Salvation*, to prove his point of how much of a rationalist and reductionist Warfield is in his stance against sacerdotalism:

23. Ibid., 105.
24. Ibid.

Misunderstanding about what actually constitutes sacerdotalism is at the heart of the controversy over the objectivity of the covenant. I said earlier that rationalism has made considerable inroads into the conservative wing of the Reformed faith, and the clear tendency of this rationalism is a reductionistic one. Instead of a robust supernaturalism that applies to all of life (seen and understood by faith only), the clear tendency of the rationalist system is to disparage the means of grace. This tendency is seen in B.B. Warfield's book *The Plan of Salvation*, which is worth quoting on this point at length.

> . . . [I]t has yet been taught in a large portion of the Church (up to today in the larger portion of the Church), that God in working salvation does not operate upon the human soul directly but indirectly; that is to say, through instrumentalities which he has established as the means by which his saving grace is communicated to men. As these instrumentalities are committed to human hands for their administration, a human factor is thus intruded between the saving grace of God and its effective operation in the souls of men; and this human factor indeed, is made the determining factor in salvation. Against this Sacerdotal system, as it is appropriately called, the whole Protestant Church, in all its parts, Lutheran and Reformed, Calvinistic and Arminian, raises its passionate protest. *In the interests of the pure supernaturalism of salvation* it insists that God the Lord himself works by his grace immediately on the souls of men, and has not suspended any man's salvation upon the faithlessness or caprice of his fellows.[25]

Contrary to Wilson's charge of rationalism against Warfield's analysis on the means of grace, Warfield demonstrates that God "in working salvation" operates upon "the human soul directly," which is a legitimate theological argument against sacerdotalism. Sacerdotalists wrongly argue that God works indirectly through the instrumentalities of the means of grace in his working out of salvation. According to Warfield, sacerdotalists mistakenly conceive that God's saving grace is communicated to men "through instrumentalities" whereby God established them as the means of grace. In doing so, sacerdotalists elevate "a human factor," which may be "intruded between the saving grace of God and its effective operation

25. Ibid., 85–86.

in the souls of men." Sacerdotalists invite "this human factor" as "the determining factor in salvation." Resultantly, they fall into sacramental legalism, which is consistent with their theological system and outlook. As we have briefly explored Warfield's critique against sacerdotalism, we should understand how Warfield comprehensively and critically examined the theological problem of sacerdotalism. His point is that sacerdotalism is closely related to legalism in soteriology, inviting a "human factor" into the arena of salvation.

Based upon the aforementioned quotation, Wilson unfairly criticizes as though Warfield denied that "God uses *any means* to accomplish His purposes in salvation." Moreover, Wilson charges Warfield's concept of "pure supernaturalism" as "a refried Gnosticism, an invisible conduit from God to man, with no contact made with contaminating earthly, incarnational influences." He misinterprets Warfield's point that "God in working salvation" operates upon "the soul directly," not through the instrumentalities of the means of grace "as a claim that God is working 'apart from means.'" To be sure, however, Wilson misunderstands and misrepresents Warfield's understanding of the sacramental efficacy, reinterpreting it in the light of the Federal Visionists' concept of covenantal sacerdotalism and baptismal regeneration, which is closer to Rome than Calvin and the Westminster Standards:

> In other words, any view that says God uses *any means* to accomplish His purposes in salvation is a corrupted or impure supernaturalism. Of course, objections crowd to mind. What about the preaching of the gospel? Are all the external means that God uses to bring the gospel to lost men a charade? The gospel, missionaries, preaching, baptism, covenant nurture–are all these just a front operation for the *real* work of saving men, which is done by God directly, behind the scenes? What Warfield thought of as "pure supernaturalism" is actually closer to a refried Gnosticism, an invisible conduit from God to man, with no contact made with contaminating earthly, incarnational influences. It is telling that in Warfield's famous table illustrating all this, he has the sacerdotalists affirming their views concerning the Church and the "consistent" Calvinists affirming things about the elect.
>
> I quote Warfield at this point knowing that as a confessional Presbyterian he had to (and did) acknowledge that God established and used means of grace within the Church. I do not want to misrepresent him as overtly denying that there are means of grace. But I do want to argue that Warfield was being inconsistent

here. I take his insistence that God works "directly" on the human soul as a claim that God is working "apart from means." But elsewhere Warfield acknowledges that God uses such means of grace. But how is this not God working "directly?"[26]

However, Warfield denied baptismal regeneration because the dogma of baptismal regeneration is robbing off Christ's meritorious works as the mediator of the New Covenant. This is the reason why Warfield boldly rejected any kind of sacerdotalism, which gives credit to the contribution to personal salvation through the works of sacraments. In fact, Warfield offers one of the best critiques against different forms of sacerdotalism in the Reformed tradition. He argued that the Roman Catholic sacerdotalism conceives that God does not work "directly and immediately" for "the salvation of men." Rather, God executes his power of saving grace "through the mediation of the Church." Thus, Warfield summarized the central problem of the Roman Catholic sacerdotalism as follows:

> The sacerdotal principle finds very complete expression in the thoroughly developed and logically compacted system of the Church of Rome. According to this system God the Lord does nothing looking to the salvation of men directly and immediately: all that he does for the salvation of men he does through the mediation of the Church, to which, having endowed it with powers adequate to the task, he has committed the whole work of salvation.[27]

In the latter part of the nineteenth century, different forms of sacerdotalism were flouring. Observing these different forms, Warfield provided a very careful critique against them. For example, there was a growing consensus among Anglican writers "in the great Protestant Church of England" by which they gave credit "to the Church rather than directly to God for salvation." Thus, Warfield provided a very short but succinct critique against the Anglican form of sacerdotalism:

> The explanation of Christianity in terms of sacerdotalism not confined in our day to the old unreformed Church from which Protestantism broke forth, precisely that it might escape from dependence on the Church rather than on God alone in the matter of salvation. A very influential, (perhaps presently the most influential, and certainly to the onlooker, the most conspicuous) party in the

26. Ibid., 86.

27. Benjamin B. Warfield, *The Plan of Salvation* (Presbyterian Board of Publication, 1915: reprint, Avinger: Simpson Publishing Company, 1989), 50.

great Protestant Church of England, and, following it, large parties in its daughter Churches, have revived it in more or less completeness of expression and certainly with no hesitancy of assertion. It is common nowadays to hear men referred by Anglican writers to the Church rather than directly to God for salvation; and to have the Church defined for them as the "extension of the incarnation."[28]

Another from of sacerdotalism, according to Warfield, may be found in Confessional Lutheranism. Warfield argued that Confessional Lutheranism similar to Roman Catholicism, views that "the grace of salvation is conveyed to men in the means of grace, otherwise not." Therefore, Warfield summarized the Confessional Lutheran form of sacerdotalism as follows:

> A modified and much milder from of sacerdotalism is inherent in Confessional Lutheranism, and is continually rising to more or less prominence in certain phases of Lutheran thought, thus creating a high church party in the Lutheran Church also. It has been the boast of Lutheranism that it represents, in distinction from Calvinism, a "conservative reformation." The boast is justified, as on other grounds, so also on this, that it has incorporated into its confessional system the essence of the sacerdotalism which characterized the teaching of the old Church. Confessional Lutheranism, like Romanism, teaches that the grace of salvation is conveyed to men in the means of grace, otherwise not. But it makes certain modifications in the sacerdotal teaching which it took over from the old Church, and these modifications are of such a far-reaching character as to transform the whole system. We do not commonly hear in Lutheran sacerdotalism much of "the Church," which is the very *cor cordis* of Roman sacerdotalism: what we hear of instead is "the means of grace." Among these "means of grace" the main stress is not laid upon the sacraments, but on "the Word," which is defined as the chief "means of grace." And the means of grace are not represented as acting *ex opera operato* but it is constantly declared that they are effective only to faith.[29]

We need to be reminded that Warfield did not deny the efficacy of sacraments, richly promised in the Bible. Rather, he safeguarded "the Holy Spirit himself" as "the true agent of all gracious operations" in the execution of saving grace, which is severely hindered in the different forms of

28. Ibid., 59.
29. Ibid., 62.

sacerdotalism, including Confessional Lutheranism. Therefore, it is worth to quote Warfield's critique against the Confessional Lutheran form of sacerdotalism:

> But it remains sufficiently sacerdotal to confine the activities of saving grace to the means of grace, that is to say, to the Word and sacraments, and thus to interpose the means of grace between the sinner and his God. The central evil of sacerdotalism is therefore present in this scheme in its full manifestation, and wherever it is fully operative we find men exalting the means of grace and more or less forgetting the true agent of all gracious operations, the Holy Spirit Himself, in their absorption with the instrumentalities through which alone he is supposed to work. It is in a truly religious interest, therefore, that the Reformed, as over against the Lutherans, insist with energy that, important as are the means of grace, and honored as they must be by us because honored by God the Holy Spirit as the instruments by and through which he works grace in the hearts of men, yet after all the grace which he works by and through them he works himself not out of them but immediately out of himself, *extrinsecus accedens*.[30]

Here, we see that Warfield respects the proper place of sacraments as the means of grace, affirming sacramental efficacy while he warns the danger of different forms of sacerdotalism, which hinder the sovereign work of the Holy Spirit in the execution of saving grace for the elect. So, in the end, Warfield invited his readers to pay attention to "God the Holy Spirit" as "our gracious Saviour," abandoning unbiblical sacerdotalism:

> It is to break away from all this and to turn to God the Holy Spirit in humble dependence upon him as our gracious Saviour, our personal Lord and our holy Governor and Leader, that evangelicalism refuses to have anything to do with sacerdotalism and turns from all the instrumentalities of salvation to put its sole trust in the personal Saviour of the soul.[31]

As such, the Federal Visionists radically reinterpret baptismal efficacy, represented by Calvin and the Westminster Standards as though they affirmed baptismal regeneration. In doing so, the Federal Visionists fail to read Calvin's baptismal theology from the broader theological context whereby Calvin insisted that baptism not as the means of salvation

30. Ibid., 62–63.
31. Ibid., 65.

but as the means of grace necessarily denies the dogmatic assumption of baptismal regeneration. Moreover, baptismal regeneration cannot be maintained in Calvin's theology because he viewed water baptism as a sign or seal of the New Covenant or the covenant of grace, carefully avoiding both the Roman Catholic and the covenantal form of sacerdotalism, represented by the monocovenantalism of the Federal Vision.

REDEMPTIVE HISTORICAL REFUTATION AGAINST REBAPTISM

In the early church, the Donatists argued that "the force and value of the sacrament" depend upon "the worth of the minister." A similar argument was made by the Anabaptists during the Protestant Reformation. They denied the authenticity of baptism when believers received baptism "by impious and idolatrous men under the papal government." Similarly, the Anabaptists urged rebaptism, invalidating baptism, received by impious or wicked ministers:

> This argument neatly refutes the error of the Donatists, who measured the force and value of the sacrament by the worth of the minister. Such today are our Catabaptists, who deny that we have been duly baptized because we were baptized by impious and idolatrous men under the papal government. They therefore passionately urge rebaptism.[32]

32. Calvin, *Institutes*, 4.15.16. In the fourth century, there was a schismatic theological and practical movement. In its initial stage it was "a North African expression of a doctrine of the church." Originally, Donatus (313–47), the schismatic Bishop of Carthage in North Africa, led the movement. Donatism was influenced by "the teachings of Tertullian and Cyprian." Donatists, after the thought pattern of Donatus, insisted that "a priest's part in sacraments" is substantially important. They argued that a priest has to be "holy and in proper standing with the church for the sacrament to valid." So, Donatists denied that a priest in sacrament is "simply instrumental." As the chief anti-Donatist, Augustine maintained that a priest is "simply instrumental" in sacraments. In addition, Donatus argued that "the church was a visible society of the elect separate from the world" while Augustine developed the biblical concept of the church as "an invisible church within the visible." V. L. Walter, "Donatism," in *Evangelical Dictionary of Theology*, ed. Walter A. Elwell, (Grand Rapids: Baker, 1984), 329–30. For the rise and emergence of Donatism in the early church, see G. L. Bray, "Donatism," in *New Dictionary of Theology*, eds. Sinclair B. Ferguson and David F. Wright (Downers Grove: InterVarsity Press, 1988), 206.

For Calvin's comprehensive and critical engagement against the Anabaptists' theology and worldview, summarized in *The Schleitheim Confession*, see John Calvin, *Treatises Against the Anabaptists and Against the Libertines*, trans and ed. Benjamin Wirt Farley (Grand Rapids: Baker, 1982), 36–158.

Refuting the argument on rebaptism of the Anabaptists, Calvin, as a masterful redemptive historian, appealed to the redemptive history in which we find the Old Testament example in the Old Covenant that God did not allow second circumcision although the Israelites sometimes received circumcision under the impious and apostate priests. Calvin noted that we receive baptism "not into the name of any man," but into the name of the Triune God (Matt. 28:19). In that sense, Calvin continued to argue that baptism is not the baptism of man but "the baptism of God," so that "it surely had enclosed in itself, the promise of forgiveness of sins, mortification of the flesh, spiritual vivification, and participation in Christ," although believers receive baptism under the ministers who are impious and apostate. As such, Calvin argued against the Anabaptists from the perspective of redemptive historical theology by which he had a careful understanding of redemptive historical continuity between circumcision and baptism:

> Thus it was no hindrance to the Jews to be circumcised by impure and apostate priests; nor was the sign therefore void so that it had to be repeated, but it was a sufficient means by which to return to the real source.
>
> Their objection that baptism ought to be celebrated in the assemblies of the godly does not have the effect of extinguishing the whole force of what is only partially faulty. For when we teach what ought to be done in order that baptism may be pure and free of all defilement, we do not abolish God's ordinance, however idolaters may corrupt it. For when in ancient times circumcision was corrupted by many superstitions, it did not cease nevertheless to be regarded as a symbol of grace. And when Josiah and Hezekiah called out of all Israel those who had forsaken God [2 Kings, chs. 22; 23; 18]. They did not summon them to a second circumcision.[33]

Calvin went on to argue that the Old Testament Israelites under the Old Covenant violated the covenant although they received circumcision as "the symbol of the covenant" (*symbolum foederis*). In that religious context, God did not command second circumcision. Rather, he invited the covenant people of Israel to *repentance* although they were circumcised "by an impious and sacrilegious hand," urging them for "only conversion of heart." Likewise, Calvin insightfully refuted the idea of rebaptism by

---

33. Calvin, *Institutes*, 4.15.16.

the Anabaptists during the Protestant Reformation, applying the concepts of covenant and redemptive history:

> For this reason, when the Lord invites the Jewish people to repentance, he enjoins no circumcision upon those who (as we have said) were circumcised by an impious and sacrilegious hand and lived for a time entangled in the same impiety; but he urges only conversion of heart. However the covenant might be violated by them, the symbol of the covenant remained ever firm and inviolable by virtue of the Lord's institution. Therefore, on the sole condition of repentance they were restored into the covenant which God had once made with them in circumcision; and which, moreover, they had received at the hand of a covenant-breaking priest, and then done their utmost to defile and render ineffectual.[34]

Based upon the biblical evidence of apparent rebaptism by Paul in Acts 19:2–7, the Anabaptists justified rebaptism for those who were baptized under the Papal authority. The Anabaptists interpreted the statement, "They were baptized in the name of Jesus" of verse 5 as rebaptism by Paul. However, Calvin persuasively argued that it was not water rebaptism but "the baptism of the Holy Spirit" (*Baptismum Spiritus sancti*), which is "the visible graces of the Spirit" (*gratias Spiritus visibiles*) provided "through the laying on of hands." It is remarkable to know how Calvin refuted the Anabaptists' rebaptismal theology in the biblical theological context of Acts 19:2–7. Calvin rightly read the formula of "the baptism of the Holy Spirit" as the visible manifestation of the Holy Spirit, which was manifested on the Day of Pentecost as "the baptism of fire and of the Spirit" (*Baptismo ignis et Spiritus*) as anticipated in Acts 1:5 by the resurrected Jesus. A similar visible manifestation of "the baptism of the Holy Spirit" was poured out upon "Cornelius, his household, and kindred" through Peter in Acts 11:16:

> I admit, for my part, that it was the true baptism of John, and one and the same as the baptism of Christ, but I deny that they were rebaptized. What, then, do the words, "They were baptized in the name of Jesus," mean? Some interpret it to mean that they were only instructed with genuine doctrine by Paul; but I prefer to understand it more simply, that it is the baptism of the Holy Spirit, that is, the visible graces of the Spirit given through the laying on of hands. It is nothing new to signify these graces by the word

---

34. Ibid., 4.15.17.

"baptism." As on the Day of the Pentecost, the apostles are said to have recalled the words of the Lord about the baptism of fire and of the Spirit [Acts 1:5]. And Peter mentions that the same thing came to his memory when he had seen those graces poured upon Cornelius, his household, and kindred [Acts 11:16].[35]

After careful examination of the literary context of Acts 19:2–7, Calvin properly argued that the baptism in the name of Jesus in verse 5 and the descension of the Holy Spirit in verse 6 are "not telling two different things." Luke just follows "the form of narration familiar to the Hebrews." So, Luke's expression of descension of the Holy Spirit in verse 6 actually is the vivid description of "the nature of the baptism," already described in verse 5. Moreover, we find another strong case against rebaptism when we consider how the original apostles were not rebaptized, although they did not have true biblical doctrines when they were baptized as the disciples of Jesus:

> And this is not out of accord with what is afterward added: "When he had laid his hands upon them, the Holy Spirit descended upon them" [Acts 19:6 p.]. For Luke is not telling two different things, but he is following the form of narration familiar to the Hebrews, who first put forward a summary of the matter and then explain it more fully. Anyone can observe this from the context itself. For he says that when they had heard these things, they were baptized in Jesus' name. And when Paul had laid his hands upon them then, the Holy Spirit descended upon them. This latter expression describes the nature of the baptism.[36]

COVENANT AND INFANT BAPTISM

Calvin was sensitive towards the rise of the Radical Reformation, initiated and advocated by the Anabaptists during the Protestant Reformation. In response to the Anabaptists' rejection of infant baptism, Calvin used very harsh language. He considered the Anabaptists as "certain frantic spirits" (*phrenetici quidam spiritus*), locating their Radical Reformation as "mad ravings." It is evident that Calvin was considering "purity of doctrine" (*doctrinae puritatem*) and "the peace of church" (*ecclesiae pace*), which are the twin pillars of the well-being of the church:

35. Ibid., 4.15.18.
36. Ibid.

But since in this age certain frantic spirits have grievously disturbed the church over infant baptism, and do not cease their agitation, I cannot refrain from adding an appendix here to refrain their mad ravings. If this may perhaps seem too long to any man, let him, I pray, ponder with himself that, in such an important matter, we ought so to esteem purity of doctrine as well as the peace of the church that we must not fastidiously take exception to anything conducive to the achievement of both.[37]

Calvin illustrated some spiritual benefits for those who receive infant baptism. They may be "engrafted into the body of the church," which is the covenant community, a *visible church*. Moreover, when baptized children mature, they will have "an earnest zeal for worshipping God," reflecting their infant baptism as "a solemn symbol of adoption." In doing so, Calvin reminded us that we need to remember God's curse on people who withhold his children with "the symbol of the covenant":

Accordingly, let those who embrace the promise that God's mercy is to be extended to their children deem it their duty to offer them to the church to be sealed by the symbol of the mercy, and thereby to arouse themselves to a surer confidence, because they see with their very eyes the covenant of the Lord engraved upon the bodies of their children. On the other hand, the children receive some benefit from their baptism: being engrafted into the body of the church, they are somewhat more commanded to the other members. Then, when they have grown up, they are greatly spurred to an earnest zeal for worshipping God, by whom they were received as children through a solemn symbol of adoption before they were old enough to recognize him as Father. Finally, we ought to be greatly afraid of that threat, that God will wreak vengeance upon any man who disdains to mark his child with the symbol of the covenant; for by such contempt the proffered grace is refused, and, as it were, forsworn [Gen. 17:14].[38]

In response to the Anabaptists, Calvin repeatedly used harsh language against them. Calvin considered infant baptism as a "holy institution of God," labeling the Anabaptists as "certain mad beasts." In dealing

---

37. Ibid., 4.16.1. I would not endorse Calvin's inflammatory languages such as "certain frantic spirits," "mad ravings," and others against the Anabaptists although I consider the harsh theological and practical context of the sixteenth-century Protestant Reformation.

38. Ibid., 4.16.9.

with the Anabaptists, Calvin deepened his understanding of redemptive history, particularly the nature of redemptive historical continuity between the Old and New Covenants. Calvin properly indicated the central theological problem of the Anabaptists that they denied that the Israelites received the blessings of eternal life under the Old Covenant, limiting their blessing only to "the temporal life" because they did not read the redemptive historical continuity between the Old and New Covenants:

> In asserting a difference between the covenants, with what barbarous boldness do they dissipate and corrupt scripture! And not in one passage only—but so as to leave nothing safe or untouched! For they depict the Jews to us as so carnal that they are more like beasts than men. A covenant with them would not go beyond the temporal life, and the promises given them would rest in present and physical benefits. If this doctrine should obtain, what would remain save that the Jewish nation was satiated for a time with God's benefits (as men fatten a herd of swine in a sty), only to perish in eternal destruction? For when we mention circumcision and the promises attached to it, they at once reply that circumcision was a literal sign and its promises were carnal.[39]

In response to the Anabaptists' argument that the Israelites under the Old Covenant received circumcision and enjoyed *only* earthly and carnal blessings, Calvin effectively argued that they also received the spiritual blessings given to the believers who received baptism under the New Covenant. The Anabaptists insisted that "circumcision was a literal sign and its promises were carnal," denying the covenantal and redemptive historical continuity between the Old and New Covenants. Responding to the Anabaptists' rejection of the redemptive historical continuity, Calvin persuasively argued that "the primary promises" for the Israelites "under the Old Testament, were spiritual and referred to eternal life." In that time of redemptive history under the Old Testament, God certainly blessed the covenant people of the Israelites "by earthly and physical benefits" as a powerful means to confirm "the hope of the promises of spiritual things." In addition to spiritual and eternal blessings, God's promise to Abraham for "the possession of the Land of Canaan" was "a clear indication of his favor." As such, Calvin, as a great redemptive historical theologian, refuted the Anabaptists' contention that God did not promise any spiritual blessings, instituting circumcision in the Old Testament:

39. Ibid., 4.16.10.

It is quite certain that the primary promises, which contained that covenant ratified with the Israelites by God under the Old Testament, were spiritual and referred to eternal life; then, conversely, that they were received by the fathers spiritually (as was fitting) in order that they might gain there-from assurance of the life to come, to which they aspired with their whole heart. But meanwhile we do not deny that he attested his good will to them by earthly and physical benefits, by which we say that the hope of the promises of spiritual things was also confirmed. For example, when God promised eternal blessedness to his servant Abraham, in order to lay a clear indication of his favor before his eyes, he added another promise concerning the possession of the Land of Canaan [Gen. 15:1, 18]. In this way we ought to understand all the earthly promises given to the Jewish nation: that the spiritual promise, as the head to which they refer, should always hold the first place. And since I have treated these matters at some length in the difference between the New and Old Testaments, I now touch them more lightly.[40]

Balthasar Hubmaier,[41] a representative exponent of the Anabaptistic theology, insisted in his treatise *On the Christian Baptism of Believers* that infant children must be free from baptism "because of their age are not yet able to understand the mystery signified in it, namely spiritual regeneration, which cannot take place in earliest infancy." In that sense, Hubmaier and the Anabaptists argued that children must be regarded only "as children of Adam until they reach an appropriate age for the second birth," which is rebirth or regeneration. As such, the Anabaptists insisted the impossibility of infant children's "spiritual regeneration" (*spiritualis regeneration*). Countering the Anabaptists' argument, Calvin insightfully demonstrated his argument for the possibility of infant children's spiritual regeneration through biblical examples. John the Baptist was one of the representative examples of infant children's spiritual regeneration through the supernatural outworking of the Holy Spirit. Luke testifies that God "sanctified in his mother's womb" (*in matris utero sanctificavit*):

40. Ibid., 4.16.11.

41. For a brief analysis of Balthasar Hubmaier's life and thought as one of the leading exponents of the Radical Reformation during the Protestant Reformation in the sixteenth century, see J. C. Wenger, "Hubmaier, Balthasar," in *Evangelical Dictionary of Theology*, ed. Walter A. Elwell (Grand Rapids: Baker, 1984), 535.

And to silence such gainsayers, God provided a proof in John the Baptist, whom he sanctified in his mother's womb [Luke 1:15]—something he could do in others. And they do not gain anything here by this mocking evasion—that it was only once, and that from this one instance it does not immediately follow that the Lord usually deals thus with infants. But we are not arguing in this way either. Our purpose is solely to show that they unjustly and wickedly shut God's power within these narrow limits to which it does not permit itself to be confined. Their other quibble has no more weight. They claim that, in accordance with the usual mode of expression of Scripture, the phrase "from the womb" is merely the equivalent of saying "from childhood." But we can clearly see that the angel, when he declared this to Zechariah, meant something else, namely, that John would, while yet unborn, be filled with the Holy Spirit. Let us not attempt, then, to impose a law upon God to keep him from sanctifying whom he pleases, just as he sanctified this child, inasmuch as his power is not lessened.[42]

In addition, Calvin argued that Christ was also sanctified by the almighty and mysterious works of the Holy Spirit "from earliest infancy in order that he might sanctify in himself his elect from every age without distinction." As such, Calvin argued that Christ's conception by the Holy Spirit is an example of infants who experience the spiritual blessings of regeneration and sanctification against the Anabaptists' rejection:

Thus, he was conceived of the Holy Spirit in order that, in the flesh taken, fully imbued with the holiness of the Spirit, he might impart that holiness to us. If we have in Christ the most perfect example of all the graces which God bestows upon his children, in this respect also he will be for us a proof that the age of infancy is not utterly averse to sanctification.[43]

Furthermore, Calvin rightly argued that the elect, without exception, experience the spiritual blessings of regeneration and sanctification "by the Spirit of God" in the present life. Mentioning 1 Peter 1:23, Hubmaier and other Anabaptists insisted that there is "no regeneration except from incorruptible seed," which is "from God's Word." However, Calvin rightly argued that infant children may be "regenerated by God's power" (*Dei virtute regenerari infants*) without hearing the Word of God:

42. Calvin, *Institutes*, 4.16.17.
43. Ibid., 4.16.18.

Howsoever this may be, we consider it incontrovertible that no one of the elect is called from the present life before being sanctified and regenerated by the Spirit of God. They counter with the objection that the Spirit in Scripture recognizes no regeneration except from incorruptible seed, that is, from God's Word [1 Peter 1:23]. In this they wrongly interpret Peter's statement, which has reference only to believers who had been taught by the preaching of the gospel. We indeed admit that to such persons the Word of the Lord is the only seed of spiritual regeneration; but we deny the inference from this that infants cannot be regenerated by God's power, which is an easy and ready to him as it is incomprehensible and wonderful to us. Besides, it would be an unsafe argument that would take from the Lord the power to make himself known to them in any way he pleases.[44]

Rejecting infant baptism, Hubmaier and other Anabaptists asserted that "Baptism is a sacrament of repentance and of faith" (*Batismum poentientiae ac fidei sacramentum esse*). Because infants cannot repent and have faith, they argued that we should not admit "infants into the fellowship of baptism, lest its meaning be made empty and fleeting." In response to the Anabaptists' argument, Calvin reasoned the validity of infant baptism through the redemptive historical continuity between circumcision and baptism whereby God commanded circumcision to the infant males of the covenant family, although circumcision was "also sign of repentance" and "the seal of the righteousness of faith." In doing so, Calvin carefully insisted that infant children may be baptized into "future repentance and faith":

But these darts are aimed more at God than at us. For it is very clear from many testimonies of Scripture that circumcision was also a sign of repentance [Jer. 4:4; 9:25; cf. Deut. 10:16; 30:6]. Then Paul calls it the seal of the righteousness of faith [Rom. 4:11]. Therefore, let a reason be required of God himself why he commanded it to be impressed on the bodies of infants. For since baptism and circumcision are in the same case, our opponents cannot give anything to one without conceding it to the other. If they have recourse to their usual way out, that the age of infancy then symbolized spiritual infants, their path is already blocked. We therefore say that, since God communicated circumcision to infants as a sacrament of repentance and of faith, it does not seem absurd if they are now made participants in baptism—unless men choose to rage openly at God's institution . . . To sum up, this ob-

44. Ibid.

jection can be solved without difficulty: infants are baptized into future repentance and faith, and even though these have not yet been formed in them, the seed of both lies hidden within them by the secret working of the Spirit.[45]

In response to the Anabaptists' rejection of infant baptism, Calvin went back to the original context of the Abrahamic Covenant in which God instituted the sacrament of circumcision for the covenant community. Reflecting on the Abrahamic Covenant, Calvin argued that God required faith and repentance before the adult Abraham received circumcision as a sign of the covenant. But Isaac, as the child of Abraham, received circumcision before he had faith and repentance "by hereditary right, according to the form of the promise":

> The Lord also, when he adopts Abraham, does not begin with circumcision, meanwhile concealing what he means by that sign, but first declares what the covenant is that he intends to make with him [Gen. 15:1]; then after Abraham has faith in the promise, the Lord makes him partaker in the sacrament [Gen. 17:11]. Why, in Abraham's case, does the sacrament follow faith, but in Isaac, his son, precede all understanding? Because it is fair that he who as a grown man is received into the fellowship of the covenant to which he had been till then a stranger should learn its conditions beforehand; but it is not the same with his infant son. The latter by hereditary right, according to the form of the promise, is already included within the covenant from his mother's womb. Or (to put the matter more clearly and briefly), if the children of believers are partakers in the covenant without the help of understanding, there is no reason why they should be barred from the sign merely because they cannot swear to the provisions of the covenant. Surely this is why God sometimes affirm that children who arise from the Israelites have been begotten and born to him [Ezek. 16:20; 23:37]. For without doubt he counts as his children the children of those to whose seed he promised to be a father [Gen. 17:7].[46]

Interpreting Ephesians 2:12, Calvin attested that adults, who grew up "outside the covenant" should not have the privilege to receive "the badge of baptism unless they first have faith and repentance, which alone can give access to the society of the covenant." However, infants who are born in the covenant family, having the right "into the inheritance of the

45. Ibid., 4.16.20.
46. Ibid., 4.16.24.

covenant," have a right to receive baptism. Likewise, Calvin persuasively argued the biblical theological reason for both adult baptism and infant baptism in light of the concept of covenant continuity:

> But he who is an unbeliever, sprung from impious parents, is reckoned as alien to the fellowship of the covenant until he is joined to God through faith. No wonder, then, if he does not partake in the sign when what is signified would be fallacious and empty in him! Paul also writes to this effect: that the Gentiles, so long as they were immersed in their idolatry, were outside the covenant [Eph. 2:12]. The whole matter, unless I am mistaken, can be clearly disclosed in this brief statement. Those who embrace faith in Christ as grown men, since they were previously strangers to the covenant, are not to be given the badge of baptism unless they first have faith and repentance, which alone can give access to the society of the covenant. But those infants who derive their origin from Christians, as they have been born directly into the inheritance of the covenant, and are expected by God, are thus to be received into baptism. To this ought to be referred the Evangelist's statement that those who confessed their sins were baptized by John [Matt. 3:6]. We think that this example ought to be observed today. For if a Turk should offer himself for baptism, we could not easily baptize him unless he gave a confession satisfactory to the church.[47]

Hubmaier and other Anabaptists appealed to John 3:5 as biblical evidence that the presupposition of water baptism is regeneration. They argued this because infants are incapable of experiencing spiritual regeneration, there is no theological and biblical reason to baptize infants. In response to the Anabaptists, Calvin wonderfully portrayed his biblical theological reasoning that John 3:5 is not a verse about water baptism after regeneration but spiritual baptism in the Holy Spirit, which is a prerequisite for entering into the Kingdom of God:

> First, they are deceived in thinking that because they hear the word "water," baptism is mentioned in this passage. For after having explained the corruption of nature to Nicodemus and taught him that men must be reborn, because Nicodemus was dreaming of physical rebirth, Christ indicates here the way in which God regenerates us, namely, through water and the Spirit. It is as if he said: through the Spirit, who in cleansing and watering faithful souls performs the function of water. I therefore simply under-

47. Ibid.

stand "water and Spirit" as "Spirit, who is water." And this is no new expression, for it agrees completely with what is in the third chapter of Matthew: "He who follows me, is he who baptizes in the Holy Spirit and in fire" [Matt. 3:11; Luke 3:16; cf. John 1:26, 33]. Therefore, just as to baptize by the Holy Spirit and by fire is to confer the Holy Spirit, who in regeneration has the function and nature of fire, so to be reborn of water and the Spirit is but to receive that power of the Spirit, which does in the soul what water does in the body. I know that others interpret it differently, but I do not doubt that this is the real meaning, because Christ's purpose is only to teach that all who aspire to the Kingdom of Heaven must put off their own nature.[48]

Meanwhile, the Federal Visionists advocate the concept of baptismal regeneration. To be consistent with their own covenantal theological paradigm, they also apply it to the arena of paedobaptism. Interestingly, Rich Lusk argues that Calvin's theology on paedobaptism is inconsistent in respect to baptismal regeneration. According to Lusk, Calvin sometimes affirmed that infant children may receive the spiritual blessings of "regeneration and justification to the moment of baptism." In another instance, Calvin argued that infant children may be baptized into "future repentance and faith," putting the emphasis on "baptism's prospective efficacy." Lusk writes as follows:

Calvin's position reveals some of the complexities involved. At times, Calvin speaks as though covenant children already belong to God from the moment of conception; their baptism, then, simply ratifies their pre-existing membership in God's covenant. At other times, as we have already seen, he ties regeneration and justification to the moment of baptism. Infants receive an age appropriate portion of that grace that will later be theirs in a fuller fashion. In still other places, he speaks of baptizing infants into "future repentance and faith" (even though he acknowledges the seed of both is already present in the infant due to the Spirit's secret work). In this context, Calvin puts the emphasis on baptism's prospective efficacy, looking ahead to the child's spiritual maturity. There is an

48. Ibid., 4.16.25. Beside Hubmaier, Servetus was another representative Anabaptists' figure who Calvin specifically responded to against his theological logic. Servetus wrote his view against infant baptism in his treatise, the *Christianismi restitutio* in 1553. Calvin in his *Institutes* argued point-by-point against Servetus' rejection of infant baptism, making a careful comparison and contrast between baptism and the Lord's Supper as to why God requires infant baptism while he withholds the Lord's Supper for children. Cf. Ibid., 4.16.31.

element of truth in each of these positions, though Calvin never quite showed how his various statements fit together into a total package. Perhaps we can do so for him.[49]

Lusk argues that infant baptism is a means of "union with Christ, new life in the Spirit, and covenant membership in the family of God." In doing so, he views water baptism as the means of *union with Christ*, which is unknown to Calvin, as well as the Westminster Standards. At the same time, Lusk insists that baptism is not "absolutely necessary for salvation in each and every case. It is *ordinarily* necessary, but there are exceptions, such as when a child of the covenant dies before baptism was possible." In this manner, Lusk tries to maintain his dogmatic presupposition of the baptismal regeneration:

> This seems to be the full picture: the covenant child from the moment of conception is not without a promise from God even though the covenantal blessings have not yet been bestowed upon him, properly speaking. We might say the unbaptized child of the covenant is *betrothed* to the Lord from conception onwards. But the *marriage*—that is, the actual covenant bonding—takes place at baptism. Or, to put it in more theological terms, God is already in the process of drawing the child to himself from the moment of conception. The examples of David (Ps. 22:9–10) and John the Baptist (Luke 1:41) show God's *in utero*, pre-sacramental work. But this work isn't complete until the child receives the sign of initiation. The child remains in a liminal, transitional state until then. The threshold into union with Christ, new life in the Spirit, and covenant membership in the family of God is actually crossed when the child is baptized. From baptism forward, the child is expected to grow in faith and repentance unto maturity as he is nurtured in the Church and in the home.
>
> This organic model allows us to do full justice to biblical teaching on baptismal efficacy, but also keeps us from saying that baptism is *absolutely* necessary for salvation in each and every case. It is *ordinarily* necessary, but there are exceptions, such as when a child of the covenant dies before baptism was possible.[50]

---

49. Lusk, "Paedobaptism and Baptismal Efficacy," 108. For the comprehensive discussion of infant baptism in relation to baptismal regeneration from the perspective of monocovenantalism by Lusk, see Rich Lusk, *Paedofaith: A Primer on the Mystery of Infant Salvation and a Handbook for Covenant Parents* (Monroe: Athanasius Press, 2005).

50. Lusk, "Paedobaptism and Baptismal Efficacy," 108–9.

Likewise, falsely affirming baptismal regeneration from Calvin's theology, Lusk insists that infant baptism is a means of "union with Christ," which is a representative component of covenantal sacerdotalism. To be consistent with the dogmatic assumption of baptismal regeneration, Lusk further elaborates his covenantal sacerdotalism, arguing that infant baptism is not only a means of "union with Christ" but also "an instrument of justification and regeneration":

> So our children belong to God before baptism and thus have a right to baptism. And yet this does not make baptism a mere symbol of a preexisting relationship. It retains its efficacy as an instrument of justification and regeneration. For Calvin, neither side of this tension can be given up: our children belong to God at conception; our children are enrolled in God's family at baptism. Calvin seemed rather satisfied to allow the paradox to go unresolved.[51]

We, however, face a major theological confusion when we deal with the baptismal theology of the Federal Vision. The Federal Visionists inject their view of baptismal regeneration into the theologies of Calvin, as well as the Westminster Standards. Lusk falsely argues that "the *ordinary necessity* of baptism for salvation is simply the teaching of the Westminster standards," mentioning Shorter Catechism 85 and the Confession 25.2 and 28.1.[52] However, the Westminster divines neither described nor af-

---

51. Lusk, *Paedofaith*, 45.

52. Lusk, "Paedobaptism and Baptismal Efficacy," 125. Unlike Lusk's claim, the Westminster divines did not maintain baptism as "the ordinary necessity for salvation," affirming baptismal regeneration in the Westminster Confession of Faith 28.1 and the Shorter Catechism Q & A 85 although they used the word, the sacraments as "effectual means of salvation." Rather, they affirmed baptism as the means of grace to adopt "into the visible Church; but also to be unto a sign and seal of the covenant of grace, of his ingrafting into Christ, of regeneration, of remission of sins, and of his giving up unto God, through Jesus Christ, to walk in newness of life." And they affirmed that God requires us to have "faith in Jesus Christ" and "repentance unto life" to avoid "the wrath and curse of God": "1. Baptism is a sacrament of the New Testament, ordained by Jesus Christ, not only for the solemn admission of the party baptized into the visible church, but also to be to him a sign and seal of the covenant of grace, of his ingrafting into Christ, of regeneration, of remission of sins, and of his giving up unto God through Jesus Christ, to walk in newness of life: Which sacrament is, by Christ's own appointment, to be continued in his church until the end of the world (WCF, 28.1).

Q. 85. What doth God require of us, that we may escape his wrath and curse due to us for sin?

A. To escape the wrath and curse of God due to us for sin, God requireth of us faith in Jesus Christ, repentance unto life, with the diligent use of all the outward means whereby

firmed "the ordinary necessity of baptism for salvation" in the Westminster Standards as Lusk argues. Rather, in fact, the Westminster divines explained that "there is no ordinary possibility of salvation" outside of "the visible church":

1. The catholic or universal church, which is invisible, consists of the whole number of the elect that have been, are, or shall be gathered into one, under Christ the Head thereof; and is the spouse, the body, the fullness of Him that filleth all in all (WCF, 25.1).

2. The visible church, which is also catholic or universal under the Gospel (not confined to one nation, as before under the law), consists of all those throughout the world that profess the true religion, together with their children; and is the kingdom of the Lord Jesus Christ, the house and family of God, out of which there is no ordinary possibility of salvation (WCF, 25.2).

The Westminster divines made a clear distinction between the invisible and visible churches, which is very crucial for the biblical view of the doctrine of church and sacraments. In doing so, they were aware that water baptism is not the ordinary necessity for salvation but a sign or seal of the covenant of grace. As such, the Westminster divines emphasized the importance of the visible church "out of which there is no ordinary possibility of salvation."[53]

Christ communicateth to us the benefits of redemption (SC, Q&A 85)."

53. The Westminster divines carefully noted that the sacraments become "means of salvation" *only* "by the working of the Holy Ghost, and the blessing of Christ" in the Larger Catechism Q. and A. 161 and the Shorter Catechism Q. and A. 19. However, we must be careful because the Westminster divines did not mean that they approved and advocated the doctrine of baptismal regeneration when they stated sacraments as "means of salvation." Rather, God can use sacraments as "means of salvation" through the sovereign work of the Holy Spirit, accompanying the proclamation of the word in his sovereign time and power. And the elect only may receive rich spiritual blessings through faith, promised in sacraments: "Q. 161. How do the sacraments become effectual means of salvation? A. The sacraments become effectual means of salvation, not by any power in themselves, or any virtue derived from the piety or intention of him by whom they are administered, but only by the working of the Holy Ghost, and the blessing of Christ, by whom they are instituted (LC, Q & A.161).

Q. 91. How do the sacraments become effectual means of salvation? A. The sacraments become effectual means of salvation, and not from any virtue in them, or in him that doth administer them; but only by the blessing of Christ, and the working of his Spirit in them that by faith receive them (SC, Q & A 91)." Furthermore, the Westminster divines carefully noted that "the word, sacraments, and prayer" as the means of grace become "effectual to the elect for their salvation." In doing so, they did not mean to affirm the

The Federal Visionsts advocate the concept of baptismal regeneration, which is neither biblical nor Reformational as we have already explored. At the same time, they teach that water baptism is a sacramental means to be united with Christ. But, they also teach that baptized children, although they are already regenerated and sanctified with the covenantal blessings of union with Christ, may fall from grace through apostasy. Lusk writes as follows:

> True, baptized children can renounce their Father and become prodigals; they can reject Jesus as their Husband and become adulterers. But having once passed through the waters of baptism, however unfaithful their actions are to that newly granted baptismal identity, they are still the actions of baptized persons. They have been sanctified by the blood of the covenant, even if they later choose to that blood and covenant (Heb. 10:29). Baptism is an act with eternal consequences for the faithful and the unfaithful. Covenant members who fall from grace can only expect God's harshest judgment. Just as the promises of salvation are for us and for our children, so the warnings of apostasy are for us and for our children as well.[54]

The Federal Vision's theological analysis on infant baptism has been shadowed by their monocovenantalism, falsely affirming baptismal regeneration. In doing so, they inject their view of baptismal regeneration into the theologies of Calvin and the Westminster Standards. Once again, their analysis on baptismal regeneration is an affirmation that they hold covenantal sacerdotalism, which is not compatible to neither Calvin nor the Westminster Standards.

SUMMARY

We have found that Calvin did not affirm baptismal regeneration in his treatise on baptismal theology. Calvin's concept of the baptism as "a sign and seal of the covenant of grace" was well adopted in the Confessional

---

dogmatic assumption of baptismal regeneration. Rather, God uses the means of grace to bestow rich spiritual blessings through the sovereign work of the Holy Spirit when the elect accept them by faith: "Q. 154. What are the outward means whereby Christ communicates to us the benefits of his mediation? A. The outward and ordinary means whereby Christ communicates to his church the benefits of his mediation, are all his ordinances; especially the word, sacraments, and prayer; all which are made effectual to the elect for their salvation" (LC, Q&A 154).

54. Lusk, "Paedobaptism and Baptismal Efficacy," 112.

statement as we see in the Westminster Standards. I have argued that baptism as the sign of the covenant in the theologies of Calvin and the Westminster Standards necessarily exclude baptismal regeneration in Calvin and the Westminster Standards.

However, the Federal Visionists have falsely argued that Calvin and the Westminster Standards taught and affirmed baptismal regeneration. I have indicated that by injecting baptismal regeneration into Calvin and the Westminster Standards, the Federal Visionists also unfairly criticized Warfield's denial of baptismal regeneration as rationalism.

Calvin as a great redemptive historical theologian defended infant baptism, refuting the Anabaptists' argument against infant baptism from the perspective of redemptive historical continuity between the Old and New Covenants. Meanwhile, the Federal Visionists reinterpret infant baptism in light of their monocovenantal dogmatic assumption, which is baptismal regeneration. Pushing it further, the Federal Visionists locate infant baptism as a sacramental means of union with Christ, which is unknown to Calvin and the Westminster Standards.

Now, let us focus on Calvin's concept of covenant and Eucharist in his own Reformation context, critically engaging with the Federal Vision if it is necessary.

5

Covenant and Eucharist

CALVIN SELF-CONSCIOUSLY VIEWED THE Lord's Supper as the sign and seal of the New Covenant in his unpacking of the Eucharistic theology in his debate against the Schoolmen's transubstantiation and the Lutheran consubstantiation. In doing so, he closely examined the Lord's Supper in light of redemptive historical and covenantal continuity and discontinuity between the Old and New Covenants, as well as the sign and seal of the New Covenant or the covenant of grace in his depiction of the spiritual presence view. Calvin's careful reading of redemptive historical and covenantal continuity and discontinuity enabled him to make a conclusion that infant children are not invited to the Lord's Supper because they are not capable to discern themselves, having faith and love.

Meanwhile, the Federal Visionists endorse paedocommunion, exclusively emphasizing redemptive historical and covenantal continuity to be consistent with their monocovenantalism. In doing so, they fail to read correctly the decisive Pauline passage, which clearly goes against paedocommunion as seen in 1 Corinthians 11:21–33.

SPIRITUAL PRESENCE AGAINST THE SCHOOLMEN'S TRANSUBSTANTIATION

Calvin tried to make a concrete balance between "physical signs" and "spiritual truth" in his analysis and understanding of the Eucharistic theology. He demonstrated a constant consciousness of this balance in his defense of the exalted Christ's spiritual presence in the Eucharist against the Schoolmen's unbiblical notion of transubstantiation. In this manner, Calvin emphasized the importance of this harmony before he proceeded the discussion on the theological problem of transubstantiation as follows:

I therefore say (what has always been accepted in the church and is today taught by all of sound opinion) that the sacred mystery of the Supper consists in two things: physical signs, which, thrust before our eyes, represent to us, according to our feeble capacity, things invisible; and spiritual truth, which is at the same time represented and displayed through the symbols themselves . . . The signification is contained in the promises, which are, so to speak, implicit in the sign. I call Christ with his death and resurrection the matter, or substance. But by effect I understand redemption, righteousness, sanctification, and eternal life, and all the other benefits Christ gives to us.[1]

Regarding the Schoolmen's view of transubstantiation as unbiblical, Calvin was very critical, arguing that they are the instruments of Satan. Mentioning Peter Lombard's view on transubstantiation, represented in *Sentences*,[2] Calvin insisted that Christ's glorified body will be contained in the realm of heaven until his return as a final judge as proclaimed by Peter in Acts 3:21 after the Pentecostal Event:

And first we must not dream of such a presence of Christ in the sacrament as the craftsmen of the Roman court have fashioned— as if the body of Christ, by a local presence, were put there to be touched by the hands, to be chewed by the teeth, and swallowed by the mouth. For Pope Nicholas dictated this form of recantation to Berengarius. But Peter Lombard, even though he toils hard to explain away this absurdity, inclines rather more to a divergent opinion.

For as we do not doubt that Christ's body is limited by the general characteristics common to all human bodies, and is contained in heaven (where it was once for all received) until Christ return in judgment [Acts 3:21], so we deem it utterly unlawful to draw it

---

1. Calvin, *Institutes*, 4.17.11.

2. Peter Lombard (1100–1159) was one of the most influential theologians in the medieval Church. Especially, his magnum opus, *Four Books of Sentences* (*Sententiarum Libri Quatuor*) became a very influential theological textbook for the Roman Catholics "until the time of the Reformation and beyond." Lombard broke new ground in the sacramental theology. Perhaps, he was the first theologian to list seven sacraments, which have been the standard view of the Roman Catholic sacramental theology. In addition, he argued that a sacrament is not only "a visible sign of an invisible grace" after Augustine but also "the effective *cause* of that grace." Cf. A. N. S. Lane, "Lombard, Peter," in *New Dictionary of Theology*, eds. Sinclair B. Ferguson and David F. Wright (Downers Grove: InterVarsity Press, 1988), 396–97.

back under these corruptible elements or to imagine it to be present everywhere.[3]

Rejecting the concept of transubstantiation, Calvin insisted that Christ bestows spiritual benefits, promised in the Bible "through his Spirit so that we may be made one in body, spirit, and soul with him." As such, we are joined "in unity" through "the Spirit of Christ," who is a channel by which believers receive all the spiritual blessings. "The radiance of Christ's Spirit" imparts to us the communion of Christ's body and blood. Meditating on Scripture, Calvin noted that believers' participation with Christ depends solely upon the power of the Spirit. He appealed to Paul arguing that Christ does not dwell with us carnally but *spiritually* as he boldly states that "Christ dwells in us only through his Spirit" in Romans 8:9. He furthermore clarified that Christ's spiritual dwelling with believers does not take away "the communion of his flesh and blood":

> And there is no need of this for us to enjoy a participation in it, since the Lord bestows this benefit upon us through his Spirit so that we may be made one in body, spirit, and soul with him. The bond of this connection is therefore the Spirit of Christ, with whom we are joined in unity, and is like a channel through all that Christ himself is and has conveyed to us. For if we see that the sun, shedding its beams upon the earth, casts its substance in some measure upon it in order to beget, nourish, and give growth to its offspring—why should the radiance of Christ's Spirit be less in order to impart to us the communion of his flesh and blood which we are now discussing [Rom. 8:9], but teaches that the Spirit alone causes us to possess Christ completely and have him dwelling in us.[4]

During the Protestant Reformation, the Roman church fought bitterly to defend the medieval doctrine of transubstantiation against the Reformers. Calvin called the doctrine as "fictitious transubstantiation" (*fictitia illa transsubstantiatio*). He argued that the Schoolmen's doctrine of transubstantiation despises "not only Scripture but even the consensus of the ancient church." Examining the concept of "conversion" in the early church in relation to the doctrine of the presence of Christ in the Eucharist, represented by Tertullian in his treatise on *Against Marcion*, Calvin noted that their intention is not to wipe out "the substance in the outward sign," but to inform that the bread in the Lord's Supper is very different from

---

3. Calvin, *Institutes*, 4.17.12.

4. Ibid.

"common bread, and is now something else." Furthermore, the early church fathers noted that the Lord's Supper is composed of "two parts, the earthly and the heavenly." They did not confuse or mix the two parts, which are fundamentally important for the biblical Eucharistic theology:

> From this proceeds that fictitious transubstantiation for which today they fight more bitterly than for all the other articles of their faith. For the first fabricators of this local presence could not explain how Christ's body might be mixed with the substance of bread without many absurdities immediately cropping up. They therefore had to take refuge in the fiction that a conversion of the bread into the body takes place; not that the body is properly made from the bread, but because Christ, to hide himself under the figure, annihilates its substance.
>
> But it is wonderful how they fell to such a point of ignorance, even of folly, that, despising not only Scripture but even the consensus of the ancient church, they unveiled that monster.
>
> Indeed, I admit that some of the old writers used the term "conversion" sometimes, not because they intended to wipe out the substance in the outward sign, but to teach that the bread dedicated to the mystery is far different from common bread, and is now something else. But they all everywhere clearly proclaim that the Sacred Supper consists of two parts, the earthly and the heavenly; and they interpret the earthly part to be indisputably bread and wine.[5]

In his rejection of the Schoolmen's doctrine of transubstantiation, Calvin noted that the doctrine did not have historical ground to be supported by the ancient church, but rather it was innovated by the medieval church whereby the doctrine has been corrupted significantly. Calvin noted that "the ancient writers" correctly recognized that "the sacred symbols of the Supper are bread and wine," although they said that "in consecration a secret conversion takes place." However, Calvin emphasized that they did not mean "by this that the elements have been annihilated" because bread and wine are "the spiritual food and drink of the soul." In doing so, Calvin found a *radical discontinuity* between the early and medieval churches in the development of the doctrine of transubstantiation:

> Surely, whatever our opponents may prate, it is plain that to confirm this doctrine they lack the support of antiquity, which they often dare oppose to God's clear Word. For transubstantiation was

5. Ibid., 4.17.14.

devised not so long ago; indeed, not only was it unknown to those better ages when the purer doctrine of religion still flourished, but even when that purity already was somewhat corrupted. There is no one of the ancient writers who does not admit in clear words that the sacred symbols of the Supper are bread and wine, even though, as has been said, they sometimes distinguish them with various titles to enhance the dignity of the mystery. For because they say that in consecration a secret conversion takes place, so that there is now something other than bread and wine, as I have just observed, they do not mean by this that the elements have been annihilated, but rather that they now have to be considered of a different class from common foods intended solely to feed the stomach, since in them is set forth the spiritual food and drink of the soul. This we do not deny.[6]

Calvin demonstrated a redemptive historical aspect of the Lord's Supper, countering the Schoolmen's idea of transubstantiation. He saw a redemptive historical significance of "the water gushing from the rock in the desert," which ultimately points to spiritual blessings in Christ (Ex.17:6). The fresh water from the rock was "a token and sign of the same thing" as wine points to and represents Jesus' blood. With redemptive historical consciousness, Calvin noted that the Israelites drank "the same spiritual drink" like believers under the New Covenant as Paul reinterprets it from a redemptive historical perspective in 1 Corinthians 10:4. Reflecting on the Israelites' episode of drinking water from the rock in the wilderness, Calvin concluded that no conversion takes place when "earthly elements" are used for "a spiritual use" because they are "seals of the promises":

> This will appear more clearly from the example of a similar sacrament. The water gushing from the rock in the desert [Ex. 17:6] was for the fathers a token and sign of the same thing as wine

---

6. Ibid. Godfrey pointedly recognizes that Calvin refuted the Roman Catholic transubstantiation as the Medieval innovation, which does not have the support from the writers of the ancient Church: "Calvin recognized that this doctrine of transubstantiation was one 'for which today they fight more bitterly than for all the other articles of their faith' (4.17.14). Calvin rejected their view utterly, showing that it was not taught in the ancient church. He labeled their novelty 'magic' and pointed out that by it they destroyed any analogy to baptism. Even Rome did not claim that the water of baptism was turned into the blood of Christ (4.17.15). Rome also did not understand the work of the Spirit in the Lord's Supper as the one who truly united the believer with Christ (4.17.16)." Godfrey, "Calvin, Worship, and the Sacraments," 382.

represents for us in the supper. For Paul teaches that they drank the same spiritual drink [1 Cor. 10:4]. And the watering place was common to people's beasts of burden and cattle. From this it is easily inferred that in earthly elements, when they are applied to a spiritual use, no other conversion occurs than with respect to men, inasmuch as to them they are seals of the promises.[7]

Calvin pointed out the importance of lifting up believers' hearts, minds, and souls to the realm of heaven where the exalted Christ reigns in both the visible and invisible worlds. He argued that the underlining theological principles of transubstantiation overlook the crucial importance of the heavenward mindset and theology. Likewise, Calvin emphatically noted that the central problem of the idea of transubstantiation undermines that "the spiritual reality is joined to bread and wine in this mystery":

> Moreover, since it is God's plan (as I often reiterate) to lift us to himself, by appropriate means, those who call us indeed to Christ, but to Christ hidden invisibly under bread, wickedly frustrate his plan by their obstinacy. For it is not possible for the human mind, leaping the infinite spaces, to reach beyond heaven itself to Christ. What nature denied to them they tried to correct by a more harmful remedy, so that by remaining on earth we may need no heavenly nearness of Christ. Here, then, is the necessity that compelled them transmute Christ's body.
>
> Even in Bernard's time, although a blunter manner of speaking had been adopted, transubstantiation was not yet recognized. And in all ages before, this comparison flitted about on everybody's lips, that the spiritual reality is joined to bread and wine in this mystery.[8]

As Calvin had very critical mindset against the Schoolmen's transubstantiation, he was equally critical to the Lutheran concept of consubstantiation, which is a theological byproduct of the notion of ubiquity. Now, let us turn our discussion to Calvin's critique against the Lutheran idea of consubstantiation.

7. Calvin, *Institutes*, 4.17.15.
8. Ibid.

SPIRITUAL PRESENCE AGAINST THE LUTHERAN CONSUBSTANTIATION

Joachim Westphal and other Lutheran figures had a vicious theological battle against Calvin in respect to the mode of the presence of Christ in the Eucharist. Calvin argued that the Lutheran concept of consubstantiation is a theological byproduct of literal interpretation whereby it requires figurative interpretation. Interestingly, Calvin noticed a distinction between moderate and literal views among the Lutherans. According to Calvin, the moderate view was the view in which they believed that "the body of Christ is with the bread, in the bread, and under the bread" while literal viewers argued that "the bread is the body":

> As for those who leave bread in the Supper and affirm that it is the body of Christ, much difference exists among them. Those who speak more moderately, although they insist upon the letter, "This is my body," still afterward abandon their rigor and say that it amounts to the same thing as that the body of Christ is with the bread, in the bread, and under the bread. Of the thing itself, which they affirm, I have already made some mention, and I must soon say more about it. Now I am only discussing the words, by which they say they are constrained not to allow the bread to be called the body, because it is the sign of the body. But if they shun every metaphor, why do they leap from Christ's simple designation to widely divergent phrases of their own? For there is a great difference between "the bread is the body" and "the body is with the bread." But they saw that this simple proposition, "the bread is the body," was untenable. Consequently, they tried to wriggle out of their difficulty by the use of these expressions.
>
> Others again, being bolder, do not hesitate to assert that, properly speaking, the bread is the body, and in this way truly prove themselves literalists.[9]

Calvin realized the importance of the validity of the *figurative interpretation* of certain biblical texts, and he insisted that it is crucial for biblical hermeneutics and theology. In the Eucharistic theology, Calvin added that *figurative interpretation* is an essential component, especially in the discussion of the mode of the presence of Jesus Christ. Calvin concretely argued that figurative or symbolical interpretation is foundational because

---

9. Ibid., 4.17.20.

"physical and visible" things represent "spiritual and heavenly" things. In like manner, Calvin wrote:

> It remains for us, therefore, to admit that, on account of the affinity which the things signified have with their symbols, the name of the thing was given to the symbol—figuratively, indeed—but not without a most fitting analogy. I pass over allegories and parables, lest someone accuse me of seeking a place to hide and of disagreeing from the present issue.
>
> I say that this expression is a metonymy, a figure of speech commonly used in Scripture when mysteries are under discussion. For you could not otherwise understand such expressions as "circumcision is a covenant" [Gen. 17:13], "the lamb is the Passover" [Ex. 12:11], "the sacrifices of the law are expiations" [Lev. 17:11; Heb. 9:22], and finally, "the rock from which water flowed in the desert" [Ex. 17:6], "was Christ" [1 Cor. 10:4], unless you were to take them as spoken with meanings transferred. Not only is the name transferred from something higher to something lower, but, on the other hand, the name of the visible sign is also given to the thing signified: as when God is said to have appeared to Moses in the bush [Ex. 3:2]; the Ark of the Covenant is called God and God's face [Ps. 84:8; 42:3]; and the dove, the Holy Spirit [Matt. 3:16]. For though the symbol differs in essence from the thing signified (in that the latter is spiritual and heavenly, while the former is physical and visible), still, because it not only symbolizes the thing that it has been consecrated to represent as a bare and empty token, but also truly exhibits it, why may its name not rightly belong to the thing?[10]

Calvin saw the core problem of the Lutheran hermeneutics and theology in respect to the presence of Jesus Christ in the Eucharist, as the denial of the figurative interpretation of the Eucharistic passage of "this is." That is the reason why they fell into consubstantiation. Countering the Lutheran concept of consubstantiation, Calvin declared the validity and importance of figurative interpretation of the passage of "this is my body" in Matthew 26:26, closely examining other important biblical passages, which require figurative interpretation to comprehend and embrace the abundant richness of spiritual blessings in the Eucharistic passages:

> But is some intransigent person, blind to all else, so insists upon the expression "this is" as to regard this mystery as separate from all the others, the answer is easy. They say that the copulative verb

10. Ibid., 4.17.21.

bears such emphasis as not to admit of a figure of speech. But if we grant this to them, to be sure, one reads the copulative verb in Paul's words, where he calls bread "a participation in the body of Christ" [1 Cor. 10:16]. But participation is something different from the body itself.

Indeed, where the sacraments are under consideration, almost the same word occurs: "This will be for you a covenant with me" [Gen. 17:13 p.]; "This will be for you a covenant with me" [Gen. 17:13 p.]; "This lamb will be the Passover for you" [Ex. 12:11; cf. ch. 12:43]. In short, when Paul says, "The rock was Christ" [1 Cor. 10:4], why is the copulative verb, according to them, less emphatic in that place than in Christ's utterance? Where John says, "The Holy Spirit was not yet, because Jesus was not yet glorified" [John 7:39, cf. Vg.], let them also reply, what is the force of the copulative verb? For if they remain true to their rule, the eternal essence of the Spirit will be destroyed, as if he received his beginning from Christ's ascension. Let them, finally, answer what the statement of Paul signifies: that baptism is "the washing of regeneration and renewal" [Titus 3:5], inasmuch as baptism is clearly unprofitable for many.

But there is nothing stronger to refute them than the statement of Paul that the church is Christ [1 Cor. 12:12]. For, having made a comparison with the human body, he adds, "So is Christ" [*ibid.*]; there he does not mean the only-begotten Son of God in himself but in his members.[11]

In response to the Lutheran concept of ubiquity represented by Westphal's *Apologia confessionis*, Calvin insisted that the resurrected body of Jesus Christ will stay "in heaven even to the Last Day." Calvin insightfully argued the bodily presence of Jesus Christ from the perspective of redemptive history with a consciousness of the principle of *sola Scriptura* as a final authority of all the doctrinal issues. In doing so, Calvin's presupposition is that the resurrected body of Jesus Christ will stay in the heavenly realm until his Second Coming. From the redemptive historical perspective, Calvin rightly and insightfully saw that "the coming of the Spirit" at the Day of the Pentecost and "the ascent of Christ are antithetical," which is a definitive biblical signature that the resurrected body of Jesus Christ will stay in heaven until the consummation day:

> But because nothing will be more effective to strengthen the faith of the pious than to have learned that the doctrine which we have

11. Ibid., 4.17.22.

put forward has been drawn from the pure Word of God, and rests upon its authority—I shall also make this plain with as much brevity as I can. Not Aristotle, but the Holy Spirit teaches that the body of Christ from the time of his resurrection was finite, and is contained in heaven even to the Last Day [cf. Acts 3:21]. Nor am I unaware that they cavalierly evade those passages which are quoted in proof of this. Whenever Christ says that he will depart [John 14:12, 28; 16:7], forsaking the world [John 16:28], they answer that this departure is nothing but a change of mortal state. But according to such reasoning, Christ would not have substituted the Holy Spirit to supply, as they say, the defect of his absence, seeing that the Spirit does not succeed him; nor Christ descend again from heavenly glory to reassume the state of mortal life. Surely, the coming of the Spirit and the ascent of Christ are antithetical; consequently, Christ cannot dwell with us according to the flesh in the same way that he sends his Spirit.[12]

In refuting the Lutheran concept of ubiquity and consubstantiation from the perspective of historical theology, Calvin appealed primarily to Augustine's Eucharistic theology for the affirmation of the spiritual presence of Christ in the Eucharist. Following Augustine's interpretation in *John's Gospel*, Calvin carefully argued that Christ's resurrected and glorified body is not on earth but in heaven. But to ask exactly which region of heaven, according to Calvin, is "a very prying and superfluous question" as Augustine already mentioned. This is another example of how Calvin was self-consciously faithful to the Reformation principle of the *sola Scriptura* as the final and ultimate authority of all the doctrinal issues:

---

12. Ibid., 4.17.26. Godfrey properly locates Melanchthon as a moderate Lutheran while he puts Westphal as a hyper-Lutheran, who is a major subject that Calvin pointedly provided a comprehensive critique of in his analysis on the problem of ubiquity and consubstantiation: "As Calvin turned to consider the Lutheran doctrine of the Lord's Supper (sections 20–34), he responded particularly to the Lutheran doctrine of ubiquity. The word 'ubiquity' is derived from the Latin 'ubique,' meaning everywhere. The doctrine states that the human nature of Christ shares in his divine attribute of omnipresence and therefore his body can be everywhere. While the Lutheran confessions did not require a belief in ubiquity, it became the standard way in which Lutherans explained how Christ's body could be in, with, and under the bread. In particular Calvin had debated in lengthy treatises the Lutheran theologian Joachim Westphal, and much of the discussion in these sections draws on that debate. Calvin had concluded that he agreed substantially with the moderate Lutherans including Melanchthon, but differed strongly with the hyper-Lutherans such as Westphal." Godfrey, "Calvin, Worship, and the Sacraments," 382.

Here (to note this also briefly) Augustine conceives of Christ as present among us in three ways: in majesty, in providence, and in ineffable grace. Under grace I include that marvelous communion of his body and blood—provided we understand that it takes place by the power of the Holy Spirit, not by that feigned inclusion of the body itself under the element. Indeed, our Lord testified that he had flesh and bones, which could be felt and seen [John 20:27].

Also, "departing" and "ascending" do not signify giving the appearance of one sending and departing, but actually doing what the words state. Shall we therefore, someone will say, assign to Christ a definite region of heaven? But I reply with Augustine that this is a very prying and superfluous question; for us it is enough to believe that he is in heaven.[13]

Again, it is interesting to find out that Calvin self-consciously adopted the Eucharistic theology, represented by Augustine, especially in respect to the spiritual presence of Christ in his response to the Lutheran consubstantiation. Following Augustine's interpretation of the spiritual presence of Christ, Calvin insisted that Christ as God in light of the second person of the trinity, is present everywhere while he, as a glorified man, stays in heaven after his ascension:

"Christ imparted immortality to his own flesh, but did not remove its nature from it. We ought not to think that it is everywhere diffused according to this fleshly form, for we ought to beware lest we so affirm the deity of the Man that we take away the reality of his body. And it does not follow that what is in God must be everywhere, as God is." The reason is soon given: "For one person is God and man, and both are one Christ: everywhere, through the fact that he is God; in heaven, through the fact that he is man." How stupid would it have been not to except the mystery of the Supper, a thing so serious and weighty, if there had been in it anything contrary to the doctrine that he was discussing? And yet, if anyone reads attentively what follows a little after, he will find that the Supper is also included under that general doctrine. For he says that Christ, the only begotten Son of God, and likewise the Son of man, is everywhere wholly present as God; that he is God dwelling in the temple of God (that is, in the church), and in some place in heaven, by reason of the measure of his true body. We

---

13. Calvin, *Institutes*, 4.17.26.

see how, in order to unite Christ with the church, God does not withdraw Christ's body from heaven.[14]

Relying on Augustine's understanding of the spiritual presence of Christ in the Eucharist, Calvin argued that Christ's "bodily presence" (*praesentia corporali*) is an *antithesis* to his "spiritual presence" (*praesentia spirituali*) after his ascension. Closely examining Augustine's interpretation of Christ's presence in Matthew 28:20, Calvin argued that Christ's prophetic message to his disciples after his resurrection is a surety that Christ will be present not physically on this earth but spiritually because his glorified body will be in heaven until his Second Coming:

> For it is, after all, restricted to majesty, which is always set over against body; and flesh is expressly distinguished from grace and power. We find the same antithesis in another passage in Augustine: that Christ withdrew his bodily presence from his disciples in order to be with them spiritual presence. There it is clear that he distinguishes the essence of the flesh from the power of the Spirit, by which we are joined to Christ, though we are otherwise separated from him by a great distance in space. He often uses the same type of expression, as when he says: "He will come again to the living and the dead in his bodily presence also, according to the rule of faith and sound doctrine. For in his spiritual presence he was also to come to them, and was to be with the whole church in the world even to the end of the age" [Matt. 28:20; cf. John 17:12]. Therefore, this discourse is directed to believers whom Christ had already begun to save in his bodily presence, and whom he with his bodily presence was to leave, so that he might save them in his spiritual presence with the Father. To understand "bodily" for "visible" presence is a quibble, since he contrasts the body to the divine power. And adding, "to save with the Father," Augustine makes it clear that He pours down his grace from heaven through the Spirit upon us.[15]

Calvin argued that the Lutheran concept of ubiquity draws out an idea of "an invisible presence" of Christ's body after his ascension. However, Calvin rightly pointed out that their argument does not have biblical warrant to support that the ascended body of Christ is invisibly present on earth. To justify the concept of ubiquity, according to Calvin, the Lutherans insisted that the ascended body of Christ is "everywhere in space but without form," and they further insisted that the glorified

14. Ibid., 4.17.28.

15. Ibid.

body of Christ is "visible in itself in heaven, yet in the Supper invisible by a special mode of dispensation." Quoting Acts 3:21, Calvin countered the Lutheran idea of ubiquity, arguing that Christ's glorified body must remain in heaven until his Second Coming as Peter proclaimed after the redemptive historical event of the Pentecost:

> And while they prate in this way, they are compelled to make Christ's double, because, according to them, it is visible in itself heaven, yet in the Supper invisible by a special mode of dispensation. But how beautifully this holds together is easy to judge, both from other passages of Scripture and from the testimony of Peter. Peter says that Christ must be received or embraced by heaven until he come again [Acts 3:21]. These men teach that he is everywhere in space but without form. They object that it is wrong for the nature of the glorious body to submit to the laws of common nature.[16]

Calvin viewed the Lutheran concept of ubiquity as "the monstrous notion" because it emphasizes Christ's body as "hidden under the bread in the Supper." Reflecting on the Scriptural passages, Calvin carefully insisted that the bodily presence of Christ was "circumscribed by the measure of a human body." The Lutherans, affirming their doctrine of ubiquity appealed to Matthew 28:20, which is Jesus' word to his disciples after his resurrection: "I am with you even to the end of the age." However, Calvin rightly interpreted the passage, arguing that Jesus' ascension into heaven is a clear indication that his body does not present "in all places, but when it passes into one, it leaves the previous one." In that sense, Calvin emphasized that Jesus' presence after his ascension is not bodily but a spiritual one:

> Now, although we concede to them what they chatter about the invisible presence, yet that immeasurableness will still not be proved, without which they will try in vain to enclose Christ under bread. Under the body of Christ can be everywhere at once, without limitation of place, it will not be credible that he lies hidden under the

---

16. Ibid., 4.17.29. Examining the Lutheran idea of ubiquity, Calvin argued that it is indistinguishable from the "insane notion of Servetus" where he argued that the body of Christ was "swallowed up by his divinity": "But this answer drags with it that insane notion of Servetus (which all godly men rightly find abhorrent), that His body was swallowed up by his divinity. I do not say that they think so. But if to fill all things in an invisible manner is numbered among the gifts of the glorified body, it is plain that the substance of the body is wiped out, and that no difference between deity and human nature is left." Ibid.

bread in the Supper. To meet this necessity, they have introduced the monstrous notion of ubiquity.

But as we have proved by firm and clear testimonies of Scripture, Christ's body was circumscribed by the measure of a human body. Again, by his ascension into heaven he made it plain that it is not in all places, but when it passes into one, it leaves the previous one.

Nor is the promise they cite, "I am with you even to the end of the age" [Matt. 28:20, Vg.], to be applied to the body.[17]

Interestingly, Calvin was not ashamed of recognizing a commonplace between himself and the Schoolmen, represented by Peter Lombard's concept of the omnipresence of Christ in his treatise on *Sentences* in light of Christ's divinity. According to Calvin, the Schoolmen developed the doctrine of transubstantiation out of the omnipresence of Christ while Lutherans developed the doctrine of consubstantiation out of the concept of ubiquity:

> There is a commonplace distinction of the schools to which I am not ashamed to refer: although the whole Christ is everywhere, still the whole of that which is in him is not everywhere. And would that the Schoolmen themselves had honestly weighed the force of this statement. For thus would the absurd fiction of Christ's carnal presence have been obviated. Therefore, since the whole Christ is everywhere, our Mediator is ever present with his own people, and in the Supper reveals himself in a special way, yet in such a way that the whole Christ is present, but not in his wholeness. For, as has been said, in his flesh he is contained in heaven until he appears in judgment.[18]

Against the backdrop of the carnal presence of Christ in the Lord's Supper, Calvin argued that the glorified body of Christ should not be brought down to us from the heavenly realm. Rather, the hearts and spirits of the community of believers should be brought up to heaven where his glorified body has been enveloped after his ascension, realizing Christ is present in his Spirit with the children of God. Thus, Calvin properly argued that the Lutheran concept of consubstantiation undermines the importance of "the secret working of the Spirit, which unites Christ himself to us." Here, we find that Calvin highly emphasized the centrality of

---

17. Ibid., 4.17.30.

18. Ibid.

the mystical works of the Spirit in relation to the union with Christ in the sacrament of the Lord's Supper:

> But greatly mistaken are those who conceive no presence of flesh in the Supper unless it lies in the bread. For thus they leave nothing to the secret working of the Spirit, which unites Christ himself to us. To them Christ does not seem present unless he comes down to us. As though, if he should lift us to himself, we should not just as much enjoy his presence! The question is therefore only of the manner, for they place Christ in the bread, while we do not think it lawful for us to drag him from heaven. Let our readers decide which one is more correct. Only away with that calumny that Christ is removed from his Supper unless he lies hidden under the covering of bread! For since this mystery is heavenly, there is no need to draw Christ to earth that he may be joined to us.[19]

Again, Calvin emphasized the mysterious nature of the spiritual presence of Christ in the Lord's Supper. He was not ashamed of recognizing that "it is a secret too lofty for either my mind to comprehend or my words to declare. And, to speak more plainly, I rather experience than understand it." Referring to John 6:53 ff., Calvin noticed that in the Lord's Supper Christ "bids me take, eat, and drink his body and blood under the symbols of bread and wine." Likewise, Calvin boldly argued that the Lutheran concept of the carnal presence of Christ in the Sacred Supper is against "Christ's heavenly majesty" and "incompatible with the reality of his human nature" when we examine it in the light of God's Word. Furthermore, Calvin persuasively contended that participation in the Lord's Supper with faith provides us with "an undoubted assurance of eternal life to our minds, but also assures us of the immortality of our flesh":

> I reject only absurd things which appear to be either unworthy of Christ's heavenly majesty, or incompatible with the reality of his human nature, since they are in necessary conflict with God's Word; for it also teaches that Christ was so received into the glory of the Heavenly Kingdom [Luke 24:26] as to be lifted above all worldly estate, and no less carefully sets off in his human nature those things which are proper to true humanity.
>
> This ought not to seem either incredible or out of accord with human reason. For as Christ's whole Kingdom is spiritual, whatever he does with his church must not be subjected to the reason of this world. Or, to use Augustine's words, this mystery, like oth-

19. Ibid., 4.17.31.

ers, is performed by men, but divinely; on earth, but in a heavenly way. Such is the presence of the body (I say) that the nature of the Sacrament requires a presence which we say manifests itself here with a power and effectiveness so great that it not only brings an undoubted assurance of eternal life to our minds, but also assures us of the immortality of our flesh. Indeed, it is now quickened by his immortal flesh, and in a sense partakes of his immortality.[20]

Refuting the unbiblical ideas of the Schoolmen's transubstantiation and the Lutheran consubstantiation, Calvin also carefully described spiritual qualifications to participate in the Lord's Supper, examining biblical passages. Let us explore Calvin's biblical theological logic for believers' spiritual qualifications to participate in the Lord's Supper."

SPIRITUAL QUALIFICATIONS TO PARTICIPATE IN THE EUCHARIST

Calvin found biblical and theological justification for infant baptism in light of covenantal continuity among the Abrahamic Covenant, Old Covenant, and New Covenant, closely examining a transition from circumcision to baptism. In such a manner, Calvin developed the concrete biblical theological justification of infant baptism over against the Anabaptists, who challenged the Reformers, rebaptizing believers who received infant baptism. Meanwhile, in the discussion of the Eucharistic theology, Calvin paid close attention to the spiritual qualifications to participate in the Lord's Supper under the New Covenant.

Calvin emphasized the importance of unity in Jesus Christ for those who partake in the Lord's Supper. The Lord's Supper, according to Calvin, is a powerful means to "quicken and inspire us both to purity and holiness of life, and to love, peace, and concord." In the Lord's Supper, Christ communicates his body to believers, making himself "completely one with us and we with him." As such, the bread in the Eucharist demonstrates the believers' unity as the body of Christ under the New Covenant. In doing so, Calvin articulated the importance of *faith and holiness* as the precondition to participate in the Lord's Supper:

> Thirdly, the Lord also intended the Supper to be a kind of exhortation for us, which can more forcefully than any other means quicken and inspire us both to purity and holiness of life, and to

20. Ibid., 4.17.32.

love, peace, and concord. For the Lord so communicates his body to us there that he is made completely one with us and we with him. Now, since he has only one body, of which he makes us all partakers, it is necessary that all of us also be made one body by such participation. The bread shown in the Sacrament represents this unity. As it is made of many grains so mixed together that one cannot be distinguished from another, so it is fitting that in the same way we should be joined and bound together by such great agreement of minds that no sort of disagreement or division may intrude. I prefer to explain it in Paul's words: "The cup of blessing which we bless is a communicating of the blood of Christ; and the bread of blessing which we break is a participation in the body of Christ. . . . Therefore . . . We . . . are all one body, for we partake of one bread" [1 Cor. 10:16–17, cf. Vg.].[21]

In the discussion of the spiritual qualifications for the participants of the Lord's Supper, Calvin paid close attention to the Pauline passage whereby he deals with the spiritual qualifications for participation in the Lord's Supper under the New Covenant. Carefully pondering upon the passage, Calvin persuasively argued that *faith and love* are dual spiritual qualifications. Calvin considered "the sacred bread of the Lord's Supper" as "spiritual food," and it is only "healthful for pious worshippers of God." In light of this, Calvin emphatically added that partaking in the Lord's Supper "without any spark of faith, without any zeal for love" is from the people who do not discern the body of the Lord in which Paul warned in 1 Corinthians 11:27–29:

We see that this sacred bread of the Lord's Supper is spiritual food, as sweet and delicate as it is healthful for pious worshippers of God, who, in tasting it, feel that Christ is their life, whom it moves to thanksgiving, for whom it is an exhortation to mutual love among themselves. On the other hand, it is turned into a deadly poison for all those whose faith it does not nourish and strengthen, and whom it does not arouse to thanksgiving and to love. Physical food, when it comes into a stomach occupied by evil humors, and is itself also vitiated and corrupted, harms rather than nourishes. So also this spiritual food, if it enters a soul corrupted by malice and wickedness, casts it down with a greater ruin—not by the fault of the food itself, but because to polluted and unbelieving men nothing is clean [Titus 1:15], however much it otherwise be sanctified by the Lord's blessing. "For," as Paul says, "any who

21. Ibid., 4.17.38.

eat and drink unworthily are guilty of the Lord's body and blood, and eat and drink judgment upon themselves, not discerning the body of the Lord" [1 Cor. 11:27 and 29, conflated]. Men of this sort who, without any spark of faith, without any zeal for love, rush like swine to take the Lord's Supper do not discern the Lord's body.[22]

Interpreting 1 Corinthians 11:28, Calvin carefully followed Paul's biblical theological logic that everyone before the table of the Lord's Supper has to examine themselves. Calvin extended this discussion further, arguing that participants in the Lord's Supper should have "inward assurance of heart upon the salvation" (*interiore cordis fiducia in salutem*), acknowledgement of inner assurance of salvation by mouth, fervent desire to imitate Christ, and sacrificial love for neighbors and others. In doing so, we can assume that Calvin was against paedocommunion because children are not able to discern for themselves whether they are spiritually qualified or not:

> On this account, Paul enjoins that a man examine himself before eating of this bread or drinking from this cup [1 Cor. 11:28]. By this (as I interpret it), he meant that each man descend into himself, and ponder with himself whether he rests with inward assurance of heart upon the salvation purchased by Christ; whether he acknowledges it by confession of mouth; then, whether he aspires to the imitation of Christ with the zeal of innocence and holiness; whether, after Christ's example, he is prepared to give himself for his brethren and to communicate himself to those with whom he shares Christ in common; whether, as he is counted a member by Christ, he in turn so holds all his brethren as members of his body; whether he desires to cherish, protect, and help them as his own members. Not that these duties both of faith and of love can now be made perfect in us, but that we should endeavor and aspire with all our heart toward this end in order that we may day by day increase our faith once begun.[23]

Meanwhile, in the medieval age, the medieval Scholastics taught that those who are "in state of grace" (*in statu gratiae*) are only worthy participants in the Lord's Supper. In doing so, they viewed "in state of grace" as a spiritual state to be "pure and purged of all sin" (*purum purgatumque omni peccato esse*). In response to them, Calvin properly argued that since sinless perfection or purity is impossible in the present world, it is not a

22. Ibid., 4.17.40.
23. Ibid.

biblical dogma to pursue, critiquing their ideas that we may expiate "our unworthiness by contrition, confession, and satisfaction":

> Commonly, when they would prepare men to eat worthily, they have tortured and harassed pitiable consciences in dire ways; yet they have not brought forward a particle of what would be to the purpose. They said that those who were in state of grace are worthily. They interpreted "in state of grace" to mean to be pure and purged of all sin. Such a dogma would debar all the men who ever were or are on earth from the use of this Sacrament. For if it is a question of our seeking worthiness by ourselves, we are undone; only despair and deadly ruin remains to us. Although we try with all our strength, we shall make no headway, except that in the end we shall be most unworthy, after we have labored mightily in pursuit of worthiness.[24]

Moreover, Calvin emphasized believers' humble attitude when they come to the table of the Lord's Supper because the spiritual worthiness consists mainly "in faith" and "in love." Furthermore, Calvin pointed out that although faith and love are not perfect, God increases them for those who come with humble and broken hearts with trust in Christ, who is "the Author of Righteousness" (*iustitiae auctorem*):

> Rather, we shall think that we, as being poor, come to a kindly giver; as sick, to a physician; as sinners, to the Author of righteousness; finally as dead, to him who gives us life. We shall think that the worthiness, which is commanded by God, consists chiefly in faith, which reposes all things in Christ, but nothing in our selves; secondly, in love—and that very love which, though imperfect, is enough to offer to God, that he may increase it to something better, inasmuch as it cannot be offered in completeness.[25]

Calvin was critical against those who claimed "a perfection of faith" (*fidei perfectionem*) as a spiritual condition to participate in the Lord's Supper. He rightly insisted that God does not require "a perfection of faith" but faith and love in Christ because it is an impossible spiritual condition to be achieved in this world as forgiven sinners. In that sense, the Lord's Supper was ordained "not for the perfect, but for the weak and feeble" to spark and stimulate "the feeling of faith and love" (*fidei et caritatis affectum*):

24. Ibid., 4.17.41.
25. Ibid., 4.17.42.

Others, agreeing with us, that worthiness itself consists in faith and love, still are far in error on the standard itself of worthiness, requiring, as they do, a perfection of faith which cannot at all be attained, and a love equal to that which Christ has shown toward us. But, by doing so, they, like those previously mentioned, drive all men from approaching this most holy Supper. For if their view obtained, no one would receive it except unworthily, since all to a man would be held guilty and convicted of their own imperfection. And it would be excessive stupidity—not to mention foolishness—to require such perfection in receiving the Sacrament as would make the Sacrament void and superfluous. For it is a sacrament ordained not for the perfect, but for the weak and feeble, to awaken, arouse, stimulate, and exercise the feeling of faith and love, indeed, to correct the defect of both.[26]

As we have already explored, Calvin's Eucharistic theology goes against paedocommunion because he set faith and love as spiritual requirements to participate in the Lord's Supper in light of 1 Corinthians 11:27–30. Calvin was sensitive about redemptive historical continuity and discontinuity in the realm of sacramental theology. He thought that infant baptism is a legitimate practice under the New Covenant in light of the covenantal continuity between the Old and New Covenants in terms of sacramental continuity between circumcision and baptism. That is the reason why Calvin was not only a great theologian but also a wonderful redemptive historical theologian, offering a sound balance between theology and redemptive history.

Meanwhile, the Federal Visionists enforce paedocommunion as biblical as paedobaptism is a legitimate sacramental practice under the New Covenant. They make their case by arguing that the Israelites under the Old Covenant ate the Passover lamb and the biblical evidence suggests that all the Israelites, without exception, participated in the eating of the Passover lamb. From the perspective of redemptive historical continuity, then, it is legitimate for children to participate in the sacrament of the Lord's Supper. As such, Leithart, as an exponent of the Federal Vision, argues that children participated in the Passover meal with adults under the Old Covenant. He ascertains that it is a decisive biblical and redemptive historical reason to include covenant children in the Lord's Supper:

26. Ibid.

Paedocommunion ritually announces that the church is continuous with Israel. All paedobaptists agree that the church is the new Israel, formed as the body of the Risen Christ. But paedocommunion reinforces this point dramatically, for it insists that the admission requirements to the church's meal are exactly the same as the admission requirements to Israel's meals.[27]

Then, Leithart interprets the first Passover context of Exodus 12:3–4 and whether covenant children were included in the eating of the Passover lamb. Examining the passage in the milieu of the general pattern of the Old Testament feasts where the Israelites ate the meals, he concludes that the "household" comprehensively embraces not only adults but also "children and servants":

> With regard to Passover, inclusion of children is not so obvious, but a strong case can be made that they were included in this feast as well. Debate focuses on Exodus 12, the account of the first Passover. Verses 3 to 4 specify how large a lamb is needed for the meal:
>
> Speak to all the congregation of Israel, saying, "On the tenth of this month they are each one to take a lamb for themselves, according to their fathers' households, a lamb for each household. Now if the household is too small for a lamb, then he and his neighbor nearest to his house are to take one according to the number of souls; according to each man's eating, you are to compute for the lamb."
>
> This regulation makes it clear that the Passover lamb had to be at least big enough to feed a household, but who is included in a "household"? Throughout the Pentateuch, "house" includes children and servants. Noah's "house" obviously included his sons and daughters-in-law (Genesis 7:1), and Abram circumcised the males in his "house" (Genesis 17:23, 27). The very first verse of Exodus tells us that Jacob's sons came to Egypt, each with his "house" (1:1). Nowhere in the Bible does the word "household" exclude children. If the lamb was to be large enough for a household, it was to be large enough for the children of the house to receive a portion. If children of the household were not allowed to eat, why was the size of the lamb specified in this way?[28]

Then, Leithart appeals to a covenantal continuity to include children in the Lord's Supper as children were included in the Old Testament feasts,

---

27. Leithart, "A Response to '1 Corinthians 11:17–34: The Lord's Supper,'" 299. For exegetical and theological argument, based upon 1 Corinthians 11:17–34 against the paedocommunion of the Federal Vision, see Knight III, "1 Corinthians 11:17–34," 282–96.

28. Leithart, "A Response to '1 Corinthians 11:17–34: The Lord's Supper,'" 299–300.

especially the Passover meal, which is equivalent to the Lord's Supper under the New Covenant. Keeping this in mind, Leithart reinterprets 1 Corinthians 11:27–30, which is a classical passage for Calvin, to go against paedocommunion. Leithart, in the debate with George Knight in relation to paedocommunion, argues that 1 Corinthians 11 does not support the antipaedocommunion position. In doing so, he disapproves Knight's argument that the Pauline passage is a decisive biblical passage against paedocommunion, saying that "Knight reasons like a Baptist":

> At the outset, two methodological points may be made. First, I was disappointed that Knight does not interact explicitly with any of the paedocommunion interpretations of 1 Corinthians 11, particularly the extended discussion in Tim Gallant's *Feed My Lambs*. Admittedly, much of this literature has been published in obscure corners of the Reformed world (Grande Prairie, Alberta!). Still, the omission was disappointing. Second, Knight's treatment of 1 Corinthians isolates that passage not only from the surrounding chapters of 1 Corinthians but also from the larger biblical context of sacred meals. He makes occasional reference to texts outside of 1 Corinthians 11, but how this chapter fits into the argument of chapters 8–11 is not explained. By concentrating on a single New Testament text, Knight ignores the Old Testament evidence detailed above. The larger redemptive historical questions, which are so central in debates about paedobaptism, are not even allowed to arise. To find a Reformed theologian reasoning about the sacraments without reference to the Old Testament is disconcerting, to say the least. I say this without pejorative intent, but simply as an accurate description of Knight's method: On this issue, Knight reasons like a Baptist.[29]

29. Ibid., 301. It is important to note that in his response to Knight, Leithart recognizes that the Westminster Standards are the confessional document, which goes against paedocommunion: "Knight has offered a careful treatment of this passage in order to defend the *Confession*'s exclusion of those who are not 'of years and ability to examine themselves.' I wish to comment on several aspects of his treatment. I agree with much that Knight has written. His exhortations about the dangers of wrong participation are to be heeded." Ibid.

We must understand that the Westminster divines had a consciousness against paedocommunion while they stated paedobaptism as a biblical practice when they formulated the difference between "the sacraments of baptism and the Lord's Supper" in the Larger Catechism Q & A 177: "Q. 177. Wherein do the sacraments of baptism and the Lord's Supper differ?

A. The sacraments of baptism and the Lord's supper differ, in that baptism is to be administered but once, with water, to be a sign and seal of our regeneration and ingraft-

Calvin used the Pauline passage in 1 Corinthians 11:28–29 as a decisive hermeneutical and theological linchpin against paedocommunion as we have already explored in detail. Calvin's hermeneutical and theological outlook was well adopted by the Westminster divines whereby they made a confessional statement against paedocommunion. However, the Federal Visionists have taken a different hermeneutical and theological road, arguing that 1 Corinthian 11:28–29 is not an anti-paedocommunion passage. Countering Knight's argument against paedocommunion, Leithart insists that Paul's major point in 1 Corinthians 11: 28–29 is not against paedocommunion. Rather, Paul made a statement about "whether I have broken faith with Christ" before the covenant community participates in the Lord's Supper, following the exegetical and theological argument made by Tim Gallant:

> But the second point requires some clarification. While Knight points to a parallel with 2 Corinthians 13, there are clues in the more immediate context of 1 Corinthians 11 that assist us in understanding what Paul expects from the Corinthians. Paul had confessed in chapter 9 that he disciplines himself so that he will not in the end be "disqualified" (9:24–27), and the word for "disqualified" (*adokimos*) is a negative adjective form of the verb for "examine" in 11:28 (*dokimazo*). Paul wants to "run" (live) in such a way that he proves himself qualified, proves himself to be in Christ. As Tim Gallant points out, "Paul continues from 9:27 to show how the Israelites in the wilderness, despite partaking of God's (sacramental and spiritual, as well as physical) bounty . . . fell into sin and judgment. . . . They did become *adokimoi*, disqualified, provoking God's wrath." This sets up the exhortation in 11:28, for Paul does not want the Corinthians to "prove unqualified" in the way that the Israelites did. Gallant concludes,
>
> > The concern of *examine* (*put yourself to the proof*) is not, then, whether I am producing the right feelings toward the elements, or know enough theology, or anything of the sort. It is rather, as the relation between the words . . . attests, to ascertain whether I am approved . . . , whether I am in the faith. . . . It has to do with *whether I have broken faith with Christ.*

ing into Christ, and that even to infants; whereas the Lord's supper is to be administered often, in the elements of bread and wine, to represent and exhibit Christ as spiritual nourishment to the soul, and to confirm our continuance and growth in him, and that only to such as are of years and ability to examine themselves."

"Putting yourself to the proof" is not a matter of introspective examination, but a manner of life. For the current debate, the central question is, as Gallant puts it, "Where does the Bible call into question whether covenant children are approved (*dokimoi*)?" Children who are within the church by baptism, and are responsive to their parents, are continually "showing themselves approved."[30]

Likewise, Leithart, as one of the major exponents of the Federal Vision, uses the Pauline passage of 1 Corinthians 11:17–34 to approve paedocommunion, which Calvin and the Westminster divines used as a decisive biblical passage to go against paedocommunion.

SUMMARY

In the Eucharistic theology, Calvin brilliantly maintained the concept of spiritual presence against the Medieval Schoolmen's transubstantiation and the Lutheran consubstantiation. Calvin refuted the Schoolmen's doctrine of transubstantiation from the perspective of historical theology, mainly appealing to the ancient church, especially Augustine. In addition, as a great redemptive historical theologian, Calvin emphasized a redemptive historical aspect of the Eucharist, explaining why Christ is present in his Spirit in the Lord's Supper over against transubstantiation and consubstantiation.

As a masterful redemptive historical theologian, Calvin carefully evaluated whether or not children are spiritually qualified to participate in the Lord's Supper under the New Covenant. Examining 1 Corinthians 11:27–30, Calvin emphasized dual spiritual qualifications for the Lord's Supper, which are *faith and love*. In that sense, I have argued that Calvin was against paedocommunion because children are not capable of discerning themselves whether they are spiritually qualified or not.

Meanwhile, the Federal Visionists insist paedocommunion as a biblical doctrine, appealing to a redemptive historical continuity between the Passover meal under the Old Covenant and the Lord's Supper under the New Covenant. They argue that pedocommunion must be legitimate under the New Covenant as children participated in the Old Testament feasts, especially the Passover meal, which is equivalent to the Lord's Supper under the New Covenant. In doing so, the Federal Visionists do not consider 1 Corinthians 11 as a decisive biblical passage for antipaedocommunion while Calvin's Eucharsitic theology as well as the Westminster Standards rightly suggest that the passage is an antipaedocommunion passage without any ambiguity.

30. Leithart, "A Response to '1 Corinthians 11:17–34: The Lord's Supper,'" 303.

Conclusion

THE SINGLE MOST IMPORTANT reason for the rise of the Federal Vision in conservative Reformed community in North America is due to the rejection of the antithesis between law and gospel in hermeneutics, theology, and praxis. I would identify the Federal Vision as *a consistent monocovenantalism* because the proponents of the Federal Vision consistently apply their monocovenantal vision into the arenas of hermeneutics, the doctrine of justification by faith, double predestination, the doctrine of church, and sacramental theology.

One of the major contributions of the Protestant Reformation was the antithesis between law and gospel, which was faithfully applied to biblical hermeneutics and theology. Calvin was a genius in his application of the antithesis between law and gospel into his biblical hermeneutics and theology, setting the great hermeneutical and theological stages for the latter Reformed covenant theology. Calvin faithfully applied the antithesis between law and gospel in his soteriology, represented by justification by faith alone (*sola fide*) and salvation by grace alone (*sola gratia*). Of course, Calvin was a covenant theologian, who emphasized believers' covenantal obedience for God's sovereign grace in personal salvation. However, Calvin located believers' covenantal obedience in response to God's salvific grace into the realm of not justification but progressive sanctification. In addition, Calvin applied the concept of union with Christ (*unio cum Christo*) in his doctrine of soteriology as a comprehensive hermeneutical tool to embrace all the soteriological blessings, including the doctrine of election, justification, and sanctification. Calvin used the concept of union with Christ to embrace the soteriological blessings of justification and sanctification as double grace (*duplex gratia*). Nevertheless, Calvin carefully maintained justification by faith alone (*sola fide*) in the hermeneutical milieu of the antithesis between law and gospel.

Reflecting on the development of twentieth century-theology, it was a period of time imbued with theological confusion due to the rise and influence of neoorthodox theology, represented by Karl Barth. Barth's existential monocovenantalism coupled with the denial of the antithesis between law and gospel, as well as the antithesis between the covenant of works and the covenant of grace, have been very influential directly and indirectly even in the Reformed and evangelical communities. The Federal Visionists, as conservative Reformed theologians and pastors, have had the consciousness of monocovenantalism with their rejection of the antithesis between law and gospel, as well as the antithesis between the covenants of works and grace, although they identify their theology not with Barth but Calvin and the Westminster Standards. With monocovenantal consciousness, they reinterpret the theologies of Calvin and the Westminster Standards, following the hermeneutical and theological pattern of monocovenantalism, represented by Norman Shepherd and others. In doing so, the Federal Visionists radically reinterpret justification by faith alone (*sola fide*) with the rejection of the antithesis between law and gospel, injecting their monocovenantalism into Calvin and the Westminster Standards. In that sense, I have suggested that the theology of the Federal Vision is not compatible to the theologies of Calvin and the Westminster Standards.

Exploring Calvin's understanding of covenant and redemptive history, I have endeavored to prove that Calvin was the forerunner of the distinction between the covenant of works and the covenant of grace, which was the defining mark of the latter Reformed orthodox hermeneutics and theology. Calvin's covenant theology is perfectly harmonious with the latter Reformed covenant theology although he did not use the term, the covenant of works (*foedus operum*) in respect to the original Adamic status in the Garden of Eden before the Fall. Most importantly, Calvin perceived the historical and logical order as not gospel and law but law and gospel as the means of eschatological heavenly blessings and inheritance. However, the Federal Visionists with their monocovenantal mindset do not maintain the historical and logical order of the law and gospel, which is foundational for Calvin's covenant theology and the depiction of redemptive history, inaugurated in Genesis 3:15 with the announcement of the primitive Gospel.

Calvin as a great redemptive historical theologian brilliantly interpreted the relationship between the Old and New Covenants. In light of redemptive historical continuity, Calvin perceived that the Old Testament believers under the Old Covenant were saved by God's grace through faith according to the principle of the covenant of grace, inaugurated in Genesis 3:15. However, Calvin viewed that in a limited sense, there is a contrast between the Old and New Covenants. He also interpreted the outward earthly blessings and curses under the Old Covenant in light of redemptive history and eschatology with the concrete implication of *typology*. Calvin persuasively argued that Israel's blessings and curses in the Promised Land, regulated by the Mosaic law, was a type of the heavenly blessing and hellish curse whereby Calvin interpreted it from the perspective of eschatology. So, Calvin envisioned the Old Covenant eschatology in his interpretation of the Old Covenant in contrast to the New Covenant. In that sense, I have argued that Calvin's hermeneutics and theology have an eschatological outlook and orientation through and through.

In addition, Calvin interpreted the Old Covenant with a designation, "the covenant of law" (*foedus legale*), contrasting to the New Covenant. Representatively, in his interpretation of Jeremiah 31 and 32, Calvin made a contrast between the Old and New Covenants, designating the Old Covenant as "the covenant of law" (*foedus legale*). In doing so, Calvin powerfully demonstrated that the Old Covenant was temporal, being governed by the principle of works for the Israelites' earthly blessings and curses, signifying the temporal character of Israel while the New Covenant was a "perpetual covenant." Remarkably, Calvin did not fall into legalism or neonomianism in his interpretation of the Old Covenant although he designated it as "the covenant of law" (*foedus legale*) in a limited sense. Calvin was able to avoid legalism or neonomianism in his interpretation of the Old Covenant because he applied the principle of "the covenant of law" (*foedus legale*) under the Old Covenant not to the level of individual salvation but to the earthly typological blessings or curses, which point to the ultimate eschatological blessings and curses. In that sense, Calvin's implication of the covenant of law in respect to the Old Covenant is a pinnacle of both redemptive historical and eschatological hermeneutics. Moreover, it became a cornerstone for the latter Reformed orthodox theologians' designation of the Old Covenant as the republication of the covenant of works with redemptive historical adjustment.

Meanwhile, the Federal Visionists reinterpret the relationship between the Old and New Covenants in light of their own monocovenantalism. They fall into covenantal legalism in their interpretation of soteriology although they emphasize the nature of sovereign grace in personal salvation under the Old and New Covenants, exclusively emphasizing the character of redemptive historical continuity without paying attention to the aspect of the contrast between the Old and New Covenant. In doing so, they fail to recognize that there is harmony between Calvin's designation of "the covenant of law" (*foedus legale*) and the Reformed orthodox theologians' designation of the Old Covenant as "a republication of a covenant of works" with redemptive historical adjustment.

We have found that Calvin expounded the doctrine of the Pauline double predestination, namely election and reprobation in light of the antithesis between law and gospel. In that sense, Calvin not only applied the antithesis between law and gospel to the doctrines of justification by faith alone (*sola fide*) and salvation by grace alone (*sola gratia*) but also to the doctrine of double predestination. In addition, Calvin's concept of covenant never vitiated the distinction between election and reprobation. In Calvin's doctrine of double predestination, there is no middle ground between election and reprobation in terms of the bestowment of soteriological blessings, applied not through common grace but saving grace.

Meanwhile, the Federal Visionists radically reinterpret the doctrine of double predestination in light of monocovenantalism whereby they reject the antithesis between law and gospel. It is true that they identify their understanding of the double predestination with those of Calvin and the Westminster Standards; however, the Federal Visionists' understanding of the double predestination is not compatible to the Pauline double predestination, faithfully expounded and adopted by Calvin and the Westminster Standards.

As a great redemptive historian and theologian, Calvin made a careful distinction between the national election of Israel and individual election within the covenant people of Israel. In doing so, Calvin located the national election of Israel as "general election" (*generalis election*) while he identified personal election unto salvation as an actual election in which he named as "a special mode of election" (*specialem electionis modum*). Likewise, Calvin made a clear distinction between "general election" and "special election," in his understanding of the Old Testament Israel as a chosen nation.

However, the distinction between the individual elect and reprobate within the covenant community of Israel in the Old Testament of Israel is decisively lacking in the election theology of the Federal Vision. The blurring between the national election of Israel and individual election unto salvation lies in the fact that the hermeneutics of the Federal Vision does not have a careful balance between continuity and discontinuity in their understanding of the relationship between the Old and New Covenants.

Calvin connected election and effectual calling as a decisive turning point from election to salvation for the elect, uniting Christ through the almighty power of the Holy Spirit. Calvin put effectual calling as a decisive means to have the assurance of election on our part. Furthermore, Calvin argued that God provides all the necessary spiritual means for those who are the elect in Christ, who may be persevered unto the end. In that sense, Calvin considered the doctrine of perseverance as "the gift of perseverance" (*dono perseverantiae*), which signifies God's sovereign grace in the process of perseverance of saints. Calvin developed and adopted the distinction between general and special calling in his analysis of God's calling. He demonstrated that general calling (*universalis vocatio*) is a universal call without exception, which includes reprobates "through the outward preaching of the word." However, special calling (*specialis vocatio*) is God's special call, which is applied to the elect alone, uniting with Christ through the inward illumination of the Holy Spirit. Likewise, in Calvin's theology, the distinction between election and reprobation is safeguarded by the distinction between general and special calling.

Meanwhile, we have found that the Federal Visionists insist that they adopt the Pauline doctrine of double predestination. However, their covenantal approach to the doctrine of election becomes a hermeneutical and theological barrier to maintain the doctrine of double predestination although they identify their view with Calvin and the Westminster Standards. The watershed between Calvin and the Federal Vision takes place in the rejection of the distinction between law and gospel, as well as the denial of the distinction between general and effectual calling. It is very important to note that in Calvin's theology the distinction between general and effectual calling is a divinely ordained means to differentiate between the elect and the reprobates. However, in the theology of Federal Vision, there is no distinction between general calling and effectual calling, which is an absolutely necessary means to interpret and maintain the Pauline doctrines of double predestination and perseverance of saints.

In his discussion and expounding of baptismal theology, Calvin never dogmatized baptismal regeneration, which was the hallmark of the medieval baptismal theology and can be summed up as meritorious sacerdotalism. We have found that Calvin, as a great redemptive historical theologian, paid special attention to the nature of redemptive historical continuity between the Abrahamic, Old, and New Covenants when he answered to the Anabaptists' critique against infant baptism. Furthermore, Calvin did not consider infant baptism as the means of union with Christ because he viewed it as the sign or seal of the covenant of grace.

Meanwhile, the Federal Visionists inject their covenantal sacerdotalism into the baptismal theologies of Calvin and the Westminster standards. They falsely argue that Calvin and the Westminster divines affirmed baptismal regeneration over against the Roman Catholic view of meritorious sacerdotalism. As the Federal Vsisionists advocate the dogmatic concept of baptismal regeneration, they also argue that water baptism is a sacramental means of union with Christ, which is alien idea to both Calvin and the Westminster Standards.

Calvin expounded spiritual presence view over against the Schoolmen's concept of transubstantiation and the Lutheran concept of consubstantiation. In doing so, Calvin defended his view in light of historical theology, as well as redemptive history. In addition, as a great redemptive historical theologian, Calvin expounded on the spiritual qualifications to participate in the Lord's Supper under the New Covenant. Closely examining biblical passages in relation to spiritual qualifications for the Lord's Supper, Calvin rightly concluded that *faith and love* are the dual spiritual qualifications. In that sense, I have argued that Calvin's Eucharistic theology necessarily goes against paedocommunion because children are not able to discern for themselves whether they are spiritually qualified or not.

Meanwhile, the Federal Visionists support paedocommunion as though it is equal to paedobaptism as a legitimate sacramental practice under the New Covenant. In the interpretation of 1 Corinthians 11:28–29, the Federal Visionists have taken a different hermeneutical and theological road than Calvin and the Westminster Standards, insisting that the passage is not an anti-paedocommunion passage but a paedocommunion one.

As such, we have revisited Calvin's covenant theology in light of contemporary discussion, particularly interacting with the Federal Vision. In doing so, we have found that the Federal Vision is not compatible to the theologies of Calvin and the Westminster Standards. The theology of the Federal Vision is deeply colored by monocovenantalism, rejecting the distinction between law and gospel, as well as the distinction between the covenant of works and the covenant of grace. In that sense, Federal

Visionists thoroughly revise biblical and systematic theology through the lens of monocovenantalism.

As we live in the global age, God invites the covenant community to proclaim the good news of the Gospel to all nations. Calvin's covenant theology provides a comprehensive biblical answer for biblical hermeneutics, theology, and praxis, which are foundational for global mission, which is the duty of the church in response to the Great Commission of the risen Jesus Christ, our only Savior and Lord until he comes back again with the Glory of Parousia.

Bibliography

PRIMARY SOURCES

Calvin

Calvin, John. *The Bondage and Liberation of the Will: A Defense of the Orthodox Doctrine of Human Choice against Pighius.* ed. A.N.S. Lane, trans G.I. Davies. In *Texts and Studies in Reformation and Post-Reformation Thought.* Vol. II. Grand Rapids: Baker, 2002.

———. *Calvin's Commentaries.* 22 vols. Various Translators. Edinburgh: Calvin Translation Society, 1863. Reprint, Grand Rapids: Baker, 1996.

———. *Calvin: Theological Treatises.* ed. & trans. J. K. S. Reid. In *The Library of Christian Classics.* London: SCM Press, 1954. Reprint, Louisville: Westminster John Knox Press, 2006

———. *Concerning the Predestination of God.* trans. J. K. S. Reid. Cambridge, James Clarke & Co., 1961. Reprint, Louisville: Westminster John Knox Press, 1997.

———. *Institutes of the Christian Religion.* ed. John T. McNeill, trans. Ford Lewis Battles. In *The Library of Christian Classics.* vols. XX–XXI. Philadelphia: The Westminster Press, 1975.

———. *Ioannis Calvini opera quae supersunt omnia.* 59 vols. eds. G. Baum, E. Cunitz, and E. Reuss. Brunswick and Berlin: C. A. Schwetschke, 1863–1900.

———. *Selected Works of John Calvin: Tracts and Letters.* 7 vols. eds. Henry Beveridge, David Constable, and Marcus R. Gilchrist. Grand Rapids: Baker, 1983.

———. *Treatises against the Anabaptists and against the Libertines.* trans & ed. Benjamin Wirt Farley. Grand Rapids: Baker, 1982.

Federal Vision

Barach, John. "Covenant and Election." In *The Auburn Avenue Theology, Pros & Con: Debating the Federal Vision*, ed. E. Calvin Beisner, 149–56. Fort Lauderdale: FL: Knox Theological Seminary, 2004.

———. "Covenant and Election." In *The Federal Vision.* eds. Steve Wilkins and Duane Garner, 15–44. Monroe: Athanasius Press, 2004.

Beisner, E. Calvin ed. *The Auburn Avenue Theology, Pros & Con: Debating the Federal Vision.* Fort Lauderdale: Knox Theological Seminary, 2004.

Horne, Mark. "Reformed Covenant Theology and Its Discontents." In *A Faith That Is Never Alone: a Response to Westminster Seminary California*, ed. P. Andrew Sandlin, 73–107. La Grange: Kerygma Press, 2007.

————. "What's for Dinner? Calvin's Continuity with the Bible's and the Ancient Church's Eucharistic Faith." In *The Federal Vision*, eds. Steve Wilkins and Duane Garner, 127–49. Monroe: Athanasius Press, 2004.

Jordan, James. "Merit Versus Maturity: What Did Jesus Do for Us?" In *The Federal Vision*, eds. Steve Wilkins and Duane Garner, 151–200. Monroe: Athanasius Press, 2004.

Leithart, Peter J. *The Baptized Body*. Moscow: Canon Press, 2007.

————. "'Judge Me, O God': Biblical Perspectives on Justification." In *The Federal Vision*, eds. Steve Wilkins and Duane Garner, 203–35. Monroe: Athanasius Press, 2004.

————. *The Kingdom and the Power: Rediscovering the Centrality of the Church*. Phillipsburg: Presbyterian and Reformed Publishing, 1993.

————. "A Response to '1 Corinthians 11:17–34: The Lord's Supper.'" In *The Auburn Avenue Theology, Pros & Con: Debating the Federal Vision*, ed. E. Calvin Beisner, 297–304. Fort Lauderdale: Knox Theological Seminary, 2004.

————. "Stoic Elements in Calvin's Doctrine of the Christian Life." *Westminster Theological Journal* 55 (1993): 31–54 (Part One); 191–208 (Part Two).

————. "Trinitarian Anthropology: Toward a Trinitarian Re-casting of Reformed Theology." In *The Auburn Avenue Theology, Pros & Con: Debating the Federal Vision*, ed. E. Calvin Beisner, 58–71. Fort Lauderdale: Knox Theological Seminary, 2004.

Lusk, Rich. "New Life and Apostasy: Hebrews 6:4–8 as Test Case." In *The Federal Vision*, eds. Steve Wilkins & Duane Garner, 271–99. Monroe: Athanasius Press, 2004.

————. "Paedobaptism and Baptismal Efficacy: Historic Trends and Current Controversies." In *The Federal Vision*, eds. Steve Wilkins and Duane Garner, 71–125. Monroe: Athanasius Press, 2004.

————. *Paedofaith: A Primer on the Mystery of Infant Salvation and a Handbook for Covenant Children*. Monroe: Athanasius Press, 2005.

————. "A Response to 'The Biblical Plan of Salvation.'" In *The Auburn Avenue Theology, Pros & Con: Debating the Federal Vision*, ed. E. Calvin Beisner, 118–48. Fort Lauderdale: Knox Theological Seminary, 2004.

Sandlin, P. Andrew ed. *Backbone of the Bible: Covenant in Contemporary Perspective*. TX: Covenant Media Press, 2004.

————. "Covenant in Redemptive History: 'Gospel and Law' or 'Trust and Obey'?" In *Backbone of the Bible: Covenant in Contemporary Perspective*, ed. P. Andrew Sandlin, 63–84. TX: Covenant Media Press, 2004.

————. "The Polemics of Articulated Rationality," In *A Faith That Is Never Alone: a Response to Westminster Seminary California*, ed. P. Andrew Sandlin, vii–xix. La Grange: Kerygma Press, 2008.

Schlissel, Steve M. "Justification and the Gentiles." In *The Federal Vision*, eds. Steve Wilkins & Duane Garner, 237–61. Monroe: Athanasius Press, 2004.

————. "A New Way of Seeing." In *The Auburn Avenue Theology, Pros & Con: Debating the Federal Vision*, ed. E. Calvin Beisner, 18–39. Fort Lauderdale: Knox Theological Seminary, 2004.

————. "A Response to 'Covenant and Salvation.'" In *The Auburn Avenue Theology, Pros & Con: Debating the Federal Vision*, ed. E. Calvin Beisner, 87–95. Fort Lauderdale: Knox Theological Seminary, 2004.

Shepherd, Norman. *The Call of Grace: How the Covenant Illumines Salvation and Evangelism*. Phillipsburg: Presbyterian and Reformed Publishing, 2000.

———. "The Covenant Context for Evangelism." In *The New Testament Student and Theology*, ed. J. H. Skilton. Phillipsburg: Presbyterian and Reformed Publishing, 1976.

———. "Faith and Faithfulness." In *A Faith That Is Never Alone: a Response to Westminster Seminary California*, ed. P. Andrew Sandlin, 53–72. La Grange: Kerygma Press, 2007.

———. "The Grace of Justification." Originally published February 8, 1979 now at http://www.hornes.org/theologia/content/norman_shepherd/the_grace_of_justification.htm.

———. "The Imputation of Active Obedience." In *A Faith That Is Never Alone: a Response to Westminster Seminary California*, ed. P. Andrew Sandlin, 249–78. La Grange: Kerygma Press, 2007.

———. "Justification by Faith Alone." *Reformation & Revival Journal* 11/2 (2002): 75–89.

———. "Justification by Faith in Pauline Theology." In *Backbone of the Bible: Covenant in Contemporary Perspective*, ed. P. Andrew Sandlin, 85–101. TX: Covenant Media Press, 2004.

———. "Justification by Works in Reformed Theology." In *Backbone of the Bible: Covenant in Contemporary Perspective*, ed. P. Andrew Sandlin, 103–20. TX: Covenant Media Press, 2004.

———. "Law and Gospel in Covenantal Perspective: The Unity of God's Salvific Plan." November 15, 2004 online at http://www.christianculture.com/cgi-local/npublisher/viewnews.cgi?category=3&id=1100539305.

———. "My Understanding of Covenant." on line at www.spindleworks.com/library/CR/shepherd.htm.

———. "The Relation of Good Works to Justification in the Westminster Standards." Westminster Theological Seminary, 1976.

———. "Thirty-Four Theses on Justification in Relation to Faith, Repentance, and Good Works." Westminster Theological Seminary, 1978.

Trouwborst, Tom. "A Response to 'The Reformed Doctrine of Regeneration.'" In *The Auburn Avenue Theology, Pros & Con: Debating the Federal Vision*, ed. E. Calvin Beisner, 187–205. Fort Lauderdale: Knox Theological Seminary, 2004.

Wilkins, Steve and Duane Garner, eds. *The Federal Vision.* Monroe: Athanasius Press, 2004.

Wilkins, Steve. "Covenant, Baptism, and Salvation." In *The Auburn Avenue Theology, Pros & Con: Debating the Federal Vision*, ed. E. Calvin Beisner, 254–69. Fort Lauderdale: Knox Theological Seminary, 2004.

———. "Covenant, Baptism, and Salvation." In *The Federal Vision*, eds. Steve Wilkins & Duane Garner, 47–69. Monroe: Athanasius Press, 2004.

Wilson, Douglas. "The Church: Visible or Invisible." In *The Federal Vision*, eds. Steve Wilkins and Duane Garner, 263–69. Monroe: Athanasius Press, 2004.

———. *'Reformed' Is Not Enough*. Moscow: Canon Press, 2002.

———. "A Response to 'Covenant and Apostasy.'" In *The Auburn Avenue Theology, Pros & Con: Debating the Federal Visio*, ed. E. Calvin Beisner, 224–32. Fort Lauderdale: Knox Theological Seminary, 2004.

———. "Sacramental Efficacy in the Westminster Standards." In *The Auburn Avenue Theology, Pros & Con: Debating the Federal Vision*, ed. E. Calvin Beisner, 233–44. Fort Lauderdale: Knox Theological Seminary, 2004.

————. "Union with Christ: An Overview of the Federal Vision." In *The Auburn Avenue Theology, Pros & Con: Debating the Federal Vision*, ed. E. Calvin Beisner, 1–8. Fort Lauderdale: Knox Theological Seminary, 2004.

SECONDARY SOURCES

Allis, Oswald T. "The Covenant of Works." In *Basic Christian Doctrines: Contemporary Evangelical Thought*, ed. Carl F. H. Henry, 96–102. New York/Chicago/San Francisco: Holt, Rinehart & Winston, 1962.

Althaus, Paul. *Die Prinzipien der deutschen reformierten Dogmatik im Zeitalter der aristotelischen Scholastik*. Leipzig: Deichert, 1914. Reprint, Darmstadt: Wissenschaftliche Buchgesellschaft, 1967.

Anderson, Marvin W. "Trent and Justification (1546): a Protestant Reflection." *Scottish Journal of Theology* 21 (1968): 385–406.

Arminius, James. *The Writings of James Arminius*. 3 vols. vols. 1 and 2 trans. James Nichols. vol. 3 trans. William Nichols. Grand Rapids: Baker, 1986.

Armour, Rollin S. *Anabaptist Baptism: A Representative Study*. Scottsdale: Herald Press, 1966.

Armstrong, E. B. B. "Calvin's Theology of the Lord's Supper Set in Historical Context and With Special Reference to his 'Short Treatise.'" M. Th. Diss., University of Aberdeen, 1994.

Augustine. *St. Augustin's City of God and Christian Doctrine*. ed. Phillip Schaff. The Nicene and Post–Nicene Fathers, vol. 2. Edinburgh: T & T Clark / Grand Rapids: Eerdmans, 1993.

————. *St. Augustin: Anti–Pelagian Writings*. ed. Phillip Schaff. The Nicene and Post–Nicene Fathers, vol. 5. Edinburgh: T & T Clark / Grand Rapids: Eerdmans, 1991.

Bahnsen, Greg L. *Theonomy in Christian Ethics: Expanded Edition with Replies to Critics*. 2d. ed. Phillipsburg: Presbyterian and Reformed Publishing, 1984.

————. "M.G. Kline on Theonomic Politics." *Journal of Christian Reconstruction* 6 (Winter 1980): 196–221.

Baker, J. Wayne. *Heinrich Bullinger and the Covenant: the Other Reformed Tradition*. Athens: Ohio University Press, 1980.

Ball, John. *A Treatise of the Covenant of Grace*. London: G. Miller, 1645.

Barker, William S. and Robert W. Godfrey, eds. *Theonomy: A Reformed Critique*. Grand Rapids: Academie Books, 1990.

Barth, Karl. *Church Dogmatics*. 4 vols. trans. G. W. Bromiley. Edinburgh: T.&T. Clark, 1974.

————. "Gospel and Law." In *God, Grace, and Gospel*, trans. J. S. McNab. 1–28. Scottish Journal of Theology Occasional Papers No. 8 London: Oliver Boyd, 1959.

————. *The Theology of Calvin*. trans. Geoffrey W. Bromiley. Grand Rapids: Eerdmans, 1995.

Bartholomew, Craig G. "Covenant and Creation: Covenant Overload or Covenantal Deconstruction." *Calvin Theological Journal* 30 (1995): 11–33.

Battles, Ford Lewis. *The Piety of John Calvin: An Anthology Illustrative of the Spirituality of the Reformer of Geneva*. Grand Rapids: Baker, 1978.

Baugh, S. M. "The New Perspective, Mediation, and Justification." In *Covenant, Justification, and Pastoral Ministry: Essays by the Faculty of Westminster Seminary California*, ed. R. Scott Clark, 137–63. Phillipsburg: Presbyterian and Reformed Publishing, 2007.

Bavaud, G. "La doctrine de la justification d´ après Calvin et le Concile de Trente." *Verbum Caro* 22 (1968): 83–92.

Bavinck, Herman. *Our Reasonable Faith: A Survey of Christian Doctrine.* trans. Henry Zylstra. Grand Rapids: Baker, 1977.

Beeke, Joel R. *Assurance of Faith: Calvin, English Puritanism, and the Dutch Second Reformation.* New York: Peter Lang, 1991.

Bell, M. Charles. "Was Calvin a Calvinist." *Scottish Journal of Theology* 36 (1983): 535–40.

Berkhof, Louis. *The History of Christian Doctrines.* Reprint, The Banner of Truth Trust, 1991.

———. *Systematic Theology.* Grand Rapids: Eerdmans, 1939. Reprint, 1988.

Berkouwer, G. C. *Faith and Justification.* trans. Lewis B. Smedes. Grand Rapids: Eerdmans, 1954.

———. *Sin.* trans. Philip C. Holtrop. Grand Rapids: Eerdmans, 1971.

———. *The Triumph of Grace in the Theology of Karl Barth.* trans. Harry R. Boer. Grand Rapids: Eerdmans, 1956.

Bierma, Lyle D. "Covenant or Covenants in the Theology of Olevianus?" *Calvin Theological Journal* 22 (1987): 228–50.

———. "The Covenant Theology of Caspar Olevian." PhD diss., Duke University, 1980.

———. *German Calvinism in the Confessional Age: The Covenant Theology of Caspar Olevianus.* Grand Rapids: Baker, 1996.

Blaising, Craig A., and Darrell L. Bock, eds. *Dispensationalism, Israel and the Church: The Search for Definition.* Grand Rapids: Zondervan Publishing House, 1992.

———. *Progressive Dispensationalism.* Wheaton: Victor, 1993.

Bogue, Carl W. "Jonathan Edwards on the Covenant of Grace." In *Soli Deo Gloria,* ed. R. C. Sproul. Nutley: Presbyterian and Reformed Publishing, 1976.

Bouwsma, William J. *John Calvin: A Sixteenth-Century Portrait.* New York: Oxford University Press, 1988.

Braaten, Carl E. and Robert W. Jensen, eds. *Union with Christ: The New Finnish Interpretation of Luther.* Grand Rapids: Eerdmans, 1998.

Bratcher, Dennis A. "The Concepts of Conditionality and Apostasy in Relation to the Covenant." Th.M Thesis, Westminster Theological Seminary, 1986.

Bray, G. L. "Donatism." In *New Dictionary of Theology,* eds. Sinclair B. Ferguson & David F. Wright, 206. Downers Grove: InterVarsity Press, 1988.

Brglez, H. A. "Saving Union with Christ in the Theology of John Calvin: A Critical Study." PhD diss., University of Aberdeen, 1993.

Brown, W. Adams. "Covenant Theology." In *Hastings Encyclopedia of Religion and Ethics,* ed. James Hastings, vol.4. New York: Charles Scribner's Sons, 1912.

Brug, John F. "The Lutheran-Catholic Statement of Justification." *Wisconsin Lutheran Quarterly* (Winter, 1984): 66–70.

Bruggink, Donald J. "Calvin and Federal Theology." *The Reformed Review* 13 (1959–1960): 15–22.

Brunner, Emil. *Die Christliche Lehre von Schöpfung und Erlösung: Dogmatik.* Band 2. Zürich: Zwingli—Verlag, 1950.

Bullinger, Heinrich. *De Testamento Seu Foedere Dei Unico et Aeterno.* Tiguri, 1534.

Burrage, Champlin. *The Church Covenant Idea: Its Origin and Its Development.* Philadelphia: American Baptist Publication Society, 1904.

Burrell, S. A. "The Covenant Idea as a Revolutionary Symbol: Scotland, 1596–1637." *Church History* 29 (1958): 338–50.

Campbell, Ken M. "God's Covenant." Th.M Thesis. Westminster Theological Seminary, 1971.

Carpenter, Craig B. "A Question of Union with Christ? Calvin and Trent on Justification." *Westminster Theological Journal* 64/2 (Fall, 2002): 363–86.

Cassidy, James J. "Calvin on Baptism: Baptismal Regeneration or the *Duplex Loquendi Modus*?" In *Resurrection and Eschatology: Theology in Service of the Church: Essays in Honor of Richard B. Gaffin Jr*, eds. Land G. Tipton and Jeffrey C. Waddington, 534–55. Phillipsburg: Presbyterian and Reformed Publishing, 2008.

Chafer, Lewis Sperry. "Dispensationalism." *Bibliotheca Sacra* 93 (1936): 390–449.

_____. *Dispensationalism*. Dallas: Dallas Seminary Press, 1951.

_____. *Systematic Theology*. 7 vols. Dallas: Dallas Seminary Press, 1948.

Chin, Clive S. "*Unio Mystica* and *Imitatio Christi*: The Two-Dimensional Nature of John Calvin's Spirituality." PhD diss., Dallas Theological Seminary, 2002.

Cho, Jinmo Timothy. "Persevere in Suffering with a Good Conscience: John Calvin's View of Christian Suffering with an Emphasis on the Relationship between Divine Preservation and the Believer's Perseverance." PhD diss., Westminster Theological Seminary, 2004.

Clark, R. Scott. "Do This and Live: Christ's Active Obedience as the Ground of Justification." In *Covenant, Justification, and Pastoral Ministry: Essays by the Faculty of Westminster Seminary California*, ed. R. Scott Clark, 229–65. Phillipsburg: Presbyterian and Reformed Publishing, 2007.

_____. "Election and Predestination: The Sovereign Expressions of God." In *Theological Guide to Calvin's Institutes*, eds. David W. Hall and Peter A. Lillback, 90–122. Phillipsburg: Presbyterian and Reformed Publishing, 2008.

———. "Letter and Spirit: Law and Gospel in Reformed Preaching." In *Covenant, Justification, and Pastoral Ministry: Essays by the Faculty of Westminster Seminary California*, ed. R. Scott Clark, 331–63. Phillipsburg: Presbyterian and Reformed Publishing, 2007.

———. *Recovering the Reformed Confession: Our Theology, Piety, and Practice*. Phillipsburg: Presbyterian and Reformed Publishing, 2008.

Coates, Thomas. "John Calvin's Doctrine of Justification." *Concordia Theological Monthly* 34 (1963): 325–34.

Cocceius, Johannes. *Summa Doctrine de Foedere et Testamento Dei*. Amsterdam, 1648.

Cooper, Karl T. "Paul and Rabbinic Soteriology: A Review Article." *Westminster Theological Journal* 44 (1972): 123–39.

Cottrell, Jack W. "Covenant and Baptism in the Theology of Huldreich Zwingli." PhD diss., Princeton Theological Seminary, 1971.

Davis, D. Clair. "A Challenge to Theonomy." In *Theonomy: A Reformed Critique*, eds. William S. Barker & W. Robert Godfrey, 389–402. Grand Rapids: Zondervan Publishing House, 1990.

———. "How did the Church in Rome Become Roman Catholicism." In *Roman Catholicism: Evangelical Protestants Analyze What Divides and Unites Us*, ed. John Armstrong, 45–62. Chicago: Moody Press, 1994.

———. "Inerrancy and Westminster Calvinism." In *Inerrancy and Hermeneutic: A Tradition, A Challenge, A Debate*, ed. Harvie M. Conn, 35–46. Grand Rapids: Baker, 1990.

Davis, Thomas J. *The Clearest Promises of God: the Development of Calvin's Eucharistic Teaching*. AMS Studies in Religion 1. New York: AMS Press, 1995.

DeJong, Peter Y. *The Covenant Idea in New England Theology.* Grand Rapids: Eerdmans, 1945.

De Kroon, Marijn. *The Honour of God and Human Salvation: Calvin's Theology According to His Institutes.* trans. John Vriend and Lyle D. Bierma. Edinburgh: T. & T. Clark, 2001.

Douglas, J. D. "Pighius, Albert." In *Evangelical Dictionary of Theology*, ed. Walter E. Elwell, 858. Grand Rapids: Baker, 1984.

Dumbrell, William J. *Covenant and Creation: An Old Testament Covenantal Theology.* Nashville, Camden & New York: Thomas Nelson Publishers, 1984.

———. "Law and Grace: The Nature of the Contrast in John 1:17." *Evangelical Quarterly* 58 (1986): 25–37.

Dunn, James D. G. "The Incident at Antioch (Gal. 2:11–18)." *Journal for the Study of the New Testament* 18 (1983): 3–57.

———. *Jesus, Paul, and the Law: Studies in Mark and Galatians.* Louisville: Westminster, 1990.

———. "The Justice of God: A Renewed Perspective on Justification by Faith." *Journal of Theological Studies* 43 (1992): 1–22.

———. "The New Perspective on Paul." *Bulletin of the John Rylands University Library of Manchester* 65 (1983): 95–122.

———. "Works of the Law and the Curse of the Law (Galatians 3:10–14)." *New Testament Studies* 31 (1985): 523–42.

———. "Yet Once More—'The Works of the Law': A Response." *Journal for the Study of the New Testament* 46 (1992): 99–117.

Ecumenical Creeds and Reformed Confessions. Grand Rapids: CRC Publications, 1988.

Edmonson, Stephen. *Calvin's Christology.* Cambridge: Cambridge University Press, 2004.

———. "Christ and History: Hermeneutical Convergence in Calvin and Its Challenge to Biblical Theology." *Modern Theology* 21 (2005): 3–36.

———. "The Biblical Historical Structure of Calvin's *Institutes.*" *Scottish Journal of Theology* 59 (2006): 1–13.

Edwards, Jonathan. *Treatise on Grace and Other Posthumously Published Writings.* ed. Paul Helm. Cambridge & London: James Clarke & Co. Ltd., 1971.

———. *The Works of Jonathan Edwards.* 18 vols. eds. Perry Miller, John E. Smith and Harry S. Stout. New Haven: Yale University Press, 1957–2000.

Eenigenburg, Elton M. "The Place of Covenant in Calvin's Teaching." *Reformed Review* 10 (1957): 1–22.

Emerson, Everett H. "Calvin and Covenant Theology." *Church History* 25 (June 1956): 136–44.

Faber, Jelle. *Essays in Reformed Doctrine.* Neerlandia / Alberta, Canada: Inheritance Publications, 1990.

Ferguson, Sinclair B. *A Heart for God: If He Can Be Known, How Can We Discover Him?* Colorado Springs: NavPress, 1987.

———. "Calvin on the Lord's Supper and Communion with Christ." In *Serving the Word of God: Celebrating the Life and Ministry of James Philip*, eds. David Stay and David Wright, 203–17. Edinburgh: Christian Focus and Rutherford House, 2002.

———. "The Doctrine of the Christian Life in the Teaching of Dr. John Owen [1616–1683]: Chaplain to Oliver Cromwell and Sometime Vice Chancellor of the University of Oxford." PhD diss., University of Aberdeen, 1979.

———. "John Murray." In *Hand Book of Evangelical Theologians*, ed. Walter J. Elwell, 168–81. Grand Rapids: Baker, 1993.

———. *John Owen on the Christian Life*. Carlisle / Edinburgh: The Banner of Truth Trust, 1987.

———. Review of *The New Testament Student and Theology*, ed. J.H. Skilton. *The Banner of Truth Magazine* (July/August, 1977), 59–63.

———. "The Teaching of the Confession." In *The Westminster Confession in the Church Today*, ed. Alasdair I. C. Heron, 28–39. Edinburgh: Saint Andrews Press, 1982.

Ferguson, Sinclair B., David F. Wright and J. I. Packer, eds. *New Dictionary Theology*. Downers Grove: InterVarsity Press, 1988.

Finger, T. N. "Merit." In *Evangelical Dictionary of Theology*, ed. Walter A. Elwell, 709–10. Grand Rapids: Baker, 1984.

Fitzer, Joseph. "The Augustinian Roots of Calvin's Eucharistic Thought." *Augustinian Studies* 7 (1976): 69–98.

Flinn, P. Richard. "Baptism, Redemptive History, and Eschatology: The Parameters of Debate." *Christianity and Civilization* 1 (Spring 1982): 111–51.

Frame, John M. *Apologetics to the Glory of God: An Introduction*. Phillipsburg: Presbyterian and Reformed Publishing, 1994.

———. *Cornelius Van Til: An Analysis of His Thought*. Phillipsburg: Presbyterian and Reformed Publishing, 1995.

———. *The Doctrine of God*. Phillipsburg: Presbyterian and Reformed Publishing, 2002.

———. *The Doctrine of the Knowledge of God*. Phillipsburg: Presbyterian and Reformed Publishing, 1987.

Fuller, Daniel P. *Gospel and Law: Contrast or Continuum? The Hermeneutics of Dispensationalism and Covenant Theology*. Grand Rapids: Eerdmans, 1980.

———. "The Hermeneutics of Dispensationalism." ThD diss., Northern Baptist Theological Seminary, 1957.

———. "A Response on the Subjects of Works and Grace." *Presbyterion* 9 (1983): 72–79.

Gaffin, Jr., Richard B. "Biblical Theology and the Westminster Standards." In *The Practical Calvinists: An Introduction to the Presbyterian and Reformed Heritage: In Honor of D. Clair Davis' Thirty Years at Westminster Theological Seminary*, ed. Peter A. Lillback, 425–42. Great Britain: Christian Focus Publications, 2002.

———. "Biblical Theology and the Westminster Standards." *Westminster Theological Journal* 65 (2003): 165–79.

———. *By Faith Not by Sight: Paul and the Order of Salvation*. Waynesboro: Paternoster Press, 2006.

———. *The Centrality of the Resurrection: A Study in Paul's Soteriology*. Grand Rapids: Baker, 1978.

———. "The Holy Spirit." *Westminster Theological Journal* 43 (1980): 58–78.

———. "Justification and Union with Christ," In *Theological Guide to Calvin's Institutes: Essays and Analysis*, eds. David W. Hall & Peter A. Lillback, 248–69. Phillipsburg: Presbyterian and Reformed Publishing, 2008.

———. *Perspectives on Pentecost: Studies in New Testament Teaching on the Gifts of the Holy Spirit*. Grand Rapids: Baker, 1979.

———. *Resurrection and Redemption: A Study in Pauline Soteriology*. ThD diss., Westminster Theological Seminary, 1969.

———. *Resurrection and Redemption: A Study in Paul's Soteriology*. Phillipsburg: Presbyterian and Reformed Publishing, 1987.

———. "Review Essay: Paul the Theologian." *Westminster Theological Journal* 62 (2000): 121–41.

———. "Systematic Theology and Biblical Theology." In *The New Testament Student and Theology*. vol.3. ed. John H. Skilton, 32–50. Phillipsburg: Presbyterian and Reformed Publishing, 1976.

———. "The Vitality of Reformed Dogmatics." In *The Vitality of Reformed Theology: Proceedings of the International Theological Congress June 20–24th 1994, Noordwijkerhout, The Netherlands*, eds. J. M. Batteau, J. W. Maris, and K. Veling, 16–50. Kampen: Uitgeverij Kok, 1994.

Gamble, Richard C. "Brevitas et Facilitas: Toward an Understanding of Calvin's Hermeneutic." *Westminster Theological Journal* 47 (1985): 1–17.

———. "Exposition and Method in Calvin." *Westminster Theological Journal* 49 (1987): 153–65.

Garlington, D. B. "The Obedience of Faith in the Letter to the Romans; Part I: The Meaning of *hupakoen pisteos* (Rom 1:5; 16:26)." *Westminster Theological Journal* 52 (1990): 201–24.

———. "The Obedience of Faith in the Letter to the Romans; Part II: The Obedience of Faith and Judgment by Works." *Westminster Theological Journal* 53 (1991): 47–72.

Garrett, Duane A. "Type, Typology." In *Evangelical Dictionary of Biblical Theology*, ed. Walter A. Elwell, 785–87. Grand Rapids: Baker, 1996.

Garcia, Mark A. "Christ and the Spirit: The Meaning and Promise of a Reformed Idea." In *Resurrection and Eschatology: Theology in Service of the Church*, eds. Lane G. Tipton & Jeffrey C. Waddington, 424–42. Phillipsburg: Presbyterian and Reformed Publishing, 2008.

———. "Imputation and the Christology of Union with Christ: Calvin, Osiander, and the Contemporary Quest for a Reformed Model." *Westminster Theological Journal* 68 (2006): 219–51.

———. *Life in Christ: Union with Christ and Twofold Grace in Calvin's Theology*. Milton Keynes/ Colorado Springs/ Hyderabad: Paternoster, 2008.

Gerrish, Brian A. "The Flesh of the Son of Man: John W. Nevin on the Church and the Eucharist." In Gerrish, *Tradition in the Modern World: Reformed Theology in the Nineteenth Century*, 49–70. Chicago: University of Chicago Press, 1978.

———. *Grace and Gratitude: The Eucharistic Theology of John Calvin*. Edinburgh: T. & T. Clark, 1993.

Glenny, W. Edward. "Typology: A Summary of the Present Evangelical Discussion." *Journal of the Evangelical Theological Society* 40 (1997): 627–38.

Godfrey, W. Robert. "Back to Basics: A Response to the Robertson-Fuller Dialogue." *Presbyterion* 9 (1983): 80–84.

———. "Calvin, Worship, and the Sacraments." In *Theological Guide to Calvin's Institutes: Essays and Analysis*, eds. David W. Hall & Peter A. Lillback, 368–89. Phillipsburg: Presbyterian and Reformed Publishing, 2008.

———. "Law and Gospel." In *New Dictionary of Theology*, eds. Sinclair B. Ferguson and David F. Wright, 379–80. Downers Grove / Leicester: InterVarsity Press, 1988.

———. "Westminster Seminary, the Doctrine of Justification, and the Reformed Confessions." In *The Pattern of Sound Doctrine: Systematic Theology at the Westminster Seminaries: Essays in Honor of Robert B. Strimple*, ed. David VanDrunen, 127–48. Phillipsburg: Presbyterian and Reformed Publishing, 2004

————. "What Really Caused the Great Divide?" In *Roman Catholicism: Evangelical Protestants Analyze What Divides and Unites Us*, ed. John Armstrong, 65–82. Chicago: Moody Press, 1994.

Gordon, T. David. "Why Israel did not Obtain Torah-Righteousness: A Translation Note on Romans 9:32." *Westminster Theological Journal* 54 (1992): 163–66.

Green, Doug. "N.T. Wright–A Westminster Seminary Perspective," March 3, 2004 at http://www.ntwrightpage.com/Green_Westminster_Seminary_Perspective.pdf.

Hagen, Kenneth. "From Testament to Covenant in the Early Sixteenth Century." *Sixteenth Century Journal* 3 (1972): 1–20.

Hahn, Scott & Kimberly. *Rome Sweet Home*. San Francisco: Ignatius, 1993.

Hall, Basil. *John Calvin: Humanist and Theologian*. London: Routledge and Kegal Paul, 1956.

————. "Calvin Against the Calvinists." In *John Calvin: A Collection of Distinguished Essays*, ed. Gervase E. Duffield, 19–37. Grand Rapids: Eerdmans, 1966.

Hall, David W. *The Legacy of John Calvin: His Influence on the Modern World*, In *The Calvin 500 Series*. Phillipsburg: Presbyterian and Reformed Publishing, 2008.

Hanna, Eleanor B. "Biblical Interpretation and Sacramental Practice: John Calvin's Interpretation of John 6:51–58." *Worship* 73 (1999): 211–30.

Hart, Trevor. "Humankind in Christ and Christ in Humankind: Salvation as Participation in Our Substitute in the Theology of John Calvin." *Scottish Journal of Theology* 42 (1989): 67–84.

Helm, Paul. *Calvin and the Calvinists*. Edinburgh: Banner of Truth Trust, 1982.

————. "Calvin and the Covenant: Unity and Continuity." *Evangelical Quarterly* 55 (1983): 65–81.

Heppe, Heinrich. *"Die Dogmatik: der Evangelisch–reformierten Kirche."* Neukirchen Kreis Moers: Neukirchener Verlag, 1958.

Hesselink, I. John. "Calvin, the Holy Spirit, and Mystical Union." *Perspectives* 13 (1998): 15–18.

Hodge, A. A. *The Confession of Faith: A Handbook of Christian Doctrine Expounding The Westminster Confession*. Reprint, The Banner of Truth Trust, 1983.

Hodge, Charles. *The Epistle to the Romans: A Commentary on Romans*. Reprint, The Banner of Truth Trust, 1975.

————. *Systematic Theology*. 3 vols. Reprint, Grand Rapids: Eerdsmans, 1995.

Hoekema, Anthony A. "Calvin's Doctrine of the Covenant of Grace." *Reformed Review* 15 (1962): 1–12.

————. "The Covenant of Grace in Calvin's Teaching." *Calvin Theological Journal* 2 (1967): 133–61.

Hoeksema, Herman. *Reformed Dogmatics*. Grand Rapids: Reformed Free Publishing Association, 1985.

Horton, Michael. "Déjà Vu All Over Again." *Modern Reformation* 13/4 (July/August, 2004): 23–30.

————. *People and Place: A Covenant Ecclesiology*. Louisville / London: Westminster John Knox Press, 2008.

————. "What Still Keeps Us Apart?" In *Roman Catholicism: Evangelical Protestants Analyze What Divides and Unites Us*, ed. John Armstrong, 245–66. Chicago: Moody Press, 1994.

Jensen, P. F. "Merit." In *New Dictionary of Theology*, eds. Sinclair B. Ferguson and David F. Wright, 422. Downers Grove/Leicester: InterVarsity Press, 1988.

————. Review of *Gospel and Law: Contrast or Continuum? The Hermeneutics of Dispensationalism and Covenant Theology*, by Daniel P. Fuller. *Calvin Theological Journal* 17 (1982): 109–12.

Jensen, Robert W. "Response to Seifrid, Trueman, and Metzger on Finnish Luther Research." *Westminster Theological Journal* 65 (2003): 245–50.

Jeon, Jeong Koo. *Covenant Theology: John Murray's and Meredith G. Kline's Response to the Historical Development of Federal Theology in Reformed Thought.* Lanham: University Press of America, 2004.

————. *Covenant Theology and Justification by Faith: The Shepherd Controversy and Its Impacts.* Eugene: Wipf and Stock Publishers, 2006.

————. "Covenant Theology and Old Testament Ethics: Meredith G. Kline's Intrusion Ethics." *Kerux* (2002): 3–33.

Johnson, Dennis E. *The Message of Acts in the History of Redemption.* Phillipsburg: Presbyterian and Reformed Publishing, 1997.

Johnson, Galen. "The Development of John Calvin's Doctrine of Infant Baptism in Reaction to the Anabaptists." *Mennonite Quarterly Review* 73 (1999): 803–23.

Jones, R. Tudur. "Union with Christ: The Existential Nerve of Puritan Piety." *Tyndale Bulletin* 41 (1990): 186–208.

Kaiser, Walter C., Jr. "The Eschatological Hermeneutics of 'Epangelicalism': Promise Theology." *Journal of Evangelical Theological Society* 13 (1970): 91–100.

————. "Leviticus 18:5 and Paul: Do This and You Shall Live (Eternally?)." *Journal of Evangelical Theological Society* 14 (1971): 19–28.

————. "The Law As God's Gracious Guidance for the Promotion of Holiness." In *Five Views on Law and Gospel.* Grand Rapids: Zondervan Publishing House, 1996.

Kang, Paul Chulhong. *Justification: The Imputation of Christ's Righteousness from Reformation Theology to the American Great Awakening and the Korean Revivals.* New York: Peter Lang Publishing, 2006.

Karlberg, Mark W. *The Changing of the Guard: Westminster Theological Seminary in Philadelphia.* Unicoi: The Trinity Foundation, 2001.

————. *Gospel Grace: The Modern-Day Controversy.* Eugene: Wipf and Stock Publishers, 2003.

————. "Justification in Redemptive History." *Westminster Theological Journal* 43 (1981): 213–46.

————. "Legitimate Discontinuities Between the Testaments." *Journal of the Evangelical Theological Society* 28 (1985): 9–20.

————. "The Mosaic Covenant and the Concept of Works in Reformed Hermeneutics: A Historical Critical Analysis with Particular Attention to Early Covenant Eschatology." PhD diss., Westminster Theological Seminary, 1980.

————. "The Original State of Adam: Tensions within Reformed Theology." *Evangelical Quarterly* 87 (1987): 291–309.

————. "Reformed Interpretation of the Mosaic Covenant." *Westminster Theological Journal* 43 (1980): 1–57.

————. "The Significance of Israel in Biblical Typology." *Journal of Evangelical Theological Society* 31/3 (1988): 257–69.

————. "Works and Grace." *New Horizons* 18/9 (1997): 23.

Kim, Jae Sung. "*Unio cum Christo*: The Work of the Holy Spirit in Calvin's Theology." PhD diss., Westminster Theological Seminary, 1998.

Kim, Seyoon. *The Origin of Paul's Gospel.* 2nd ed. Tübingen: J. C. B. Mohr (Paul Siebeck), 1984.

———. *Paul and the New Perspective: Second Thoughts on the Origin of Paul's Gospel.* Grand Rapids: Eerdmans, 2002.

Kendall, R. T. *Calvin and English Calvinism to 1649.* Oxford: Oxford University Press, 1979.

Kennedy, Kevin Dixon. "Union with Christ as Key to John Calvin's Understanding of the Extent of the Atonement." PhD diss., Southern Baptist Theological Seminary, 1999.

———. *Union with Christ and the Extent of the Atonement in Calvin.* Studies in Biblical Literature 48. New York: Peter Lang, 2002.

Kevan, Ernest F. *The Grace of Law: A Study in Puritan Theology.* Reprint, Grand Rapids: Baker, 1976.

———. *Moral Law.* Phillipsburg: Presbyterian and Reformed Publishing, 1991.

Klassen, William. *Covenant and Community.* Grand Rapids: Eerdmans, 1968.

Kline, Meredith G. "Covenant Theology under Attack." *New Horizons* 15/2 (1994): 3–5.

———. *God, Heaven and Har Magedon: A Covenantal Tale of Cosmos and Telos.* Eugene: Wipf and Stock Publishers, 2006.

———. "Gospel until the Law: Romans 5:13–14 and the Old Covenant." *Journal of the Evangelical Theological Society* 34/4 (1991): 433–46.

———. *Kingdom Prologue: Genesis Foundations for a Covenantal Worldview.* Overland Park: Two Age Press, 2000.

———. "Of Works and Grace." *Presbyterion* 9 (1983): 85–92.

Knight III, George W. "1 Corinthians 11:17–34: The Lord's Supper: Abuses, Words of Institution and Warnings with An Addendum on 1 Corinthians 10:16–17." In *The Auburn Avenue Theology, Pros & Con: Debating the Federal Vision,* ed. E. Calvin Beisner, 282–96. Fort Lauderdale: Knox Theological Seminary, 2004.

Kolb, Robert. "Contemporary Lutheran Understanding of the Doctrine of Justification: A Selective Glimpse." In *Justification: What's at Stake in the Current Debates,* eds. Mark Husbands and Daniel J. Trier, 153–76. Downers Grove: InterVarsity Press, 2004.

Küng, Hans. *Justification: The Doctrine of Karl Barth and a Catholic Reflection.* trans. Thomas Collins, Edmund E. Tolk, and David Granskou. Philadelphia: The Westminster Press, 1981.

Kuyper, Abraham. *The Work of the Holy Spirit.* trans. Henri De Vries. Chattanooga: AMG Publishers, 1995.

Lane, A. N. S. "Calvin's Doctrine of Assurance." *Vox Evangelica* 11 (1979): 32–54.

———. *Justification by Faith in Catholic–Protestant Dialogue: An Evangelical Assessment.* Edinburgh: T. & T. Clark, 2002.

———. "Lombard, Peter." In *New Dictionary of Theology,* eds. Sinclair B. Ferguson & David F. Wright, 396–97. Downers Grove: InterVarsity Press, 1988.

———. "The Quest for the Historical Calvin." *Evangelical Quarterly* 55 (1983): 95–113.

———. "Twofold Righteousness: A Key to the Doctrine of Justification? Reflections of Article 5 of the Regensburg Colloquy (1541)." In *Justification: What's At Stake in the Current Debates,* eds. Mark Husbands and Daniel J. Trier, 205–24. Downers Grove: InterVarsity Press, 2004.

Lang, August. *Der Heidelberger Katechismus und vier verwandte Katechismen.* Reprint, Darmstadt: Wissenschaftliche Buch-gesellschaft, 1967.

Lee, Irons. "Raised for Our Justification." *Modern Reformation* (March/April 1996): 25–28.

Letham, Robert W. A. "The *Foedus Operum:* Some Factors Accounting for Its Development." *Sixteenth Century Journal* 14 (1983): 457–67.

Lillback, Peter Alan. "The Binding of God: Calvin's Role in the Development of Covenant Theology." PhD diss., Westminster Theological Seminary, 1985.

———. *The Binding of God: Calvin's Role in the Development of Covenant Theology.* Grand Rapids: Baker, 2001.

———. "Calvin's Covenantal Response to the Anabaptist View of Baptism." *Christianity and Civilization* 1 (1982): 185–232.

———. "Calvin's Interpretation of the History of Salvation: The Continuity and Discontinuity of the Covenant." In *Theological Guide to Calvin's Institutes: Essays and Analysis,* eds. David W. Hall and Peter A. Lillback, 168–204. Phillipsburg: Presbyterian and Reformed Publishing, 2008.

———. "Ursinus' Development of the Covenant of Creation: A Debt to Melanchthon or Calvin?" *Westminster Theological Journal* 43 (1981): 247–88.

———. "Calvin's Covenantal Response to the Anabaptist View of Baptism." *Christianity and Civilization* 1 (1982): 185–232.

———. "Ursinus' Development of the Covenant of Creation: A Debt to Melanchthon or Calvin?" *Westminster Theological Journal* 43 (1981): 247–88.

Linden, David H. Review of "Justification by Faith Alone," by Norman Shepherd. In *Reformation & Revival Journal* 11/2 (Spring, 2002) online at http://www.grebeweb .com/linden/shepherd_review.htm.

Luther, Martin. *Die Martin Luthers Werke: kritische gesamtausgabe.* Weimary: H. Böhlau, 1883–1993.

———. *Luther's Works,* 55 vols. eds. Jaroslav Pelikan and Helmut T. Lehmann. Philadelphia: Fortress Press / Muhlenberg Press, 1957–1986.

Machen, J. Gresham. *The Christian Faith and the Modern World.* London: Hodder and Stoughton Limited, 1936.

———. *The Christian View of Man.* Reprint, Carlisle / Edinburgh: The Banner of Truth Trust, 1995.

———. *Christianity and Culture.* Reprint, Carlisle / Edinburgh: The Banner of Truth Trust, 1969.

———. *God Transcendent.* ed. Ned B. Stonehouse. Carlisle / Edinburgh: The Banner of Truth Trust, 1982.

———. *Machen's Notes on Galatians.* ed. John H. Skilton. Philadelphia: Presbyterian and Reformed Publishing, 1972.

———. *The New Testament: An Introduction to Its Literature and History.* ed. W. John Cook. Carlisle / Edinburgh: The Banner of Truth Trust, 1997.

———. *The Origin of Paul's Religion.* Reprint, Grand Rapids: Eerdmans, 1976.

———. *What is Christianity?: And Other Addresses.* ed. Ned B. Stonehouse. Grand Rapids: Eerdmans, 1951.

———. *What is Faith?* New York: The Macmillan Company, 1925.

Macleod, Donald. "Covenant Theology." In *Dictionary of Scottish Church History & Theology,* ed. Nigel M. De S. Cameron, 214–18. Downers Grove: InterVarsity Press, 1993.

———. *W. Stanford Reid: An Evangelical Calvinist in the Academy.* Montreal & Kingston: McGill-Queen's University Press, 2004.

Marcel, Pierre. "The Relation between Justification and Sanctification in Calvin's Thought." *Evangelical Quarterly* 27 (1955): 132–45.

Marshall, I. Howard. "Sanctification in the Teaching of John Wesley and John Calvin." *Evangelical Quarterly* 34 (1962): 75–82.

McComiskey, Thomas E. *The Covenant of Promise: A Theology of the Old Testament Covenants.* Grand Rapids: Baker, 1985.

McCoy, Charles S. "The Covenant Theology of Johannes Cocceius." PhD diss., Yale University, 1956.

McCoy, Charles S. and Wayne Baker J. *Fountainhead of Federalism: Heinrich Bullinger and the Covenant Tradition.* Louisville: Westminster John Knox Press, 1991.

McDonnell, Kilian. *John Calvin, the Church, and the Eucharist.* Princeton: Princeton University Press, 1967.

McGiffert, Michael. "From Moses to Adam: the Making of the Covenant of Works." *Sixteenth Century Journal* 19/2 (1988): 131–55.

———. "Grace and Works: the Rise and Division of Covenant Divinity in Elizabethan Puritanism." *Harvard Theological Review* 75/4 (1982): 463–502.

McGowan, A. T. B. "Calvin on Limited Atonement." In *The Federal Theology of Thomas Boston,* 48–53, 56–58. Rutherford Studies in Historical Theology. Edinburgh: Paternoster and Rutherford House, 1997.

———. "Justification and the *ordo salutis.*" In *Justification in Perspective,* ed. Bruce L. McCormack, 147–63. Grand Rapids: Baker, 2006.

McGrath, Alister. *Iustitia Dei: A History of the Christian Doctrine of Justification.* 2 vols. Cambridge, London: Cambridge University Press, 1986.

———. *Justification by Faith: What It Means for Us.* Grand Rapids: Zondervan Publishing House, 1988.

———. *A Life of John Calvin.* Cambridge: Basil Blackwell Ltd., 1990

McLelland, Joseph C. "Covenant Theology: A Re-evaluation." *Canadian Journal of Theology* 3 (1957): 184–97.

McWilliams, David B. "The Covenant Theology of the Westminster Confession of Faith and Recent Criticism." *Westminster Theological Journal* 53 (1991): 109–24.

Melanchthon, Philip. *Corpus Reformatorum: Philippi Melanchthonis Opera quae supersunt omnia.* eds. C. G. Bretschneider and H. E. Bindseil. Halle, 1834ff.

———. *Loci Communes (1555).* ed. and trans. Clyde L. Manschreck. Oxford University Press, 1965.

Mendenhall, George E. "Ancient Oriental and Biblical Law." *The Biblical Archaeologist* 17/2 (1954): 26–46.

———. "Covenant Forms in Israelite Tradition." *The Biblical Archaeologist* 17/3 (1954): 50–76.

Metzger, Paul Louis. "Mystical Union with Christ: An Alternative to Blood Transfusions and Legal Fictions." *Westminster Theological Journal* 65 (2003): 201–14.

Milne, Douglas J. W. "A Barthian Stricture on Reformed Theology: The Unconditionality of the Covenant of Grace." *The Reformed Theological Review* 55/3 (1996): 121–33.

Milner, Benjamin Charles. *Calvin's Doctrine of the Church.* Leiden: E. J. Brill, 1970.

Moller, Jens G. "The Beginnings of Puritan Covenant Theology." *Journal of Ecclesiastical History* 14 (1963): 46–67.

Moltmann, Jürgen. "*Föderaltheologie.*" In *Lexicon für Theologie und Kirche,* 4:190–92. Freiburg: Verlag Herder, 1960.

———. *God in Creation: A New Theology of Creation and the Spirit of God.* trans. Margaret Kohl. San Francisco: Harper and Row, 1985.

———. *Theology of Hope.* trans. James W. Leitsch. New York: Harper and Row, 1967.

————. *The Trinity and the Kingdom.* trans. Margaret Kohl. San Francisco: Harper and Row, 1981.

Moo, Douglas J. "Israel and Paul in Romans 7:7–12." *New Testament Studies* 32 (1986): 122–35.

————. "'Law,' 'Works of the Law' and Legalism in Paul." *Westminster Theological Journal* 45 (1983): 73–100.

Mosser, Carl. "The Greatest Possible Blessing: Calvin and Deification." *Scottish Journal of Theology* 55 (2002): 36–57.

Muller, Richard A. *After Calvin: Studies in the Development of a Theological Tradition.* Oxford: Oxford University Press, 2003.

————. "Calvin and the 'Calvinists': Assessing Continuities and Discontinuities Between the Reformation and Orthodoxy." *Calvin Theological Journal* 30 (1995): 345–75.

————. *Christ and the Decree: Christology and Predestination in Reformed Theology from Calvin to Perkins.* The Labyrinth Press, 1986. Reprint, Grand Rapids: Baker, 2008.

————. "Covenant and Conscience in English Reformed Theology: Three Variations on a 17th Century Theme." *Westminster Theological Journal* 42 (1980): 308–34.

————. "The Covenant of Works and the Stability of Divine Law in Seventeenth-Century Reformed Orthodoxy: A Study in the Theology of Herman Witsius and Wilhelmus À Brakel." *Calvin Theological Journal* 29 (1994): 75–101.

————. *Dictionary of Latin and Greek Theological Terms: Drawn Principally from Protestant Scholastic Theology.* Grand Rapids: Baker, 1985.

————. "The Hermeneutic of Promise and Fulfillment in Calvin's Exegesis of the Old Testament Prophecies of the Kingdom." In *The Bible in the Sixteenth Century*, ed. David C. Steinmetz, 68–82. Duke Monographs in Medieval and Renaissance Studies 11. Durham: Duke University Press, 1990.

————. "A Note on 'Christocentrism' and the Imprudent Use of Such Terminology." *Westminster Theological Journal* 68 (2006): 253–60.

————. *The Unaccommodated Calvin: Studies in the Foundation of a Theological Tradition.* New York: Oxford University Press, 2000.

Murray, John. *Christian Baptism.* Phillipsburg: Presbyterian and Reformed Publishing, 1980.

————. "The Calling of the Westminster Assembly." *The Presbyterian Guardian* 11/2 (1942): 26–28.

————. "The Christian Doctrine of Vicarious Atonement: The Origin of the Idea of Vicarious Atonement, II." *The Homiletic Review* 102/2 (1931): 93.

————. *Collected Writings of John Murray: The Claims of Truth.* vol.1. The Banner of Truth Trust, 1976.

————. *Collected Writings of John Murray: Select Lectures in Systematic Theology.* vol.2. The Banner of Truth Trust, 1977.

————. *Collected Writings of John Murray: Life (by Iain H. Murray), Sermons and Reviews.* vol.3. The Banner of Truth Trust, 1982.

————. *Collected Writings of John Murray: Studies in Theology.* vol.4. The Banner of Truth Trust, 1983.

————. *The Covenant of Grace: A Biblico-Theological Study.* Phillipsburg: Presbyterian and Reformed Publishing, 1988.

————. "Dr. Machen's Hope and the Active Obedience of Christ." *The Presbyterian Guardian* 3 (1937): 163.

———. "The Epistle to the Romans." vols.1 & 2. In *The New International Commentary on the New Testament,* ed. Gordon D. Fee. Grand Rapids: Eerdmans, 1968.

———. *The Imputation of Adam's Sin.* Phillipsburg: Presbyterian and Reformed Publishing, 1959.

———. "Is Infant Baptism Scriptural?" *The Presbyterian Guardian* 5 (1938): 227–29.

———. *Principles of Conduct: Aspects of Biblical Ethics.* Grand Rapids: Eerdsmans, 1991.

———. *Redemption: Accomplished and Applied.* Grand Rapids: Eerdsmans, 1989.

———. "The Theology of the Westminster Standards." *The Calvin Forum* 9 (1944): 111–15.

———. "The Westminster Confession of Faith and the Salvation of Infants." *The Presbyterian Guardian* 3 (1936): 120–21.

———. "Why We Baptize Infants." *The Presbyterian Guardian* 5 (1938): 143–44.

———. "The Work of the Westminster Assembly." *The Presbyterian Guardian* 11/3 (1942): 37–38.

Nevin, John Williamson. "Doctrine of the Reformed Church on the Lord's Supper." *Mercersburg Review* 2 (1850): 421–548. Reprint in *The Mystical Presence and other Writings on the Eucharist,* eds. Bard Thompson and George H. Bricker. Philadelphia: United Church Press, 1966.

———. *The Mystical Presence: A Vindication of the Reformed or Calvinistic Doctrine of the Holy Eucharist.* ed. Augustine Thompson. New York: Lippencott, 1846. Reprint, Eugene: Wipf and Stock Publishers, 2000.

Niesel, Wilhelm. *The Theology of Calvin.* trans. Harold Knight. Philadelphia: Westminster Press, 1956.

Nygren, Anders. *Commentary on Romans.* trans. Carl C. Rasmussen. Philadelphia: Muhlenberg Press, 1949.

Oberman, Heiko. *The Dawn of the Reformation. Essays in Late Medieval and Early Reformation Thought.* Edinburgh: T. & T. Clark, 1986.

———. "The 'Extra' Dimension in the Theology of John Calvin." *Journal of Ecclesiastical History* 21 (1970): 43–64.

———. *Forerunners of the Reformation.* Philadelphia: Fortress Press, 1981.

———. *The Harvest of Medieval Theology: Gabriel Biel and the Late Medieval Nominalism* Cambridge: Harvard University Press, 1963.

———. *The Reformation: Roots and Ramifications.* Edinburgh: T. & T. Clark, 1994.

———. "The Tridentine Decree on Justification in the Light of Late Medieval Theology." In *Journal for Theology and the Church 3, Distinctive Protestant and Catholic Themes Revisited,* ed. Robert W. Funk, 28–54. New York: Harper & Row, 1967.

Old, Hughes Oliphant. "Biblical Wisdom Theology and Calvin's Understanding of the Lord's Supper." In *Calvin Studies VI,* ed. John H. Leith, 111–36. Colloquium on Calvin Studies, Davidson College and Davidson Presbyterian Church, 1992.

Olevianus, Caspar. *An Exposition of the Symbole of the Apostles.* trans. John Fielde. London, 1581.

———. *A Firm Foundation: An Aid to Interpreting the Heidelberg Catechism.* trans. and ed. Lyle D. Bierma. Grand Rapids: Baker, 1995.

———. *De Substantia Foederis Gratuiti inter Deum et Electos.* Geneva, 1585.

Oliphint, K. Scott, ed. *Justified in Christ: God's Plan for Us in Justification.* Mentor, 2007.

Orthodox Presbyterian Church. *Justification: Report of the Committee to Study the Doctrine of Justification.* Willow Grove: The Committee on Christian Education of the Orthodox Presbyterian Church, 2007.

Osborne, G. R. "Type, Typology." In *Evangelical Dictionary of Theology*, ed. Walter A. Elwell, 1117–119. Grand Rapids: Baker, 1984.

Osterhaven, M. Eugene. "Calvin on the Covenant." *Reformed Review* 33 (1980): 136–49.

Owen, John. *Biblical Theology*. trans. Stephen P. Westcott. Pittsburg: Solideo Gloria Publications, 1994.

———. *An Exposition of the Epistles to the Hebrews*. 7 vols. eds. William H. Goold. London, Johnstone & Hunter, 1855. Reprint, Grand Rapids: Baker, 1980.

———. *The Works of John Owen*. 16 vols. ed. William H. Goold. The Banner of Truth Trust, 1977.

Parker, T. H. L. "The Approach to Calvin." *Evangelical Quarterly* 16 (1944): 165–72.

———. *A Biography of Calvin*. Philadelphia: Westminster John Knox, 2007.

———. *Calvin: An Introduction to his Thought*. Louisville: Westminster John Knox, 1995.

———. "Calvin's Central Dogma Again." *Sixteenth Century Journal* 18 (1987): 191–99.

———. "Calvin's Doctrine of Justification." *Evangelical Quarterly* 24 (1952): 101–7.

Pelagius. *Pelagius's Expositions of Thirteen Epistles of St Paul: Text*. In *Texts and Studies: Contributions to Biblical and Patristic Literature*, vol. 9, ed. J. Armitage Robinson. 2 vols. London: Cambridge University Press, 1922, 1926.

Perrin, Nicholas. "A Reformed Perspective on the New Perspective," Review of *Justification and the New Perspectives on Paul: A Review and Response*, by Guy Prentiss Waters. *Westminster Theological Journal* 67 (2005): 381–89.

Peter, Carl J. "Merit." In *The Dictionary of Theology*, eds. Joseph A. Komonchak, Mary Collins and Dermot A. Lane, 652–53. Wilmington: Michael Glazier, Inc., 1987.

Peterson, Robert A. "Calvin's Doctrine of the Atonement." PhD diss., Drew University, 1980.

———. *Calvin's Doctrine of the Atonement*. Phillipsburg: Presbyterian and Reformed Publishing, 1983.

Phillips, Richard D. "A Response to 'Sacramental Efficacy in the Westminster Standards.'" In *The Auburn Avenue Theology, Pros & Con: Debating the Federal Vision*, ed. E. Calvin Beisner, 245–53. Fort Lauderdale: Knox Theological Seminary, 2004.

Pipa Jr., Joseph A. "A Response to 'Covenant, Baptism, and Salvation.'" In *The Auburn Avenue Theology, Pros & Con: Debating the Federal Vision*, ed. E. Calvin Beisner, 270–81. Fort Lauderdale: Knox Theological Seminary, 2004.

Piper, John. *Counted Righteous in Christ: Should We Abandon the Imputation of Christ's Righteousness*. Wheaton: Crossway Books, 2002.

———. *Desiring God: Meditations of a Christian Hedonist*. Sisters: Multnomah Books, 1996.

———. *The Justification of God*. Grand Rapids: Baker, 1983.

———. *Love Your Enemies: Jesus' Love Command in the Synoptic Gospels & the Early Christian Paraenesis*. Grand Rapids: Baker, 1991.

Pitkin, Barbara. *What Pure Eyes Could See: Calvin's Doctrine of Faith in Its Exegetical Context*. New York: Oxford University Press, 1999.

Poole, David N.J. *The History of the Covenant Concept from the Bible to Johannes Cloppenburg "De Foedere Dei."* San Francisco: Mellen Research University Press, 1992.

Pope, E. A. "New England Calvinism and the Disruption of the Presbyterian Church." PhD diss., Brown University, 1963.

Potter, Mary Lane. "The 'Whole Office of the Law' in the Theology of John Calvin." *Journal of Law and Religion* 3 (1985): 117–39.

Poythress, Vern S. *The Shadow of Christ in the Law of Moses.* Phillipsburg: Presbyterian and Reformed Publishing, 1991.

———. *Understanding Dispensationalists.* 2d. ed. Phillipsburg: Presbyterian and Reformed Publishing, 1994.

Preus, James S. *From Shadow to Promise.* Cambridge: Belknap Press, 1969.

Pruett, Gordon E. "A Protestant Doctrine of the Eucharistic Presence." *Calvin Theological Journal* 10 (1975): 142–74.

Puckett, David L. *John Calvin's Exegesis of the Old Testament.* Louisville: Westminster John Knox Press, 1995.

Rainbow, Jonathan H. "Double Grace: John Calvin's View of the Relationship of Justification and Sanctification." *Ex Auditu: An International Journal of Theological Interpretation of Scripture* 5 (1989): 99–105.

Räisänen, Heikki. "Galatians 2:16 and Paul's Break with Judaism." *New Testament Studies* 31 (1985): 543–53.

———. *Jesus, Paul and Torah: Collected Essays.* trans. David E. Orton. Journal for the Study of the New Testament Supplement Series 43. Sheffield: JSOT, 1992.

———. "Legalism and Salvation by the Law: Paul's Portrayal of the Jewish Religion as a Historical and Theological Problem." In *The Pauline Literature and Theology*, ed. S. Pedersen, 63–83. Göttingen: Vandenhoeck and Ruprecht, 1980.

———. *Paul and the Law.* 2nd ed. Tübingen: J. C. B. Mohr (Paul Siebeck), 1983.

———. "Paul's Conversion and the Development of His View of the Law." *New Testament Studies* 33 (1987): 404–19.

———. *The Torah and Christ: Essays in German and English on the Problem of the Law in Early Christianity.* ed. Anne-Marit Enroth. Helsinki, 1986.

RCUS. "Report of the Special Committee to Study Justification in Light of the Current Justification Controversy: Presented to the 258th Synod of the Reformed Church of the United States." May 10–13, 2004 online at http://www.trinityrcus.com/Articles/reportshepherd1.htm.

Reid, W. Stanford. "Bernard of Clairvaux in the Thought of John Calvin." *Westminster Theological Journal* 41 (1978–1979): 127–45.

———. "Justification by Faith According to John Calvin." *Westminster Theological Journal* 42 (1980): 290–307.

Ridderbos, Herman N. *The Coming of the Kingdom.* Phillipsburg: Presbyterian and Reformed Publishing, 1962.

———. *Paul: An Outline of His Theology.* Grand Rapids: Eerdmans, 1975.

———. *When the Time Had Fully Come: Studies in New Testament Theology.* Jordan Station, Ontario: Paideia Press, 1982.

Ritschl, Albrecht. *The Christian Doctrine of Justification and Reconciliation.* trans. H. R. Mackintosh and A. B. Macaulay. Edinburgh: T. & T. Clark, 1900.

Ritschl, Otto. *Dogmengeschichte des Protestantismus.* 4 vols. Göttingen: Vandenhoeck & Ruprecht, 1908–1927.

Robbins, Carl D. "A Response to 'Covenant and Election.'" In *The Auburn Avenue Theology, Pros and Cons: Debating the Federal Vision*, ed. E. Calvin Beisner, 157–61. Fort Lauderdale: Knox Theological Seminary, 2004.

Robbins, John W. *A Companion to the Current Justification Controversy.* Unicoi: The Trinity Foundation, 2003.

Robertson, O. Palmer. *The Christ of the Covenants.* Phillipsburg: Presbyterian and Reformed Publishing, 1980.

———. *The Current Justification Controversy*. Unicoi: The Trinity Foundation, 2003.

———. "Current Reformed Thinking on the Nature of the Divine Covenants." *Westminster Theological Journal* 40 (1977): 63–76.

———. "Genesis 15:6: New Covenant Expositions of an Old Covenant Text." *Westminster Theological Journal* 42 (1980): 259–89.

———. Review of *Gospel and Law: Contrast or Continuum*, by Daniel P. Fuller. *Presbyterion* 8 (1982): 84–91.

Rohr, John v. "Covenant and Assurance in Early English Puritanism." *Church History* 34 (1965): 195–203.

———. *The Covenant of Grace in Puritan Thought*. Atlanta, Georgia: Scholars Press, 1986.

Rollock, Robert. *Select Works of Robert Rollock*. 2 vols. ed. William M. Gunn. Edinburgh: The Woodrow Society, 1844 &1849.

Rolston, Holmes III. *John Calvin versus the Westminster Confession*. Richmond: John Knox Press, 1972.

———. "Responsible Man in Reformed Theology: Calvin Versus the Westminster Confession." *Scottish Journal of Theology* 23 (1970): 129–56.

Ryrie, Charles C. *Dispensationalism*. Revised and Expanded. Chicago: Moody Press, 1995.

———. *The Grace of God*. Chicago: The Moody Bible Institute, 1963. Reprint, Moody Press, 1975.

Sanders, E. P. "The Covenant as a Soteriological Category and the Nature of Salvation in Palestinian and Hellenistic Judaism." In *Jews, Greeks and Christians: Religious Cultures in Late Antiquity*, eds. Robert Hamerton-Kelly and Robin Scroggs, 11–44. Leiden, 1976.

———. *Jesus and Judaism*. Philadelphia: Fortress Press, 1985.

———. *Jewish Law from Jesus to the Mishnah: Five Studies*. London: SCM Press / Philadelphia: Trinity Press International, 1990.

———. *Paul*. Oxford / New York: Oxford University Press, 1992.

———. *Paul and Palestinian Judaism*. Philadelphia: Fortress Press, 1977.

———. *Paul, the Law and the Jewish People*. Philadelphia: Fortress Press, 1983.

Santmire, H. Paul. "Justification in Calvin's 1540 Romans Commentary." *Church History* 33 (1964): 294–313.

Saucy, Robert L. *The Case for Progressive Dispensationalism: The Interface Between Dispensational & Non-Dispensational Theology*. Grand Rapids: Zondervan Publishing House, 1993.

Schaff, Philip. *The Creeds of Christendom*. 3 vols. Grand Rapids: Baker, 1977.

Schenck, L. B. *The Presbyterian Doctrine of Children in the Covenant*. New Haven, 1940.

Schreiner, Susan Elizabeth. *The Theatre of His Glory: Nature and the Natural Order in the Thought of John Calvin*. Durham: Labyrinth Press, 1991.

Schrenk, Gottlob. *Gottesreich und Bund im älteren Protestantismus, vornehmlich bei Johannes Cocceius*. Gütersloh: Bertelsmann, 1923.

Scofield, Cyrus I., ed. *The New Scofield Reference Bible. The Holy Bible Containing the Old and New Testaments. Authorized King James Version*. ed. E. Schuyler English. New York: Oxford, 1967.

———, ed. *The Scofield Reference Bible. The Holy Bible Containing the Old and New Testaments. Authorized Version*. New and Improved ed. New York: Oxford, 1917.

Shedd, William G. T. *Dogmatic Theology*. 3 vols. New York: Charles Scribner's Sons, 1888.

Shepherd, Victor V. *The Nature and Function of Faith in the Theology of John Calvin.* Macon: Mercer University Press, 1983.

Silva, Moisés. *Explorations in Exegetical Method: Galatians as a Test Case.* Grand Rapids: Baker, 1996.

———. "Is the Law against the Promises? The Significance of the Galatians 3:21 for Covenant Continuity." In *Theonomy: A Reformed Critique*, eds. William S. Barker & W. Robert Godfrey, 153–67. Grand Rapids: Zondervan Publishing House, 1990.

Smith, Morton H. "The Biblical Plan of Salvation with Reference to the Covenant of Works, Imputation, and Justification by Faith." In *The Auburn Avenue Theology, Pros and Cons: Debating the Federal Vision*, ed. E. Calvin Beisner, 96–117. Fort Lauderdale: Knox Theological Seminary, 2004.

Sproul, R. C. *Faith Alone: Evangelical Doctrine of Justification.* 2d. Print. Grand Rapids: Baker, 1996.

———. *Grace Unknown: The Heart of Reformed Theology.* Grand Rapids: Baker, 1997.

Steinmetz, David C. "Calvin and the Patristic Exegesis of Paul." In *The Bible in the Sixteenth Century*, ed. David C. Steinmetz, 100–18. Durham: Duke University Press, 1990.

———. *Calvin in Context.* New York: Oxford University Press, 1995.

———. "The Scholastic Calvin." In *Protestant Scholasticism: Essays in Reassessment*, eds. Carl R. Trueman and R. S. Clark, 16–30. Carlisle: Paternoster Press, 1999.

Stek, John H. "Biblical Typology Yesterday and Today." *Calvin Theological Journal* 5 (1970): 133–62.

———. "'Covenant' Overload in Reformed Theology." *Calvin Theological Journal* 29 (1994): 12–41.

———. "A New Theology of Baptism? Baptism: a Sign of Grace or Judgment?" *Calvin Theological Journal* 1 (1966): 69–73.

Stoute, D. A. "The Origins and Early Development of the Reformed Idea of Covenant." PhD diss., Cambridge, 1979.

Strehle, Stephen. *Calvinism, Federalism, and Scholasticism: A Study of the Reformed Doctrine of the Covenant.* Basler und Berner Studien zur historischen und systematischen Theologie 58. Bern: Peter Lang, 1988.

———. *The Catholic Roots of the Protestant Gospel: Encounter between the Middle Ages and the Reformation.* Studies in the History of Christian Thought 60. Leiden: E. J. Brill, 1995.

Strickland, Wayne G. ed. *The Law, the Gospel and the Modern Christian: Five Views.* Grand Rapids: Zondervan Publishing House, 1993.

Strimple, Robert B. "Roman Catholic Theology Today." In *Roman Catholicism: Evangelical Protestants Analyze What Divides and Unites Us*, ed. John Armstrong, 85–117. Chicago: Moody Press, 1994.

Sungenis, Robert A. *Not by Faith Alone: The Biblical Evidence for the Catholic Doctrine of Justification.* Santa Barbara: Queenship Publishing Company, 1997.

Swierenga, R. P. "Calvin and the Council of Trent: A Reappraisal. Part II." *Reformed Journal* 16 (1966): 19–21.

Tamburello, Dennis E. *Union with Christ: John Calvin and the Mysticism of St. Bernard.* Louisville: Westminster John Knox Press, 1994.

Tavard, George H. *The Starting Point of Calvin's Theology.* Grand Rapids: Eerdmans, 2000.

Thompson, William M. "Viewing Justification Through Calvin's Eyes: An Ecumenical Experiment." *Theological Studies* 57 (1996):447–66.

Tinker, Melvin. "Language, Symbols and Sacraments. Was Calvin's View of the Lord's Supper Right?" *Churchman* 112 (1998): 131–49.

Torrance, James B. "Calvin and Puritanism in England and Scotland—Some Basic Concepts in the Development of 'Federal Theology.'" In *Calvinus Reformator,* 264–77. Potchefstroom University for Christian Higher Education, 1982.

———. "The Concept of Federal Theology—Was Calvin a Federal Theologian." In *Calvinus Sacrae Scripturae Professor,* ed. W. H. Neuser, 15–40. Grand Rapids: Eerdmans, 1994.

———. "Covenant or Contract?: A Study of the Theological Background of Worship in Seventeenth-Century Scotland." *Scottish Journal of Theology* 23 (1970): 51–76.

———. "The Covenant Concept in Scottish Theology and Politics and Its Legacy." *Scottish Journal of Theology* 34 (1981): 225–43.

———. "Strengths and Weaknesses of the Westminster Theology." In *The Westminster Confession,* ed. Alisdair Heron, 40–54. Edinburgh: Saint Andrews Press, 1982.

Torrance, Thomas Forsyth. *Calvin's Doctrine of Man.* London: Lutterworth Press, 1949.

———. *The Hermeneutics of John Calvin.* Edinburgh: Scottish Academic Press, 1988.

Trinterud, Leonard J. "The Origins of Puritanism." *Church History* 20 (1951): 37–57.

Trueman, Carl R. and R. S. Clark, eds. *Protestant Scholasticism: Essays in Reassessment.* Carlisle: Paternoster Press, 1999.

Trueman, Carl R. "Is the Finnish Line a New Beginning? A Critical Assessment of the Reading of Luther Offered by the Helsinki Circle." *Westminster Theological Journal* 65 (2003): 231–44.

Trumper, Tim J. R. "Covenant Theology and Constructive Calvinism." Review of *Covenant Theology: John Murray's and Meredith G. Kline's Response to the Historical Development of Federal Theology in Reformed Thought,* by Jeong Koo Jeon *Westminster Theological Journal* 64/2 (2002): 387–404.

Turretin, Francis. *Institutes of Elenctic Theology.* 3 vols. trans. George Musgrave Giger and ed. James T. Dennison, Jr. Phillipsburg: Presbyterian and Reformed Publishing, 1992 & 1994.

Tylenda, Joseph N. "Calvin on Christ's True Presence in the Lord's Supper." *American Ecclesiastical Review* 155 (1966): 321–33.

———. "Calvin and Christ's Presence in the Supper—True or Real." *Scottish Journal Of Theology* 27 (1974): 65–75.

———. "A Eucharistic Sacrifice in Calvin's Soteriology?" *Theological Studies* 37 (1976): 456–66.

Ursinus, Zacharias. "*Summa Theologiae.*" In *Der Heidelberger Katechismus,* ed. August Lang. Leipzig, 1907. Reprint, Darmstadt: Wissenschaftliche Buchgesellschaft, 1967.

Van Devender, John A. *Discussion Points: Federal Vision.* Unpublished Paper, 2005.

VanDrunen, David. "Inaugural Lecture: The Two Kingdoms and the *Ordo Salutis*: Life beyond Judgment and the Question of a Dual Ethic." *Westminster Theological Journal* 70 (2008): 207–24.

———. "Where We Are: Justification under Fire in the Contemporary Scene." In *Covenant, Justification, and Pastoral Ministry: Essays by the Faculty of Westminster Seminary California,* ed. R. Scott Clark, 25–57. Phillipsburg: Presbyterian and Reformed Publishing, 2007.

Van Gemeren, Willem A. "Israel as the Hermeneutical Crux in the Interpretation of Prophecy." *Westminster Theological Journal* 45 (1983): 132–44.

———. "Israel as the Hermeneutical Crux in the Interpretation of Prophecy, II." *Westminster Theological Journal* 46 (1984): 254–97.

——. "The Law is the Perfection of Righteousness in Jesus Christ: A Reformed Perspective." In *Five Views on Law and Gospel*, ed. Wayne G. Strickland, 13–58. Grand Rapids: Zondervan Publishing House, 1996.

Van Til, Cornelius. *Common Grace and the Gospel*. Phillipsburg: Presbyterian and Reformed Publishing, 1972.

——. "Covenant Theology." In *New 20th—Century Encyclopedia of Religious Knowledge*, ed. J. D. Douglas, 240–41. 2d ed. Grand Rapids: Baker, 1991.

——. *The Defense of the Faith*. 3d. ed. Phillipsburg: Presbyterian and Reformed Publishing, 1967.

——. *The Great Debate Today*. Phillipsburg: Presbyterian and Reformed Publishing, 1971.

——. *The Intellectual Challenge of the Gospel*. Phillipsburg: Presbyterian and Reformed Publishing, 1980.

——. *An Introduction to Systematic Theology*. Phillipsburg: Presbyterian and Reformed Publishing, 1974.

——. *The Sovereignty of Grace: An Appraisal of G. C. Berkouwer's View of Dordt*. New Jersey: Presbyterian and Reformed Publishing, 1969.

Venema, Cornelis P. Review of *The Binding of God: Calvin's Role in the Development of Covenant Theology*. Texts and Studies in Reformation and Post-Reformation Thought, ed. Richard M. Muller, by Peter A. Lillback. *Mid-America Journal of Theology* 13 (2002): 201–9.

——. Review of *The Call of Grace: How the Covenant Illuminates Salvation and Evangelism*, by Norman Shepherd. *Mid-America Journal of Theology* 13 (2002):232–48.

——. "Calvin's Doctrine of the Last Things: The Resurrection of the Body and the Life Everlasting." In *Theological Guide to Calvin's Institutes: Essays and Analysis*, eds. David W. Hall and Peter A. Lillback, 441–67. Phillipsburg: Presbyterian and Reformed Publishing, 2008.

——. *The Gospel of Free Acceptance in Christ: An Assessment of the Reformation and the New Perspectives on Paul*. Edinburgh / Carlisle: The Banner of Truth Trust, 2006.

——. "The Twofold Nature of the Gospel in Calvin's Theology: The 'Duplex Gratia Dei' and the Interpretation of Calvin's Theology." PhD diss., Princeton Theological Seminary, 1985.

von Rad, Gerhard. *Genesis: A Commentary*. rev. ed. Philadelphia: The Westminster Press, 1972.

——. *Theologie Des Alten Testaments*. Band I and II. München: Chr. Kaiser Verlag, 1958 & 1965.

Vos, Antonie. "Scholasticism and Reformation." In *Reformation and Scholasticism: An Ecumenical Enterprise*, eds. Willem J. van Asselt and Eef Dekker, 99–119. Grand Rapids: Baker, 2001.

Vos, Geerhardus. *Biblical Theology: Old and New Testaments*. Grand Rapids: Eerdmans, 1948. Reprint, 1988.

——. *The Pauline Eschatology*. Reprint, Phillipsburg: Presbyterian and Reformed Publishing, 1994.

——. *Redemptive History and Biblical Interpretation*. ed. Richard B. Gaffin. Phillipsburg: Presbyterian and Reformed Publishing, 1980.

——. *The Teaching of the Epistle to the Hebrews*. ed. Johannes G.Vos. Phillipsburg: Presbyterian and Reformed Publishing, 1956.

Wallace, Ronald S. *Calvin's Doctrine of the Word and Sacrament.* Edinburgh: Oliver & Boyd, 1953. Reprint, Edinburgh: Scottish Academic Press Ltd, 1995.

———. *Calvin, Geneva, and the Reformation: A Study of Calvin as Social Reformer, Churchman, Pastor and Theologian.* Edinburgh: Scottish Academic Press, 1988.

———. "A Christian Theologian: Calvin's Approach to Theology." *Scottish Bulletin of Evangelical Theology* (1987):123–50.

Wallis, Wilber. Review of *Gospel and Law: Contrast or Continuum,* by Daniel P. Fuller. *Presbyterion* 8 (1982): 72–82.

Walter, V. L. "Donatism." In *Evangelical Dictionary of Theology,* ed. Walter A. Elwell, 329–30. Grand Rapids: Baker, 1984.

Walton, John H. *Covenant.* Grand Rapids: Zondervan Publishing House, 1994.

Warfield, Benjamin B. *The Plan of Salvation.* Presbyterian Board of Publication, 1915. Reprint, Avinger: Simpson Publishing Company, 1989.

Wawrykow, Joseph. "John Calvin and Condign Merit." *Archiv für Reformationsgeschichte* 83 (1992): 73–90.

Waters, Guy Prentiss. The Federal Vision and Covenant Theology: A Comparative Analysis. Phillipsburg: Presbyterian and Reformed Publishing, 2006.

———. Justification and the New Perspectives on Paul: A Review and Response. Phillipsburg: Presbyterian and Reformed Publishing, 2004.

Watson, P. S. "Merit." In *A Dictionary of Christian Theology,* ed. Alan Richardson, Philadelphia: The Westminster Press, 1969.

Weir, David A. *The Origins of the Federal Theology in Sixteenth-Century Reformation Thought.* Oxford: Clarendon Press, 1990.

Weis, James. "Calvin versus Osiander on Justification." *Springfielder* 30 (1965): 31–47.

Wenger, J. C. "Hubmaier, Balthasar." In *Evangelical Dictionary of Theology,* ed. Walter A. Elwell, 535. Grand Rapids: Baker, 1984.

Wenger, Thomas L. "The New Perspective on Calvin: Responding to Recent Calvin Interpretations." *Journal of Evangelical Theological Society* 50 (2007): 311–28.

Westerholm, Stephen. *Israel's Law and the Church's Faith: Paul and the Recent Interpreters.* Grand Rapids: Eerdmans, 1988.

Westminster Seminary California Faculty. "Our Testimony on Justification: A Summary of the Statement from the Faculty of Westminster Seminary California." *Modern Reformation* 13/4 (July/August, 2004): 37

Westminster Theological Seminary. *Westminster Statement on Justification.* Unpublished Doctrinal Statement of Westminster Theological Seminary. Philadelphia, 1980.

White, R. Fowler. "Covenant and Apostasy," In *The Auburn Avenue Theology, Pros and Cons: Debating the Federal Vision,* ed. E Calvin Beisner, 206–23. Fort Lauderdale: Knox Theological Seminary, 2004.

Wilcox, Peter. "Conversion in the Thought and Experience of John Calvin." *Anvil* 14 (1997): 113–28.

———. "Evangelisation in the Thought and Practice of John Calvin." *Anvil* 12 (1995): 201–17.

Wiley, David N. "The Church as the Elect in the Theology of Calvin." In *John Calvin and the Church: A Prism of Reform,* ed. Timothy George, 96–117. Louisville: Westminster John Knox Press, 1990.

Williams, George H. *The Radical Reformation.* Philadelphia: The Westminster Press, 1975.

Williamson, G. I. *The Westminster Confession of Faith: For Study Classes.* Phillipsburg: Presbyterian and Reformed Publishing, 1964.

Willis-Watkins, E. David. "A Reformed Doctrine of the Eucharist and Ministry and Its Implications for Roman Catholic Dialogues." *Journal of Ecumenical Studies* (1981): 295–305.

————. "The *Unio Mystica* and the Assurance of Faith according to Calvin." In *Calvin: Erbe und Auftrag, Festschrift for W. H. Neuser,* ed. Willem van't Spijker, 77–84. Kampen: Kok Pharos Publishing House, 1991.

Wingard, Charles. "The Doctrines of Grace." *New Horizons* 18/5 (1997): 6–9.

Witsius, Hermannus. *De Oeconomia Foederum Dei cum Homnibus Libri Quattuor.* Utrecht, 1694.

Woolsey, Andrew Alexander. "Unity and Continuity in Covenantal Thought: A Study in the Reformed Tradition to the Westminster Assembly." 2 vols. PhD diss., University of Glasgow, 1988.

Wright, N. Thomas. *The Climax of the Covenant: Christ and the Law in Pauline Theology.* Minneapolis: Fortress Press, 1991.

————. "The Paul of History and the Apostle of Faith." *Tyndale Bulletin* 29 (1978): 61–88.

————. *What Saint Paul Really Said.* Grand Rapids: Eerdmans, 1997.

Würbenhorst, Karla. "Calvin's Doctrine of Justification: Variations on a Lutheran Theme." In *Justification in Perspective,* ed. Bruce L. McCormack, 99–118. Grand Rapids: Baker, 2006.

Young, Edward J. "Confession and Covenant." In *Scripture and Confession: A Book about Confessions Old and New,* ed. John H. Skilton, 31–66. Phillipsburg: Presbyterian and Reformed Publishing, 1973.

Zens, Robert M. *Professor Norman Shepherd on Justification: A Critique.* Th.M. thesis, Dallas Theological Seminary, 1981.

Zuck, Lowell H. "Anabaptist Revolution Through the Covenant in Sixteenth Century Continental Protestantism." PhD diss., Yale University, 1954.